D0047072

$2

QUANTITATIVE METHODS FOR HISTORIANS

Quantitative Methods for Historians

A GUIDE TO RESEARCH, DATA, AND STATISTICS

Konrad H. Jarausch and Kenneth A. Hardy

The University of North Carolina Press
CHAPEL HILL AND LONDON

©1991 The University of North Carolina Press
All rights reserved
Manufactured in the United States of America

The paper in this book meets the guidelines for permanence and
durability of the Committee on Production Guidelines for Book
Longevity of the Council on Library Resources.

03   02   01   00   99   7   6   5   4   3

Library of Congress Cataloging-in-Publication Data

Jarausch, Konrad Hugo.
   Quantitative methods for historians : a guide to research, data,
and statistics / by Konrad H. Jarausch and Kenneth Hardy.
      p.   cm.
   Includes bibliographical references and index.
   ISBN 0-8078-1947-6 (alk. paper).—ISBN 0-8078-4309-1 (pbk. :
alk. paper)
   1. History—Statistical methods.   I. Hardy, Kenneth.   II. Title.
D16.17.J37   1991
907'.2—dc20
                                                                    90-40746
                                                                       CIP

Contents

Preface   xiii

1   **The Scope of Quantitative History**   1

Definition and Debate   1

Varieties of Quantitative History   4

Information Sources and Learning Aids   8

2   **Historians and Computers**   12

Historical Applications   13

Micro- and Macrocomputers   16

Data-base and Statistical Software   19

3   **The Formalized Research Process**   25

The Problem of Quantifiability   25

Formal Research Procedure   28

Implications for Project Design   32

4   **Creating a Data Set**   37

Making Material Machine-readable   37

Organizing a Codebook   42

Entering the Data   45

Establishing a System File   47

5   **Managing a Data Base**   50

Working with Program Packages   50

Correcting Errors   53

Modifying the Data   55

Linking Records   58

6   **Data, Information, and Statistics**   63

Statistical Reasoning   64

Drawing a Sample   68

Levels of Measurement   74

Statistical Hypothesis Testing   76

7   **Statistics for Questions about One Variable**   82

Descriptive Statistics   83

Inferential Statistics   98

Software Notes   102

8   **Statistics for Questions about Two Variables**   104

Nominal Dependent Variables   105

Ordinal Dependent Variables   112

Continuous Dependent Variables   118

A Continuous Dependent and a Categorical Independent Variable   126

A Continuous Independent and a Categorical Dependent Variable   132

A Continuous Independent and an Ordinal Dependent Variable   136

Software Notes   138

9   **Statistics for Questions about Many Variables**   140

   Single Continuous Dependent Variables   147

   Single Categorical Dependent Variables   160

   Single Ordinal Dependent Variables   166

   Software Notes   169

10   **Advanced Techniques**   171

   Extensions of Multiple Regression Models   171

   Multiequation Regression Models   174

   Latent Variable Measurement   176

   Grouping Similar Cases   180

   Software Notes   183

11   **Interpretation and Theory Formation**   185

   The Need for Analytical Control   185

   Quantification and Theory   189

   History and the Social Sciences   191

   Hypotheses and Model Building   194

12   **The Role of Quantitative Methods in History**   198

   National Styles of Quantification   199

   Current Problems   204

   Potential Solutions   208

   The Quantitative Challenge   212

   Appendix A. The Fort Moultrie and New England
Data Sets, by Dale Steinhauer   215

   Fort Moultrie Soldiers   215

New England Counties 224

Appendix B. Choosing Statistical Techniques for
Bivariate Relationships 229

Selected Bibliography 231

Index 241

Tables

6.1 Characteristics of Soldiers at Fort Moultrie, Charleston Harbor, S.C., 1850   65

7.1 Frequency Distribution for Values of Occupational Category   84

7.2 Frequency Distribution for Age in Years   92

8.1 Crosstabulation for Variables X and Y   106

8.2 Chi-square Test for Variables X and Y   108

8.3 Bivariate Nominal Measures of Association for Some Example Tables   111

8.4 Birthplace and Prior Occupation of Fort Moultrie Soldiers   113

8.5 Bivariate Ordinal Measures of Relationship for Some Example Tables   115

8.6 Tests for Relationship between Occupational Category and Military Rank   117

8.7 Wilcoxon Scores for Military Rank by Marital Status   119

8.8 Relationship between Value of Real Estate and Age   128

8.9 Real Estate Holdings of Fort Moultrie Officers and Soldiers   131

8.10 Example Relationship between Age and Voting Democratic   133

8.11   Logistic Regression of Rank on Value of Real
       Property   137

9.1a   Multiple Regression of Value of Real Estate on Age
       and Rank   159

9.1b   Multiple Regression of Value of Real Estate on Age,
       Rank, and Their Interaction   159

9.2   Multiple Logistic Regression of Marital Status on
       Age and Birthplace   166

9.3   Ordered Dependent Variable Multiple Logistic
       Regression of Occupational Status on Real Property
       and Marital Status   168

10.1   Example Data for a Stylized Cluster Analysis   181

Figures

7.1 Bar Chart for Frequency of Occupational Category 86

7.2 Histogram for Age 88

7.3 Ideal Shapes for Frequency Distributions of
Continuous Variables 90
    7.3a Symmetric Distribution 90
    7.3b Positively Skewed Distribution 90
    7.3c Negatively Skewed Distribution 91
    7.3d Bimodal Distribution 91

7.4 Location of Measures of Central Tendency for Some
Ideal Distributions 94
    7.4a Symmetric Distribution 94
    7.4b Positively Skewed Distribution 94
    7.4c Negatively Skewed Distribution 95
    7.4d Bimodal Distribution 95

7.5 Interquartile Range for a Nonsymmetric
Distribution 96

7.6 Box Plot of Age of Soldiers at Fort Moultrie 98

8.1 Scatterplots of Possible Relationships between Two
Continuous Variables 120
    8.1a Positive Linear Relationship 120
    8.1b Negative Linear Relationship 120
    8.1c No Relationship 121
    8.1d Curvilinear Relationship 121

8.2   Two Scatterplots for Relationships with Different
      Strengths   123
      8.2a   Scatterplot of Y versus X for r = .90   123
      8.2b   Scatterplot of Y versus X for r = .75   123

8.3   Scatterplot of Value of Real Estate versus Soldier's
      Age   127

8.4   Two Examples of Relationships between
      Quantitative Dependent and Categorical
      Independent Variables   129
      8.4a   No Relationship   129
      8.4b   Relationship   129

9.1   Alternative Three Variable Causal Diagrams for
      Two Variables Directly Causing a Third   143

9.2   Four Variable Causal Models for Spurious and Chain
      Relationships   145

9.3   Plot of Hypothetical Relationship between Income
      and Education for Whites and Blacks   146
      9.3a   Whites   146
      9.3b   Blacks   146

10.1 Causal Diagram with Exogenous and Endogenous
      Variables   175

10.2 Causal Diagram of a Multiequation Model with
      Latent Variables   179

Preface

In response to a much lamented training deficit, this volume offers practical and theoretical guidance for the application of quantitative methods in historical research. It is designed for students of history and the neighboring disciplines who are curious about the possibilities of quantification and want to learn more about its recent development. In attempting to meet the distinctive needs of methodological context, computer experience, and statistical literacy, this book seeks to render research design transparent, to help with establishing data bases, and to provide enough statistical information so that analytical procedures can be applied responsibly. In order to facilitate use, the text follows the normal steps of research practice: It begins with the definition of a problem, proceeds to building a data set, goes on to statistical methods, and concludes with interpreting the results. The computer will be "demythologized" by building upon a widely available program package (SAS), but alternative programs such as SPSS will be discussed in the software notes as well. For easier comprehension, examples of quantitative work are not treated separately but are integrated at key points into the text. Suggestions for further reading are presented in a selected bibliography which also serves as a reference list for citations in social science style.

Tested in classroom and self-study, this introduction rests on broad transatlantic experience with quantitative methods. Under the title *Quantitative Methoden in der Geschichtswissenschaft,* the original version, published in 1985, was coauthored by the historical software expert Manfred Thaller, the economic statistician Gerhard Arminger, and the German social historian Konrad H. Jarausch. When favorable reviews suggested an English language edition, the text was not just translated but fundamentally recast in order to fit the particular needs of Anglo-American scholars. As copresident of the International Commission for the Application of Quantitative Methods in History (INTERQUANT), Konrad Jarausch of the University of North Carolina at Chapel Hill has rewritten the introductory and concluding chapters as well as produced new data-base sections. As director of the statistical laboratory of the Institute for Research in Social Science at the University of North Carolina, Kenneth Hardy has penned fresh statistical chapters. As a doctoral student in nineteenth-century American history, Dale Steinhauer has compiled two U.S. data sets, listed in appendix A, which provide a consistent empirical basis for the examples in data processing and statistical analysis. Indebted to countless conversations on both sides of the Atlantic, this interdisciplinary volume itself reflects the cooperative style and international discourse on quantitative methods in history.

While intended as a working introduction, this book, in important respects, tries to go further and offer fresh impulses to scholars who have some prior quantitative experience. For novices the text starts with background information on the scope of quantitative history and historical computing, but the general chapters also critically reflect on the proper role of quantitative methods in history for the more advanced readers. While the data-base section concentrates on the basics of formalized research necessary for quantitative work, it discusses the coding process and more complicated problems of data transformation and linkage as well. The statistical parts systematically build upon the traditional fundamentals and introduce new analytical techniques for qualitative variables which are especially important for historians. The pioneering texts of two decades ago opened up exciting vistas for quantification. But the subsequent rapid development of hardware and software as well as of methods and research has outdated many earlier formulations, demanding a new attempt at synthesis. To silence postmodernist doubts, the present volume intends to convey a broader and more mature concept of quantitative methods as they become increasingly useful and essential for historical research.

Since research is a discourse with other scholars, the authors wish to acknowledge some of their many debts in writing this introduction. The Institute for Research in Social Science at the University of North Carolina, directed by J. S. Reed and A. Beza, provided both stimulation and support. American colleagues such as L. Stone and T. B. Alexander facilitated the initial steps into quantification, while European scholars such as G. Arminger, W. H. Schroeder, and M. Thaller fostered further progress. Other historians in the American Historical Association's quantitative methods committee and the International Commission for the Application of Quantitative Methods in History expanded methodological horizons. Finally, friends such as E. Johnson and W. Kamphoefner made valuable suggestions for improving the text. In the spirit of *docendo discimus*, we dedicate this volume to our students, whose insistent questions have prompted ever more intelligible answers.

QUANTITATIVE METHODS FOR HISTORIANS

I

The Scope of Quantitative History

Even after one generation of use, quantitative methods are still controversial in historical research and writing. Scholars continue to react more emotionally than rationally to the possibilities and problems of quantification in history. Because of math phobia or hostility against technology, humanists tend to charge the computer with reductionism and oversimplification. Fascinated with technical gadgets or scientific advances, social scientists make counterclaims of innovative research and accuse traditionalists of obfuscation. Some of this ritualized debate is based on ignorance and distortion, since detractors rarely have any firsthand experience in quantitative work while statistical zealots are often impatient with older methods which they have left behind. Much controversy is also due to contradictory ideographic or nomothetic conceptions of the purpose and method of historical research. Gradually this recognition began to lead, as in the case of the civilized exchanges between Robert Fogel and G. R. Elton (1983), to a "more ecumenical view." But just when it seemed that quantitative techniques had been accepted in the profession, a fresh wave of postmodernist, feminist, and populist criticism started to call their legitimacy once again into question. In order to dispel old misunderstandings and to counter fresh misconceptions, it is necessary to take a closer look at the actual role of quantification in history: What is quantitative history, which are its topical varieties, and how can one learn more about it?

DEFINITION AND DEBATE

Unfortunately, there is no clear and simple definition of "quantitative history." Instead, three overlapping uses recur in the literature.

First, quantification refers to works with tables and graphs that measure and count evidence. This is simply a more rigorous and *formalized description* of the past which has been practiced since the ancient Greeks. It is only a small step from saying that someone was "tall," "many" soldiers were killed in battle, or people experienced a "severe" famine to expressing these attributes in numbers to make them comparable over time and between cases. Second, beyond describing events, figures offer more *analytical possibilities* than regular words due to their formal properties. The large variety of statistical procedures makes it possible to evaluate causative connections through testing hypotheses in a more stringent way. The rhetoric of statistical analysis can be a great help in clarifying and falsifying interpretations. Finally, most quantitative historians also *use the computer* for handling their data and describing or analyzing it statistically. To be sure, small data sets can be investigated with a scratch pad or pocket calculator. Moreover, there is a rapidly growing field of formalized historical research such as textual analysis or data basing which does not involve statistics. But the former does not exclude the computer, while the latter often also involves word counting and eventually shades over into statistical analysis.

As a response to the deficits of philological techniques for analyzing mass data, quantitative methods impressively extend historical tools in certain areas of research. To begin with, the computer makes it possible to handle much greater masses of evidence than by laboriously sorting and resorting a card file filled with confusing and overlapping references. With a self-indexed data base, a scholar can make the computer quickly find all the relevant text passages for a specific purpose. Moreover, quantification permits greater precision of statements. When confronted with a manuscript census list, the historian no longer has to scan a portion of thousands of entries (which might be unrepresentative) in order to get a qualitative impression (or "feel") of the evidence. Instead, one can draw a statistical sample and with great confidence describe the general properties of an enormous number of individual cases quite accurately. Finally, the greatest advantage of quantitative analysis is the increased clarity and complexity of explanations which it makes possible. Far from oversimplifying the past, quantification allows the systematic consideration of a larger number of causative factors by defining and testing their relationship statistically. In a cross-disciplinary context, Eric Monkkonen argues that "quantitative history gives depth and subtlety to positivist social science while giving public policy implications to historical research" (1984). The data handling, precise description, and interpretative complexity of quantitative history can therefore remedy a double deficit, namely, the lack of time perspective in social science and lack of generality in history.

The practice of quantitative methods has, nevertheless, shown certain shortcomings which have resulted in a number of often justified criticisms. The initial overselling by cliometric zealots who wanted to reduce the entire analytical universe to a series of equations has created a backlash which stresses that quantitative methods have failed to live up to expectations. Indeed, there has been no total historiographical revolution and proponents have had to show greater modesty in their claims. For many readers quantitative research also remains boring and inaccessible. Tedious tables and formulas are certainly not as entertaining as juicy gossip about royal mistresses. But the arcana of classical philological criticism are not self-evident either. Improved training might demystify statistics, elegant style can make even numbers come to life, and well-designed graphs are often more intuitively intelligible than a convoluted narrative. Another widespread charge is that quantitative results are trivial, since they prove only what has been known already. While there is an element of truth in the contention that quantitative conclusions are rarely so surprising that they have not been anticipated in some older account, the elimination of other, equally plausible explanations through a confirmed hypothesis represents significant scholarly progress. Objections also rest on different sets of priorities: For a scholar interested in the motivation behind President Lincoln's Gettysburg address, quantitative methods appear irrelevant, whereas for a colleague fascinated by the causes of the Great Depression, they are imperative. Such real or imagined defects have prompted, in Lawrence Stone's phrase, a programmatic "revival of narrative" seeking to recreate popular mentalities (1979). In spite of their stridency, most criticisms of numerical antiquarianism or statistical dehumanization are groundless, since they invalidate the misuse of quantification rather than its proper application as an additional tool in historical research.

VARIETIES OF QUANTITATIVE HISTORY

Arguments about the merits of quantitative methods are likely to continue until their contribution to historical understanding has become so substantial as to preclude further debate. In several important research fields quantitative methods have already profoundly reoriented the entire agenda (Possekel 1990). For example, the first area to be transformed by quantification was economic history. In the 1950s and 1960s the study of economic development moved from the collection of descriptive time series to neoclassical economic analysis, called *econometrics*. This "new economic history" quickly became so rigorously statistical and vigorously theoretical that it has moved largely out of history departments into economics departments at the universities. Less interested in particular businesses or the economic life of one town, cliometricians such as D. North (1981) turned to the general and the lawlike analysis of entire economies. Preoccupied with questions of economic growth, scholars analyzed the importance of railroads "counter-factually" by asking, What if they had not been built? (R. Fogel 1964) or investigated the profitability of antebellum slavery in the South (Fogel and Engerman 1974). Provoking much controversy, these innovative works changed the terms of the debate from a focus on individuals to factors, from questions of entrepreneurship to models of development, from an occasional illustrative table to long strings of complex equations. Propelled by the theoretical and anti-contextual bent of modern economics, the transformation of economic history has been astonishingly complete, so that quantitative methods have come to dominate perhaps even excessively. But when somewhat rehistoricized and reculturalized, the stringency of the statistical and pronouncedly theoretical orientation of this cliometrics still holds promise for the explanation of a considerable part of economic development.

Another major research area radically transformed by quantitative methods has been *historical demography*. The compilation and investigation of vital statistics, initiated by mercantilist governments in the eighteenth century, has been greatly facilitated by the computer, since it involves large masses of data on "life events" such as births, deaths, and the like. The necessary older summary statistics have become easier to compute from aggregate figures or individual cases. Moreover, entire new categories of sources such as parish books or civil registers could now be transformed into machine-readable form in order to be processed statistically. Much effort went into the reconstruction of national demographic histories, such as those at the Princeton Population Research Center or the Cambridge Group for Population Research, in order to explain the "population transition" from preindustrial high mortality/nuptiality/birthrate to postindustrial stability on a much lower level (Laslett 1965; Wrigley and Schofield 1981). Inspired by the case study approach of the French journal *Annales*, another set of researchers concerned itself with "family reconstitution" in order to detect local and regional patterns of inheritance and reproductive activity. Somewhat at the borders of the historical discipline and sometimes housed in independent institutes, this quantitative demographic history developed a set of sophisticated measures and explanations of population development. But it also spurred the emergence of a nonquantitative, anthropologically oriented "family history," which explores the affective, economic, and sexual dimensions of family life in the past and in turn challenges demographers to develop more complex accounts of motivation (Maynes 1981 and Hareven 1978). One of the more exciting subfields has been the quantitative investigation of human health and disease (e.g., Bourdelais and Raulot 1987).

Closer to traditional historical concerns was the emergence of a *new political history* on the basis of quantitative methods. Encouraged by the triumph of behavioralism in political science a generation earlier, during the 1960s some American political historians began to consider whether similar concepts and survey methods might not also be applied to the study of the evolution of the political system in the past. Eventually three distinctive subfields developed out of this impetus. First, many voting or electoral studies (like the work of Lee Benson [1964]) analyzed the rich evidence of U.S. election data through the last couple of hundred years. Second, there was also much research on parliamentary behavior of representatives on the basis of "roll-call" analysis of legislative voting (by scholars such as T. B. Alexander [1967]). Finally, a cluster of analyses of the collective biographies of political elites (legislators, senators, etc.) sought to link socioeconomic background variables with political decisions on the state as well as national level (W. O. Aydelotte [1977] for Great Britain). The lively debates of the new political historians brought forth such concepts as the notion of "critical elections" in which party affiliation realigned or argued in "ethnocultural" terms of electoral loyalties. Many other political historians continued to write about power, patronage, and sectional conflict, rejecting the "new political history" as retrospective political science. But one of the pioneers of this recasting of political history, Allan Bogue, concludes persuasively: "Even if some of the criticisms are valid, much of the work of the social science historians will stand; and our conception of the political past of the United States will remain substantially altered by their efforts" (1983). This new political history has recently also found a home in Western European election, parliamentary, or elite studies, demonstrating that its methodological impulses are proving fruitful beyond the United States.

A final area of historical inquiry which has been greatly stimulated by the introduction of quantitative methods is the *new social history*. Propelled by radical democratic or Marxist concerns, this recent and most dynamic sector of historical inquiry shifted attention away from traditional elites to the often mute masses and addressed the power of social structures or customs rather than of political events. Obviously not all of the agenda, as defined by new journals such as P. Stearns's *Social History* or H.-U. Wehler's *Geschichte und Gesellschaft*, was amenable to quantification, especially when touching on collective beliefs or cultural customs. But many other concerns did and do involve quantification. For instance, the Tillys' work on collective violence is based on extracting a strike statistic from newspaper accounts (before governments collected such figures) and on analyzing the causative impact of such factors as urbanization, industrialization, and the like (1975). Stephan Thernstrom's (1964 and 1973) or Michael Katz's (1975) exemplary studies of social mobility or of class structure in nineteenth-century cities such as Newburyport or Hamilton analyze manuscript census data quantitatively. Fritz Ringer's (1979) or my own (1982) work on educational expansion and opportunity tests contemporary assertions of elitism against educational statistics in part derived from matriculation records. A complete listing of subtopics of expanding social historical fields, such as women or crime, would go on and on. In contrast to econometrics, the more open-ended subject matter and the less developed links to sociological theory have allowed quantifiers to dominate only a part of the field and forced them into a healthy dialogue with their qualitatively oriented colleagues. While they have also reshaped the research agenda through prosopography or case studies, quantitative social historians have been compelled to maintain greater methodological balance in their work.

Though quantitative methods have not nearly invaded all of historical writing, they have revitalized research significantly. To mention just a few areas, psychohistory, intellectual history, political biography, or diplomatic history have hardly been touched by quantification. But the impact of the quantitative revolution on those fields where statistics could be applied with profit has been profound. It has produced much innovative research which has answered many of the old questions and raised new ones. During the last three decades, quantification in history has also reached a certain maturity. Even skeptics admit that the civil war among historians has ended in the triumph of some of the revolutionaries within the guild. Tentative beginnings in the 1950s gave way to exciting departures during the 1960s when quantitative methods were programmatically hailed as saviors or denounced as destroyers of the profession. In the 1970s the quantitative movement succeeded in institutionalizing itself and in transforming the research agenda in a variety of fields through major substantive contributions. During the 1980s the quantitative wave seemed to have crested and receded somewhat, since trendsetting scholars turned to "softer" innovative methodologies and returned from analytical to narrative history. Due to the rise of deconstruction, the surge of feminism, and the arrival of everyday history, quantitative history is no longer the latest fad in the 1990s. Older buzzwords such as coefficients, models, and modernization have been replaced by new "in" terms like textuality, gendering, or experience and so on. But in contrast to debilitating self-doubts, research practice demonstrates that quantitative methods are here to stay in an increasing portion of historical works. Repeated surveys of the United States, Britain, and Germany (Sprague 1978 and Johnson 1988) reveal that quantification has been accepted by a major sector of the profession as a practical and worthwhile addition to historical methods to be applied as a matter of course. Hence it is necessary for productive historians to have some grasp of its procedures in order to understand its limitations and possibilities.

INFORMATION SOURCES AND LEARNING AIDS

Historians wishing to inform themselves about quantitative methods can turn to a growing number of institutionalized sources of information. Although they are a minority within the profession and may well remain so in the immediate future, quantifiers are now represented in most larger departments of history. Many colleges also offer some introductory course in quantitative methods for historians, while others force students to gather such skills in neighboring departments. Better training is provided by short courses at the Inter-University Consortium for Political and Social Research (Michigan), formerly at the Newberry Library and now at Northwestern (Chicago), or in other summer schools. Organizational progress has been even more impressive. While the original quantitative methods committee of the American Historical Association still provides some impulses, a separate vigorous scholarly organization did spring up during the 1970s, aptly named the Social Science History Association. The annual meetings of the SSHA in early November are the most sophisticated interdisciplinary forum for the discussion of advanced quantitative work anywhere. Historical data-base development is the central concern of the newly founded Association for History and Computing (AHC), based in Britain but rapidly expanding throughout Europe. Since the early 1980s an International Commission for the Application of Quantitative Methods in History (INTERQUANT) holds cross-national workshops and sponsors a program at every International Congress of Historical Sciences meeting. Much of the advance of quantitative scholarship has finally come from a spate of innovative journals such as the *Journal of Interdisciplinary History* (published at Tufts), *Social Science History* (sponsored by the SSHA), *Historical Methods* (having grown out of a technical newsletter), *Historical Social Research* (supported by the German QUANTUM group), and the latest entries such as *Histoire et Mesure* (produced in Paris) and *History and Computing* (published by Oxford University Press).

Interested students can also consult a considerable introductory literature. While they still contain some relevant information, the once exciting introductions by Edward Shorter (1971) or Charles Dollar and Richard Jensen (1971) now seem curiously out of date. Somewhat more useful is Roderick Floud's text (first released in 1973 and updated in 1979), but its British economic history perspective emphasizes concerns different from the needs of most American researchers. A series of interesting anthologies of the early 1970s (Aydelotte, Bogue, and Fogel, *The Dimensions of Quantitative Research in History*; Lorwin and Price, *The Dimensions of the Past*; or Rowney and Graham, *Quantitative History*) contain some pioneering work that is still valuable. While the show debates between William Aydelotte and Jack Hexter (in Aydelotte 1971) or Robert Fogel and G. R. Elton (1983) produced the expected fireworks, several special issues of journals provide more up-to-date insight into the current discussion without and within quantitative history: Theodore K. Rabb's essay collection on the new histories in the *JIH* of 1983, Peter Smith's issues on quantification and epistemology in the *HM* of 1984–85, and Jarausch's own survey of "quantitative history in international perspective" in the *SSH* of 1984. For the data-base ferment one might want to consult also Peter Denley and Deian Hopkin's collection on *History and Computing*

(1987) as well as Heinrich Best's abstracts of the Cologne Computer Conference of September 1988. Though the dynamic development of quantitative methods prevents the emergence of an immutable "canon," the continuing debate is producing enough practical experience with techniques and consensus on the interpretative implications of procedures to make another attempt at synthesis necessary and possible. The present introduction therefore intends to present the diverse possibilities of quantitative methods not in the breathless enthusiasm of initial discovery but in the somewhat chastened confidence of mature experience.

"Should I dare to quantify or not?" Unfortunately, there is no clearcut and generally applicable answer to this crucial question. The decision for or against quantitative methods depends above all upon the specific research problem confronted by the scholar. Since quantitative methods have no magic powers nor is the computer a futuristic toy, a rational choice presupposes a realistic knowledge of the advantages or disadvantages of quantification. Only when one understands the concrete workings as well as the intellectual implications of quantitative techniques can one decide whether the investment of time and energy into learning them is likely to yield enough interpretative insights to make it worthwhile. This text seeks to help historians choose responsibly by presenting the major steps of quantitative research from question to data to statistics to results. Its minimal goal is to convey a better *understanding* of the growing number of quantitative articles and monographs. Its maximal aim is to inspire the practical *application* of quantitative techniques in the reader's own research. This volume, therefore, strives to provide passive access to and active command of growing fields of historical research which have fundamentally transformed our vision of the past during the last two decades. Since anthropological *mentalité* history has become the latest fashion, quantitative methods can only be justified when producing superior actual or potential results. Historians cannot escape the tension between humanistic qualitative hermeneutics and quantitative social science approaches by embracing one and discrediting the other, since in principle they must use all methods available for the study of the past. Perhaps one ought to hearken back to the Enlightenment thinkers who used both approaches without compunction. The progressive Göttingen historian August Ludwig von Schlözer, for instance, defined statistics as "frozen history" and history as "statistics come alive."

2

Historians and Computers

During the last decade the relationship between historians and computers has improved dramatically. In the 1960s and 1970s this subject was somewhat mysterious and emotional, fraught with strong feelings. Traditional scholars wedded to their pencil and notepad were suspicious of the dehumanizing effect of a device about which they knew little or nothing. More adventurous historians who had managed to conquer electric typewriters sometimes held exaggerated expectations of the unlimited possibilities of "time machines." With the near universal spread of microcomputers, this emotionalism has vanished and a more sober working relationship has emerged. Few conservative practitioners would now want to give up the convenience of word processing. But while that help is welcome, the prevalent use of the PC with its laser printer as a glorified typewriter underuses the potential of computers for information management or for statistical applications. In contrast to promotional hype, the actual arrival of such advances as integrated work stations with optical disks, scanners, network connections, etc., has been slower than assumed, making predictions hazardous. But continued breakthroughs in function and price suggest that computers will play an ever increasing role in research, regardless of the feelings of many historians. Due to rapid changes in design, the following remarks can only present an interim report touching on some of the major computer uses in the field of history, discussing several basic hardware issues, and presenting a survey of current software choices.

HISTORICAL APPLICATIONS

Most often historians use the computer for *word processing*. Once dependent upon such features as electronic composing, editing, merging of documents, or automatic footnoting, few scholars are willing to return to pen and paper or clumsy typewriters and to make changes by correction fluid or paste and scissors. Especially handy for writing are built-in spelling checkers or thesauruses, not to mention the advantages of variable style sheets. If combined with laser printers, PC word processing permits the production of attractive final copies free from secretarial errors (shifting the responsibility for all mistakes to the author). Though originally conceived for office use, most continually updated packages such as WordStar, Microsoft Word, or WordPerfect offer enough features to be attractive to scholars. Moreover, specific academic programs such as Nota Bene provide even more foreign language characters and other exciting possibilities (see McWilliams 1983 or Rinearson 1986). Contained within word processors are also simple textual analysis functions such as word counts, search and replace commands, and the like. It is no exaggeration to say that the arrival of sophisticated word processors has revolutionized writing, so much so that critics are beginning to find special computer mistakes such as leftover words and sentence fragments. Since the PC increases ease and speed of composition, humanists are gradually overcoming their suspicions and accepting computers as working tools.

A growing number of historians is also employing computers for electronic *communication*. Connected by modem or more sophisticated campus networks to a central computer, even PCs can participate in the mysteries of e-mail. Convinced by superior convenience, scholars are sending messages and manuscripts to colleagues around the globe via such mail networks as BITNET or EARN. Independent of the vagaries of the postal service, this form of information exchange functions quickly, especially across great distances. Many historians also enjoy electronic access to library catalogues either locally, such as the combined UNC/Duke/State listings in North Carolina, or nationally, such as the OCLC or

RLIN catalogues (Falk 1989). Verification of bibliographic entries as well as browsing of holdings is greatly facilitated by a PC connection. Once data bases such as the Medieval and Early Modern Data Bank (MEMDB) become locally available on-line, historians will be able to call up information on their personal screens (Carlin 1989). The growing emphasis on electronic publishing by scholarly journals and university presses is also accelerating interest in electronic communication. Finally, the PC can serve as a terminal for communicating with the mainframe for the use of powerful programs of textual analysis such as SPIRES or the employment of big statistical program packages such as SAS or SPSS-X. While historians presently using e-mail are still in the minority, they do so irrespective of methodological preference or research orientation and their number increases every day.

Beyond communication, personal computers can serve as instruments for *data storage* and management. Some historians have already traded their unwieldy card files for the electronic information retrieval capacity of their PCs. Several word-processing features such as alphabetizing, indexing, and the creation of bibliographies already support the perusal of files. Moreover, the spread of hard disks or laser disks makes the storage of enormous amounts of information possible (if properly backed up against unexpected crashes). Part of regular word processing consists of managing files, such as combining chapters into a book manuscript, entering documents or tables into texts, appending bibliographies, and the like. Initially intended for creating mailing lists, most commercial data bases such as dBase IV are not designed for historical research, since their fields are too small and circumscribed. Bibliographic library programs such as REF 11 are somewhat more useful, since they allow the reproduction of complete book or article titles with some rudimentary indication of content. But the full potential of electronic data bases for historians becomes available only through more powerful programs such as FYI 3000, which allow searching not only by headings but also by key concepts within the text. Whatever program one uses, a crucial limitation of data basing is the need to tag significant passages or terms with some kind of descriptor which can be called up. Moreover, much thought needs to go into establishing relationships between files, if they are to be used as an integrated data base. With special software, the electronically stored texts can be analyzed linguistically (see the techniques presented by S. Hockey [1980]). New source material is also becoming available in prepackaged form prepared by scholarly data banks, such as the currency conversion data of the MEMDB. While many historians have been somewhat reluctant to move into this area, data basing holds great potential for facilitating their work. (For an overview of current software, cf. Brand [1984 and later].)

The most complex application of computers to historical research is their use for *statistical analysis*. Employing not only electronic data sorting, quantitative techniques exploit the microprocessor's great computational speed as a kind of super calculator capable of thousands of steps per second. This capacity has put both rudimentary and high-powered statistical techniques, once limited to a small circle of initiates, at the disposal of regular researchers. One drawback is that the information usually needs to be prepared and entered in some systematic form by being tagged or coded so that the statistical software commands will recognize and address it correctly. In quantitative work, the PC is initially employed for data entry in order to create a file and only then serves as a calculator in its own right. Commercial spreadsheet programs such as Lotus 1-2-3 were usually intended for accounting purposes and offer only the most rudimentary facilities for quantitative analysis. The historian therefore needs to resort to statistical program packages, largely designed for social scientists, and arrange his information to their specifications (for an introduction, see Lefkowitz [1985]). Another obstacle to the use of these packages is the limited power of many first- or second-generation PCs, which is often exceeded by these programs. One must either upgrade one's microcomputer by adding memory, disk storage, and a math chip or use larger computers with their vastly greater capacity and complexity. Because word processing and e-mail have become commonplace, the following comments will try to provide further guidance for data basing and statistics, those capacities least used by historians.

MICRO- AND MACROCOMPUTERS

In the computer-literate 1990s, it is hardly necessary any longer to introduce the basic features of hardware. Such quaint contraptions as the card-sorting machine of the German-American census official H. Hollerith, which made the leap from mechanical to electrical computation, evoke only a bemused smile. Gone are the days of overheated rooms filled with glowing vacuum tubes, miles of electrical cable, and clattering card readers which marked the first generation of machines. No longer do futuristic movies have evil computers like HAL, bent on ruining mankind. Though words like micro, mini, mainframe, and supercomputer have become common currency, it is important to recall that PCs are basically giant banks of electrical switches, without any innate intelligence, which can either be turned on or off. This binary character requires all information to be reduced to combinations of 1 plus 0 impulses, complicating every design. In spite of rapid technological changes, the basic structure of most computers has become stable. The brains of these machines are the microprocessors whose memory is divided into preprogrammed ROM (Read Only Memory) and accessible RAM (Random Access Memory), now measured in kilobytes or megabytes. Based on some operating system such as DOS, UNIX, or VMS, commands are entered through input devices such as keyboards and perhaps eventually voice. Programs and files are stored either on portable diskettes or large capacity hard disks. Output can be directed to screens, printers, plotters, or other devices (Norton 1983). With greater understanding of these basic features, more and more historians are becoming comfortable with such machines.

When trying to use computers, scholars face a complicated choice of whether to work on institutional mainframes or with their own PCs. For simple tasks, microcomputers have many advantages. Not only are they already familiar as word processors, but they also tend to be cheap (once the purchase outlay is absorbed, the running costs are negligible). Even most clones of major manufacturers are relatively reliable, and many universities offer some basic repair service for their own machines. Since it tends to be designed for secretaries and/or students, PC software is initially easy to use. Most programs are also interactive, responding immediately to the user's command and thereby facilitating corrections and experimentation in procedures. Finally, it is more efficient to work within the comfortable environment of one's own office without the noise and competition of a computer center. Unfortunately, PCs also have their share of disadvantages as well. Their chief drawback is the limited size of their central processor and their storage devices. Most statistical software needs considerable memory in order to run its calculations, and data bases in text form quickly exceed machine limits since word storage takes up much more room than keeping numbers. Hence most normal micros are limited to modest data sets. A couple of thousand cases with ten variables still run relatively quickly, but even doubling both parameters will slow down the processing considerably. Initially much of the PC software was also somewhat amateurish, confining the researcher to simplistic procedures without the option to employ more complex and powerful strategies. Finally, there is the vexing problem of compatibility between diskette sizes, operating systems, printers, and the like. With the arrival of the more powerful third generation of micros, based on 32-bit processors, some of these irritations have started to wane. Since they tend to do well with data entry, pilot runs, or smaller data sets, personal computers are in many ways ideal for the cottage-industry style of historical research (Jensen 1983 and McCaa 1984).

For larger and more complicated tasks, bigger IBM, DEC, or other computers will continue to play a central role. The greatest edge of these monstrous machines is in power and speed. Instead of fitting a large problem into a small PC, the historian can follow the question and the data without worrying about processing capacity. Another advantage of the mainframes is the exceedingly complex software which they offer. If a procedure exists at all, it is available there. Finally, most computer centers also provide "de-bugging" advice on software problems and statistical questions which is often invaluable in overcoming some technical hurdle. Unfortunately, the difficulties in working on mainframes are also correspondingly greater. Users initially need to learn a job control language which tends to differ from vendor to vendor. Moreover, runs generally create direct costs levied on a research account. In earlier years, when such charges were computed only for accounting purposes, this was not much of a problem, but more recently many computer centers have started to demand "hard money," which severely limits the researcher in the questions pursued. Often access to mainframes is unnecessarily difficult, requiring frequent trips to another building and becoming quite competitive during peak times. As a result of institutional preference, historical jobs usually receive low priority, making for long delays in getting results (turnaround time). Finally, mainframes tend to be down at the most inconvenient moments, such as in the middle of a large run, rendering their use somewhat unpredictable. The shift from cards to terminals for commands or data entry and the emergence of some kind of interactive batch processing has widened many of the traditional bottlenecks. But anyone who has worked on a mainframe and hunted for paper print-out in dozens of anonymous boxes has some kind of horror story to tell (see Jarausch, Arminger, and Thaller 1985).

Due to their complementary strengths, macro- and microcomputers can best be used to supplement one another. In the ideal arrangement, the PC is employed for data entry and initial pilot studies. When exploring a big data set or manipulating a large data bank, the micro merely serves as a terminal for communicating with the mainframe, thereby circumventing the problems of computer centers. This division of labor presupposes a stable line for up- or downloading data and the mastery of the appropriate communication software. In less than ideal cases, the researcher can still do the preparatory work on a PC and then take the diskettes to the computer center to have them read onto a mainframe tape. For serious statistical use, an IBM or compatible microcomputer needs a minimum of a 10 MHz cpu, 640 k or more of RAM, a hard disk with at least 40 megabytes or more, and a mathematical coprocessor. These requirements transcend all first-generation "XT" and even many second-generation "AT" PCs. A more ideal configuration would include a 20 MHz 80386 processor, a math coprocessor, a high capacity (1.44 Mb) diskette, and a fast 80 megabyte hard disk. Before embarking upon a large data-base or quantitative project, historians should investigate their institutional infrastructures to find out what kind of machines are available and how they can communicate with each other. When buying or upgrading equipment, it is crucial to go beyond the word-processing capacity and to include some communication facility such as a modem. To round out a historical work station, other features can be added such as a scanner (to read printed documents) or an optical laser disk (for permanent storage of large amounts of information). But one needs to resist commercial hype and insist on testing precisely those applications for which the machines will be used. Serious computer magazines (*Byte*), institutional consultants, or knowledgeable colleagues are the best sources of experience and advice.

DATA-BASE AND STATISTICAL SOFTWARE

The rapid development of program packages has fortunately exempted historians from the necessity to learn basic programming. Since pushing a button will have no magic result, a computer needs a series of precise instructions, called programs, which tell it what to do. Some programmers work in *assembly* language, written in cryptic ciphers to manipulate specific memory locations and processor circuits. More accessible are the *compiler programming* languages like BASIC, FORTRAN, COBOL, PASCAL, or C. Most sophisticated are the *command* languages or ready-made programs that solve standard problems. They are easy to use since their commands are formulated in something resembling plain English. Historians will need to learn a smattering of the relevant PC operating system (DOS for IBM and clones) or job control language for mainframes, expressed in semi-intelligible terms. Similarly, some understanding of communication protocols is vital for modem or network use. Menu-driven software further customizes instructions for specific applications, rendering user access even easier—at least that is the theory. While word-processing programs have grown quite elaborate, commercial data-base software and statistical packages are less easily adapted to scholarly uses. During the last few years some daring humanists have gradually developed their own text-based data bank programs. Moreover, mainframe statistical packages, created for the social sciences, have been "downsized" for microcomputers so that they can now be employed on both levels. Since data-base and statistical software are central to research, historians need to understand their basic structure, their potential, and their limitations.

Source-oriented data processing is one of the most promising approaches to the interface between history and informatics, statistics and linguistics. In contrast to the higher formalization demanded by quantification, this approach attempts to preserve as much information contained within a document as possible, using the computer for both storage and analysis. Building upon humanities computing in editing and information retrieval, historical data bases go beyond linguistic textual analysis. In principle, the purpose of source-oriented data processing is fourfold:

1. to handle large amounts of data, searching and retrieving according to complex criteria;
2. to reorder great quantities of information quickly, producing registers;
3. to present source material either in a full edition or in a compressed form such as a thematic map or temporal curve; and
4. to facilitate complex mergers of data, such as lists of names, linking one source with another.

In effect, the computer is used as a storage, sorting, and linking device, allowing endless querying of the data in the original wording. Unfortunately, this application is relatively new and still developing rapidly, making for many unforeseen problems. While there are some leading programs, often derived from linguistics, the available packages are much less standardized, unified, or widely distributed than statistical software. Since scholars have to take a more active role in adapting routines to their own particular project needs, there is much repetition of solutions and incompatibility between systems. In spite of greater difficulty, this data-base approach is attractive to many historians (especially in the medieval and colonial periods), since it retains much of the original texture of a source such as the Domesday book (cf. the methods presented in Denley and Hopkin [1987]).

Techniques of source-oriented data processing vary according to the degree of formalization. The simplest approach consists of entering a document such as a will verbatim, adding a system of markers which signal the special meaning of each significant word:

Furthermore I leave to my [P [R son] [N John]] who has been borne by my late [P [R wive] [N Judy]], whom The Lord may grant eternal blessings, on the [DB 18th February 1745] [IP the meadow]. . . .

In this preedited notation P indicates a person, R a relation, N a name, DB a date of birth, and IP some immobile property, allowing systematic retrieval and easy editing of the original text. A more formal approach enters structured input, rearranging the original wording (e.g., of a marriage register) into fields divided by mnemonic abbreviations:

groom$John/Smith#the younger/6 APR 1739/occupation = blacksmith
bride$Joan/McArburn/22 DEC 1745/status = illegitimate

This procedure has the advantage of being convertible into machine-readable form for statistical analysis but needs a more elaborate flagging during input. Historians interested in building data bases have three kinds of software available: Commercial programs work reasonably well for structured input of a source like a student register if units have similar amounts of information, fields have the same length, and the material consists of independent entries. Preedited sources can better be handled through concordance-oriented software based on a keyword in context listing (KWIC). Such programs produce either a lengthy printout of original text with additional words of context (Oxford Concordance Program) or an interactive concordance listed on the screen and limited to only specified contexts (Brigham Young Concordance). Most elaborate is the emerging historical data-base software such as the KLEIO program produced by Manfred Thaller of the Max Planck Institute at Göttingen in Germany. (For further information, see the discussion in Jarausch, Arminger, and Thaller [1985] as well as Thaller [1989].)

In contrast to the linguistic inspiration of data-base programs, *statistical software* is designed for social scientists, agronomists, or doctors dealing with quantitative problems. Its purpose is to offer scholars an impressive array of data management and analytical procedures in relatively simple form without burdening them with detailed knowledge of a programming language such as FORTRAN or PASCAL. Instead of requiring the mastery of complex mathematical formulas, statistical packages proceed by a plain language cookbook approach, providing basic recipes which only need to be applied to a particular case. Connected by some general system features, they essentially consist of separate subroutines for specific purposes which can be customized through a few standard specifications. Researchers employ commands to order certain operations, such as calling up a data set and defining or transforming the data, and to use a specific procedure, such as crosstabulating two variables (explained in chapters 5 and 8). Their profitable use rests on two essential prerequisites which must always be remembered. First, the data, such as the U.S. census listing for Fort Moultrie, have to be regular enough to be coded either numerically or as short character strings (see below, chapter 4 and appendix A):

Erving, John	50 Male	Lt. Colonel	MA
Elisa	35 Female		MA
William	17 Male (?)		MA

Second, the researcher has to be basically familiar with the analytical purpose, assumptions, and limitations of the statistical procedure employed. The computer will obediently run any routine ordered—no matter whether it is appropriate for the particular variable or illuminating for the problem at hand. Though not specifically designed for historical material, these statistical packages, once mastered, offer powerful analytical tools (Jendrek 1985).

While all statistical software is functionally similar, historians have found some leading programs more useful than others. The highly touted commercial spreadsheets, developed for manipulating columns of figures, usually lack sophisticated data management functions and complex analytical procedures. For both micro and mainframe use, a convenient and capable starting point might be P-STAT; another possibility is the statistically advanced but somewhat difficult BMDP. More popular is SYSTAT, which runs on a variety of micro- and minicomputers including IBM micros and their clones, Apple Macintoshs, and DEC VAXs. This package requires programming in BASIC for more complicated data transformation and file management tasks and suffers from some weaknesses in data-basing functions, date and time arithmetic, and maximum number of variables handled in one file and some narrowness when powerful statistical routines are required. But SYSTAT performs straightforward data entry, transformation, and analyses well and is quite easy to use (see SYSTAT 1984). Since their on-campus support and documentation tend to be more extensive, researchers would nevertheless be well advised to concentrate on two other, even better known packages which have IBM PC, mini-computer, and IBM mainframe versions.

Many historians prefer the popular SPSS-X, the Statistical Package for the Social Sciences, or its PC variant, SPSS/PC. SPSS's manuals are easy to read for nonstatisticians and nonprogrammers, its command language is the closest of the three to standard English, and its data transformation procedures are more user-friendly. But the variety of statistical techniques offered is somewhat limited (Norusis 1988a and 1988b). Most complex and powerful is SAS. The SAS system has a more complete array of simple and advanced statistical routines and its tools for complex file input and database management are definitely superior. It has excellent character and date/time manipulation capabilities and can import files from many common data-base management programs found on PCs, minis, and mainframes (SAS Institute 1985a, 1985b, and 1985c). For very special problems of linear modeling which transcend the all-purpose packages, there are programs like GLIM and LISREL. Due to fierce commercial competition, the main packages are being continually revised to include more advanced data transformations and statistical routines or eliminate "bugs" in previous versions. Preference is not a matter of religious faith but rather of convenience—in handling such problems as missing values or character strings—and of local support, since novice users are dependent upon the constant advice and clarification of their campus computer user-service organizations (Jarausch, Arminger, and Thaller 1985; Lefkowitz 1985).

In dealing with computer hardware and software, historians should steer between the Scylla of ignorance and the Charybdis of zealotry. Not knowing about the availability of certain devices or programming options often exacts a high cost in wasted labor and unexplored analytical avenues. But getting caught up in computer hype for its own sake tends to fixate a scholar's attention on technical innovation or software advances to the detriment of intellectual results. In spite of the rapid pace of development, there is no need for constant worry about having the latest gadget or using the most up-to-date program. Instead, it is crucial to ask whether a specific machine or software is doing the job for which it was acquired. Innovation has come in spurts with periods of relative quiescence, marked by detail refinement, in between. There is no need to throw away a particular configuration or version of a program for the sake of technical finesse, unless it has begun to hamper rather than help research. The time and money required for buying newer machines or learning the latest release of a program need to be weighed carefully against their real rather than presumed benefits. Whenever possible, scholars should test the solution of the problem which interests them concretely by asking colleagues or checking with other campus experts. Conferences by organizations such as the AHC or SSHA and the leading journals communicate positive as well as negative experiences. While computers produce impressive results and their future potential may be even more breathtaking, scholars should remember that hardware and software are only tools, not ends in themselves. In historical research, the intellectual question must always be dominant.

3

The Formalized Research Process

In order to realize the potential of historical computing, a formalized research process is essential. Already the establishment of computer data bases requires much systematic planning. Even more than linguistic analysis, the quantitative exploration of such files in tables and graphs yields its full benefits only when based upon a structured and controlled research design. Though in principle similar to hermeneutic or philological interpretation of texts, formalized research demands a more systematic and self-conscious approach, not leaping instinctively from document to insight, but rather carefully considering the implications of each investigative step. That is not to say that an occasional quotation or table cannot be used as illustration without much methodological awareness. But data bases and quantitative methods can only make their full contribution to historical understanding when they are applied to appropriate questions in a formal manner. Since reams of computer printout do not automatically yield compelling results, historical computer users must be willing to risk confrontation with some of the central elements of social scientific thinking. According to the recent introduction by Kenneth R. Hoover (1988), the importance of such a structured research design can hardly be overstated. Hence the uninitiated may well ask: What are quantifiable questions, how does formalized research proceed, and what are its implications for project planning?

THE PROBLEM OF QUANTIFIABILITY

At the beginning a researcher often wonders what constitutes a quantifiable historical problem. In order to make a wise decision, a student needs to consider the nature of the question, the quality of the sources, and the characteristics of the data. The term quantitative *methods* already indicates that quantification never ought to be an end in itself but rather a tool to increase historical understanding. While large areas of historical inquiry (such as diplomacy, war, ideas, biography, etc.) resist formalization, problems concerning the composition and differences of groups, trends of development, and their relations among one another seem especially suited to quantitative analysis. The fundamental *priority of the substantive question* is sometimes honored more in the breach than in the observance. Since there is no finite list of "quantifiable" topics, researchers will continually need to experiment in order to expand the territory of quantitative history. This exploratory impetus is necessary because the rapid development of data bases has made possible the scaling of source obstacles which yesterday still seemed insurmountable. But there is a danger of getting caught up in the excitement of innovation so that the logic of data processing begins to dominate the intellectual agenda and inhibits actual analysis. To guard against such tunnel vision, scholars should take great pains to develop a clear set of questions out of the secondary literature on their topics that will structure and direct their research. For the neophyte the safest path is to derive a historical problem out of a debate which already uses quantitative methods and to tackle sources which have previously proven amenable to being quantified.

The application of quantitative methods also depends upon the *quality of the sources*. The criteria of traditional source criticism apply to quantitative work, perhaps in an even more stringent way. The basic issue of reliability troubles both process-produced statistics and nonstatistical mass data. Though sources already in statistical form invite quantification, they need to be used very carefully, according to the complaint by the British statesman Disraeli that "there are lies, damned lies and statistics." Since figures are always collected with a specific and often political purpose in mind, it is essential not to adopt them on faith but to investigate their origin and intention in order to make some judgment on their likely accuracy. As will become clear later, categorization is the interpretative Achilles heel of many seemingly innocuous tables, since it rests on qualitative decisions of what belongs together or apart. The problem of completeness also bedevils quantitative historians, especially in mass verbal data. Simply put, the survival chances of information about the elites are vastly higher than of documentation about the poor. Hence otherwise appealing sources often contain a considerable amount of "missing data" which, when it exceeds 10 percent of the total, might well invalidate an entire analysis if all the missing cases turn out to belong to one category. Though there are compensatory statistical techniques (such as inferential reasoning from other attributes), no amount of fancy manipulation can make up for nonexistent information. A final consideration is the need for representativeness of the sources. For instance, using a city directory will allow a scholar to make inferences about the stable and employed population of a city (which is likely to own houses), but it will be a poor guide for migration history, since the transients are likely to be severely underrepresented, if not missing altogether (Crew 1979). If the sources are too voluminous to be used in their entirety, sampling makes it possible to work with a fraction and still arrive at conclusions about the whole. But even sophisticated techniques (such as marginal fitting) cannot make up for an unrepresentative source base (Clubb and Scheuch 1980).

Ultimately, quantifiability is also governed by the *characteristics of the data set* to be created. According to Charles Tilly, it makes sense to quantify only when dealing with a large enough number of cases (1972). Many statistical procedures are sensitive to the tyranny of small numbers and produce misleading results if the sample is too small. A rule of thumb indicates that there ought to be at least 10 times as many observations as there are variables. Especially when interpreting percentages, it is obvious that with 20 cases a shift of 1 individual creates a change of 5 percent. While a limited number of cases with many attributes might still need to be studied quantitatively, in general it is preferable to have over 100 cases at the very minimum, since otherwise it is faster to tabulate by hand. At the other extreme, however, there is no need to give in to the historian's weakness for studying whole populations, since a sound sample of smaller size will provide equally reliable results in much less time. The cases to be investigated also have to differ in some respects while still being comparable in others. For instance, if one is investigating the making of apple cider, it makes sense to compare varieties of apples (golden delicious vs. Granny Smith) but there is no point in looking at oranges. Finally, the cases also need to have enough regularity of information to be measured or at the very least to be categorized. Studying the social determinants of nineteenth-century literacy through signatures on wills is greatly simplified when there are standardized documents with the same information, such as the amount of the bequest, the occupation of the heirs, and so on (Graff 1979). The above criteria may seem to restrict the application of quantitative methods severely. But the impressive breadth of quantitative work (sketched in the initial chapter), the great variety of sources (from obituaries to business ledgers), and the astounding diversity of data sets (textual to statistical) indicate that these conditions hardly need to hamper the imagination of quantitative historians.

FORMAL RESEARCH PROCEDURE

While historians implicitly follow a certain sequence in their research, quantitative methods require an explicitly self-conscious and controlled approach. In stylized form, this process involves four distinctive steps which need to be more formalized in quantitative than in qualitative research (Hoover 1988). From a historical question about a problem, one derives a hypothesis. Out of primary sources of indicators with measurable attributes, one develops a data set. Instead of relying on intuition, one tests the quality of the presumed relationship between causes and effects with statistics. In place of a concluding impression, one confirms, modifies, or rejects the initial hypothesis and relates the results to the existing literature. An example taken from Michael Kater's (1983) and my own recent work with G. Arminger (1989) on the social and professional sources of Nazi support before the seizure of power might illustrate the essential sequence. The broad-ranging debate on the causes of Hitler's dictatorship (recently summarized by Ian Kershaw [1985]) provided the starting assumption, known as the "lower middle class" hypothesis of Nazism:

hypothesis	data set	statistics	interpretation
lower middle class people joined the Nazi party more than others before 1933	NSDAP main membership file in the Berlin Document Center	crosstabulations, categorical modeling	while lower middle class occupations are somewhat over-represented, early Nazi membership depends more on sex, age, or religion

The appropriate sources to investigate this claim were the cards of the NSDAP *Hauptkartei*, the main file of over 10 million party members during the Third Reich, from which a systematic sample of about 20,000 individuals was drawn. Instead of merely perusing some of the individual entries, the authors used contingency tables to compare all the pre- and post-1933 Nazi joiners statistically and employed loglinear modeling to evaluate the relative importance of various factors. While the result confirmed that there was some connection between occupation and early Nazi membership (workers joined less often), other social attributes such as gender (fewer women), age (more young people), or religion (less Catholics) had a stronger influence on the outcome.

How does this formalized research process work in practice? At the risk of anticipating the discussion of the following chapters, it is necessary to stress the essential steps involved. Historians often begin their thinking with something as informal as a special interest in an area or perhaps a hunch about a possible connection between events. While this general sense of question suffices for qualitative digging through diaries, correspondence, and archival documents, it is too imprecise to be proven or disproven statistically. Instead, quantitative research requires a clear statement about a relationship between factors, called a *hypothesis*, which can be expressed in a formal, logical way. The strength and direction of influence of changes in one variable on another must be specified unmistakably. Moreover, it must be possible to find measurable or categorizable indicators for this assertion so that it can be tested statistically. In social science jargon this is sometimes called "operationalizing" a hypothesis. Without a guiding hypothesis even the most impressive data set or statistical procedure is meaningless (Jendrek 1985). In the above example, the lower middle class hypothesis of Nazism was selected out of a number of competing explanations in the literature. It was relatively easy to test, since its operationalization only required investigating the social structure of the pre- and post-1933 Nazi party membership.

Instead of bits and pieces of suggestive evidence, quantitative research requires a *firm data base*. A one-line quote from a poem might be more touching than pages upon pages of statistics—but how does anyone know that it describes more than the state of mind of the author? Therefore it is necessary to construct a representative data set which consists not of occasional and haphazard note cards but of systematic entries with qualities relevant to the hypothesis. Its observations are considered "cases" and their main properties called "variables," the attributes of which are in turn known as "values." As the basic unit for which data are recorded, *cases* can be individuals, towns, transactions, votes, or any other foci of analysis. Providing information, *variables* describe a distinctive feature of a case, whereas *values* illustrate their variation from observation to observation. This formal internal structure not only makes it possible to enter documents into a computer as a data set but also allows them to be examined statistically in order to test the relationship between factors (i.e., variables). In the Nazi study, the content of the membership file structured the data set, since the cards contained only the name (thereby also the sex), party number and entry date, birthdate, residence, and occupation of the member. The case was an individual; a variable could be, for instance, the date of party entry, while a value might be the year 1925, 1926, and so on.

In place of immersion in the sources followed by a sudden insight, quantitative research demands the *testing of a suggested relationship* with statistical procedures. While statistics cannot "prove" the metaphysical "truth" of any statement, they can help examine the nature of the connections between variables assumed in a given hypothesis. Basically, this procedure involves rejecting the null hypothesis, which states that chance might have produced the same result. The kind of mathematical techniques to be used in testing a given relationship between variables are determined by the four levels of measurement: (1) *Nominal* measures assume only that categories are exclusive and exhaustive. For instance, Nazi members can be either male or female, but not both. (2) *Ordinal* measures are rank-ordered categories, implying some hierarchy of value. One might, for example, assume that college professors and industrialists were members of the elite, store clerks and craftsmen members of the middle class, and industrial workers part of the proletariat and rank them accordingly in a descending scale. (3) *Interval* measures demand a standard unit of measurement which remains constant in size. For instance, the Nazi party joining date, expressed in years, could be considered in this light, since it begins around 1920 and extends to early 1945. (4) Finally, *ratio* measures are intervals based on a true zero point. Population figures of a Nazi's place of residence would fulfill this requirement, since some party members came from hamlets with only a handful of people while others hailed from large cities with several million inhabitants. Until the last decade or so it was generally true that the higher the level of measurement, the more powerful were the statistical procedures which could be applied, but more recently statisticians have developed sophisticated analytical techniques for categorical variables as well.

In contrast to a general sense of meaning, quantitative research necessitates the *stringent interpretation* of the statistical results. The importance of this last step cannot be overemphasized. All too often scholars drown in a mass of confusing printout without coming to grips with the original hypothesis. In principle, there are three ascending levels of formality: Even the most simple procedure will already yield *descriptive* statements about the data set. Especially in cases where the research is path-breaking, such basic information about the structure or development of masses of data will already constitute considerable scholarly progress. More *analytically* promising, however, is the testing of the initial hypothesis. The confirmation, rejection, or more likely modification of the original statement about the relationship among variables ought to be the normal aspiration of a quantitative historian, since it uses the powers of the method more adequately. More demanding and possible only in a minority of cases where the data are strong enough to support theory is *model building*. The combination of several hypotheses into one model is likely to do the complexity of historical processes greater justice than the testing of a single hypothesis. However, it can only be achieved in fortunate circumstances where the data base includes enough factors and there is already a preexisting theoretical framework. Because of the dearth of information in the membership file and the lack of elaborated theory, the above Nazi study had to be content with modifying the lower middle class hypothesis and suggesting the importance of other factors, some of which (like religion) have to be investigated further in more complex data sets.

IMPLICATIONS FOR PROJECT DESIGN

This formalized process has important implications for actual research practice. The different vocabulary involved indicates the need for more planning than in traditional historical investigation. It is no longer enough to develop a detective's eye for clues and to possess a vivid imagination for putting the pieces together. Instead, generalized interest in a problem must be focused on a particular question, usually derived from existing literature. One needs to proceed from an explicit hypothesis which can be expressed as the influence of several "independent" variables (possible causes) upon one "dependent" variable (possible effect) contained in the same data set. Often it will be useful to sketch the probable relationships graphically:

independent variables:	*intervening* variables:	*dependent* variable:
	Versailles peace	
	Great Depression	
lower middle class	presidential regime	
birthdate (age)		
sex		NSDAP membership
religion		before 1933
military service		
prior politics		

Some variables may not be included in the data set (such as military service or prior political affiliation) and therefore cannot be evaluated (they might require a different investigation). Others might be closely associated with each other (religion and prior politics, for example, since Catholics tended to belong to the Center Party while the German Nationalists were overwhelmingly Protestant). In that case they might exert little influence independent from each other and one might be substituted for the other. There might also be intervening variables, such as the political hatred against the Versailles peace treaty, the economic effect of the Great Depression, or the instability of the presidential regime, which, though not changing the effect of sex or age, might impinge differently on distinctive social strata and so on (see also Childers 1983).

By providing orientation, such a conceptual map facilitates careful *sampling* of an original source. Taking a part of the data need not falsify the results at all—if the selection adequately reflects the whole. Samples only have to be representative, so that every variable studied is present in the same proportion as in the original population. Such representativeness can be insured by selecting cases randomly, that is, giving every entry the same chance to be included in the subset as in the entirety. This principle forbids taking only the interesting outliers that deviate from the norm, because impressionistic browsing falsifies the conclusions. While the statistical procedures will be discussed in chapter 6 below, it is important to note that reliable samples can be drawn in a variety of ways. Random sampling, generated by computer, is most accurate but requires running case numbers, often impossible in historical sources. Systematic selection by pulling out every tenth or fiftieth case is technically easier and can still accurately represent a document. But taking a certain letter of the alphabet can be quite dangerous since names are ethnically, racially, and religiously biased, making for potential distortions. When a particular part of the population, such as blacks, is only marginally present in a source, it is sometimes necessary to stratify a sample by including a disproportionate number in the data set and afterwards restoring the balance by weighting the rest. In general, the size of the sample is more dependent upon the number of variables to be investigated than upon the total number of cases. When done correctly, sampling can save historians endless hours of labor and nevertheless yield highly accurate results (Kalton 1983).

The formalized process necessitates continual checking of research progress. The stylized sequence of hypothesis-data-statistics-interpretation is not a rigid set of stairs but rather an ascending plane with many opportunities to loop back to the beginning. To put the matter more bluntly, each stage interacts with the others. In order to arrive at the most convincing results, it is always necessary to feed back information from one step to another in order to hone the investigative procedure. The data structure will affect the formulation of the hypothesis; the level of measurement will condition the statistical procedures to be used; both of these will influence the interpretation of the results, and so on. Such a self-correcting research design is best achieved through a *pilot study* of a small but representative part of the entire project. Taking less than 10 percent of all cases and refining the codebook, working out data entry, running some simple frequencies or other statistics, and taking a look at their results will make it possible to revise the overall approach in order to avoid pitfalls. Quantitative research is a "hands-on" process in which many problems become clear only in actual implementation. Often one finds a better solution merely in the middle of the study. In order to channel this learning back into the overall design, it helps to start with a part of the data set so as to clarify procedures. Gaining experience with the data and the programs also produces unexpected insights which ultimately facilitate the interpretative analysis. Only after satisfactory completion of such a pilot study should the production phase of any quantitative project be begun (Thaller 1982).

A pilot study allows greater candor about the relation of means to ends in research. By gaining actual experience in implementing project aims with the computer, the scholar can become more *realistic* about the amount of time and money available for the completion of the task. It is a common mistake of novices to spend three-quarters of their effort on searching out documentation and making it machine-readable while shortchanging the statistical hypothesis testing as well as the interpretation of the results. Employing a pilot study will yield more reliable estimates about the resources required to achieve the desired goal and keep the project from bogging down in the data gathering stage. Repeated analytical checks can identify the point from which the results no longer change substantially, allowing one to cease collecting information and to move on to analysis. If the scholar is in need of outside support, a pilot study will also demonstrate the feasibility of the approach and convince a funding agency that the research is likely to succeed. While the proliferation of PCs has decreased the need for massive funding, some financial assistance will usually still facilitate quantitative work. Finally, a pilot study will provide valuable hands-on experience for the project director, making it possible to instruct research assistants and supervise their efforts fruitfully. It is not enough to write a convincing grant application and then to let the staff flounder about without adequate direction. Nothing is more distressing than a project that failed to meet its promise due to unrealistic expectations.

Finally, quantitative work also requires more *documentation* than a qualitative study. It is vital to keep some kind of written record of the countless little decisions about data and statistics involved. Tables and graphs often have a deceptive objectivity which hides repeated subjective choices. While clear at the moment when they are made, these incremental changes tend to be forgotten at a later time, and their collective impact on the outcome can be considerable. Where to put borderline cases in coding (Is a master craftsman lower middle class or upper lower class?) is one such conundrum. At crucial junctures information from an internal project log must also be communicated to the reader in the ensuing presentation, be it manuscript or publication. While not every last little step needs to be retraceable, quantitative work should in principle be highly replicable. All the information which is necessary to check a table with a desk calculator or to rerun a more complex statistical procedure needs to be included if one is to avoid quantitative shamanism. That does not mean explaining chi-square for the n'th time to the weary audience, but it does involve communicating the critical decisions in transforming sources into a data set and in statistical testing so that their logic can be understood. Compared to the mysterious chemistry of "intuition," quantitative reasoning needs to remain explicitly accessible.

While it drastically reduces the complexity of reality, social scientific thinking promises greater clarity than traditional hermeneutics. By limiting the explanatory universe only to stated variables, quantitative research formulates a problem more stringently than humanistic reasoning by "insight." This reductionism makes it possible to probe the relationship between factors more deeply and to link the results via conceptual generalization. But formalized analysis loses some of the feel for the indeterminateness of the human condition. Its scientific character rests on the systematic nature of the procedure rather than on some higher kind of objectivity, since the stylization of a problem involves many qualitative decisions. Instead of engaging in an interminable debate over the priority of generalization or intuition, the researcher needs to draw on both in a self-critical fashion. While postmodern philosophical doubts have eroded the objectivity claims of social science, they need not invalidate the utility of systematic methods. Drawing inspiration from the richly textured insights of the humanities, quantification derives much of its conceptual strength from the procedures and theories of the social sciences. In its best examples, formalized historical research can, to a degree, aspire to reconcile both modes of inquiry.

4

Creating a Data Set

After becoming familiar with computers and establishing a research plan, a scholar faces the challenge of transforming an unwieldy source into a usable data set. Historians often become interested in formal analysis when discovering a mass record such as a shipping list, marriage register, poll book, or personnel file which promises exciting insights—if it could only be analyzed! Hermeneutic researchers react predictably, but problematically: Some scholars simply ignore an unmanageable source, declaring it unimportant and thereby impoverishing research. Others browse so as to "get a feel" for the document, but their impressions risk grave errors if the data are not uniform. More conscientious historians tend to select a record segment, small enough to be probed in detail but often quite unrepresentative of the whole. Finally, well-meaning researchers sometimes employ inadequate techniques such as endless card files or pencil lists which require laborious sorting and limit the exploration of variables. Such questionable procedures might have been inevitable as long as there were no alternatives, but with the maturation of historical computing, they have become inexcusable. Once convinced of the potential benefits of a more stringent approach, a researcher will wonder about how to make a source machine-readable, how to organize a codebook, and how to enter the data into the computer. These seemingly practical questions have important interpretative implications as well.

MAKING MATERIAL MACHINE-READABLE

In order to use the computer in analysis, historians must make their sources machine-readable. While textual data bases can preserve the original words, their contents have to be *coded* for quantitative analysis. The information must be formalized into cases (such as individuals), variables, or values and systematically translated into mnemonic or numerical form. For example, the 1850 census of Fort Moultrie, close to Charleston, South Carolina, contains the following entries on soldiers:

Name	Age	Sex	Occupation	Birthplace
Erving, John	50	Male	Lieut. Colonel	Massachusetts
Luther, Roland	35	Male	Captain	Pennsylvania
Wild, T. B. I.	28	Male	1st Lieut.	Maine

While the age of the residents can be entered directly into the computer as a number, the other variables such as sex, occupation, and birthplace need to be transformed into letter abbreviations or numbers. This is a simple operation for gender since there is only one alternative, with males usually assigned "M" or 1 and females "F" or 2. With occupation, there will be little dispute since the military hierarchy has clear ranks, in which major or above would receive a "MJ" or 9, captain a "CA" or 8, and 1st lieutenant a "FL" or 5. Birthplace requires a more complicated regional listing of states, such as Massachusetts = MA or 3, Pennsylvania = PA or 9, and Maine = ME or 2 (for the mid–nineteenth century). Items like civilian jobs create more problems due to competing conceptions of classification, but one could follow schemata of leading researchers such as S. Thernstrom (1964, 1973). The result is a mixture of character codes or a set of numbers for each entry:

$$01 \quad 50 \quad M \quad MJ \quad MA \quad or \quad 01 \quad 50 \quad 1 \quad 9 \quad 03$$
$$06 \quad 35 \quad M \quad CA \quad PA \quad or \quad 06 \quad 35 \quad 1 \quad 8 \quad 09$$
$$07 \quad 28 \quad M \quad FL \quad ME \quad or \quad 07 \quad 28 \quad 1 \quad 5 \quad 02$$

Underlining the importance of conceptual clarity, practical experience suggests a number of simple rules to make coding useful. (1) Above all, codes must be *clear* and unambiguous, assigning one character or number to one attribute value. Researchers should avoid combinations such as male white 60-year-olds or female black 38-year-olds, rather separating these clusters into three distinctive variables of gender, race, and age. (2) Whenever possible, codes should be *systematic,* providing for an orderly progression within a scheme. Grouping related occupations such as carpenter, cabinetmaker, joiner, etc., next to each other makes them easier to work with than if they are spread out. (3) At the same time, codes should be *complete,* reproducing all distinctions potentially important for a study. In classifying the soldiers of Fort Moultrie, all basic military ranks used in the 1850s should be included, even if they do not crop up among the first cases, since adding subdivisions after using up available numbers becomes impossible. (4) Nonetheless, codes need to be *efficient,* since the simpler the scheme, the smaller the effort! Obsessed with the desire for accuracy, some historians spend weeks developing overly elaborate systems to account for every possible variant, losing sight of their analytical purpose in the process. (5) Finally, codes also ought to be *replicable,* since it is vital to be able to trace the assignment of values if any question arises about the correctness of a decision. Running case numbers should be used so that the data point unmistakably to the original entry in the event of a discrepancy. Since binary computers cannot tolerate ambiguity, such rules reduce complex word structures into simple character or number strings (see Jarausch, Arminger, and Thaller 1985).

As much historical information is qualitative, designing coding schemes often involves categorical decisions which may predetermine the final interpretation. As illustrated in the Fort Moultrie study, some codes for variables such as sex are so self-evident that they evoke little discussion. A substantial number also draw on preexisting schemes, such as the list of states of the union at a given date. Since it would be a waste of time to reinvent an alphabetical lineup of counties, historians should follow as many of the extant categorizations as possible, provided they help achieve the analytical purposes of their studies. It is surprising how much government officials and observers have counted and classified, creating useful contemporary schemes. Often codes developed by later scholars working on related problems can also be helpful starting points if questions are similar and prejudices are accounted for. Such complex *preexisting* codes have the further benefit of making research results comparable. But many issues of classification remain controversial since they involve contradictory perceptions of social space based on incompatible theories or ideologies. Instead of vainly striving for the Holy Grail of the perfect scheme, the historian would be wiser to enter information as close to the original as possible in order to allow multiple reclassification later. One of the great strengths of the computer is its ability to sort and reclassify data endlessly, which permits the investigator to discover social fault lines empirically rather than predetermining them on the basis of ideology. In investigating Nazi support, one should first compare party membership with the original occupations and only then combine these entries into broader groups, since often the key differences occur within rather than between broader categories (Kater 1983).

Researchers face particular challenges when ordering variables based on perception. Classifying occupations into strata presents special problems such as the multiplicity of job titles, which often exceeds one-third of all cases in a data set, with bakers differentiated from pastry chefs, bread makers, and the like. Many census terms such as storekeeper are ambiguous and cover a wide range of positions from peddler to captain of commerce. Often the meaning of designations changes over time so that the physician, for example, evolves from a primitive barber-surgeon to a sophisticated, specialized doctor. Most obstacles can be overcome by proceeding *hierarchically*. If one enters occupations textually, one can sort them alphabetically and assign discrete codes before combining them via software into broader categories in successive steps of abstraction:

   1. generic occupation: pastry chef, bread maker = baker
  21. stratum: baker, shoemaker, carpenter = artisan
321. class: artisan, tradesman, farmer = old middle class

While there may be hundreds of generic occupations, there are likely to be only several dozen strata and at most a handful of classes. Such a nesting scheme is easy to use, facilitates the reassignment of occupations, and allows analytical statements of both concreteness and generality. Another solution to the occupational dilemma is the adoption of *multiple* codes for different dimensions of a single bit of information. Professions might be classified according to economic function (agriculture, commerce, industry, etc.), social status (upper, upper middle, lower middle, etc.), or political power (elite, intermediary, mass). Multidimensional coding permits the exploration of various lines of social division. By combining existing schemes with fresh insights in hierarchical and flexible codes, historians can overcome even the most difficult coding obstacles (Hershberg 1975–76; Hubbard and Jarausch 1979; and Jarausch 1988).

A final source of frustration during the coding process is the problem of missing information. If there is insufficient data on a variable, a case should be classified in a residual category of "none of the above." Especially with rank-ordered variables, this assignment may prove statistically problematic, since the catchall value does not fit the hierarchy. Completely absent values are even more troublesome, since the machine cannot distinguish between a lack of data on age or an infant at birth, aged 0 years. Computing the former as the latter when figuring out average age would drastically falsify the result. A researcher sometimes can use other sources to fill in the gaps in the record but at other times runs into a stone wall. While it is tempting to interpolate, informed guesses should never be entered into the data set as "facts." If there are no data at all, one has no choice but to leave the coding field blank or to assign a value which lies clearly outside the normal range so that it can be excluded during subsequent calculations. As long as the ambiguous or missing information remains well under 10 percent for a given variable, it is unlikely to have a drastic effect on the distribution of the remaining values. But when as much as one-third of the fields are empty, the resulting conclusions are seriously weakened, since all absent values might cluster at one end of the scale. Especially with social data, documentation for the lower strata is often scarce, leading to serious distortions of the record. During analysis the historian should therefore not just put the missing data aside but probe it particularly carefully through comparison with other variables for any inherent bias that might skew the rest of the pattern.

ORGANIZING A CODEBOOK

For the sake of clarity, individual codes for a data set must be combined into a *codebook*. In effect, this is a systematic list of variables and coding instructions precisely documenting all decisions that translate words into characters or numbers. The Fort Moultrie example begins with a short and memorable variable name, such as race, age, sex, rank, etc. Then follows the location of the information on the computer line, expressed in terms of columns since numbers might otherwise be mistaken for each other. The next entry is a detailed description of the actual coding assignment for a variable such as rank, ranging in increasing importance from 0 = none all the way up to 9 = major and above. Finally, there are instructions for special cases such as age: "Those infants who are under the age of one and whose age is given as a fraction are considered to be zero years old." Useful for identifying source abbreviations, comments can also explain difficult decisions, especially if coding takes a long time so that their rationale might be forgotten. In principle, a codebook should include the following:

Fort Moultrie Codebook (see appendix A)

Variable name	Cols.	Description	Notes
ID	1–2	numbers, beginning with 01 which are assigned sequentially to each case as it appears in the census	
AGE	4–5	the age of each person as given in the census, beginning with 01	infants less than one are considered as zero
SEX	7	1 = male 2 = female	
RANK	8	0 = no rank 1 = private and fifer	civilians enlisted men

Such codebooks aid the scholar in making the research process transparent. They illustrate the translation of a project's intellectual aims into practical decisions. By formalizing a diffuse source into defined variables, they make it possible to "operationalize" and thereby test a hypothesis. But their application requires the keeping of a careful *diary* of all implementation choices in order to insure consistency. Since a data set is only as good as the classifications on which it is based, it is crucial to keep a list of all doubtful cases so that they can be resolved in a uniform way. Difficult choices should not be made impulsively on the spot but rather reserved for later consideration in order to produce as rational and defensible a decision as possible. Whenever an assignment is changed, this practice must be noted with the case number so that the prior entries can be corrected later. Another advantage of a detailed set of instructions is the possibility of turning over the routine coding chores to research assistants. Since most of the large projects employ student labor, it is crucial to make a codebook clear enough to facilitate correct choices by semi-informed staff. A coding diary will also help keep track of who worked on what portion of the data so that inferior performance can be checked afterwards. Finally, during the coding process researchers tend to gain valuable experience in handling the data. If recorded carefully, these insights not only help to resolve disputed cases but also aid later collaborators in understanding the rationale of earlier participants who have left the project. Good record keeping is therefore not a bureaucratic drudgery but an essential requirement (cf. Thaller 1982).

Recurrent mistakes suggest that coding should be viewed not as a fixed product but as a *self-correcting process*. The gain in computer manipulability of numbers is often accompanied by an information loss. Combining pastry chefs, bread makers, and others into one number for bakers reduces the texture of the source. Much of this difficulty can be circumvented by entering data as close to the original wording as possible and using the computer to combine it into bigger groups. Premature aggregation also prevents later recombination. Dividing cities into groups according to the number of inhabitants, such as 1 = under 5,000, 2 = under 100,000, etc., makes it impossible to answer questions about villages with less than 2,000 or medium-sized towns with 10,000 to 50,000. Often this obstacle can be overcome by coding only a small part of the material and then examining the initial data with simple descriptive or analytical statistics. Such a pilot study will reveal some of the discontinuities of the data, enabling the researcher to construct categories that reflect significant differences rather than mechanical preconceptions. Often preliminary analysis of a part of the evidence yields new questions which require a restructuring of the codes. If only one-tenth of the information has been entered, it is easy to alter the categories; but when the process is virtually complete, repeating all the steps tends to be prohibitive. Hence coding results depend upon intellectual clarity as well as upon technical accuracy. It cannot be overemphasized that the historical question determines the utility of any code. At the same time, the best codebook is worthless if it is not applied intelligently.

Ultimately, coding is a necessary evil which can be both gratifying and maddening. A researcher will gain some pleasure from transforming verbal documents into orderly columns of figures. But most scholars chafe at the repetitiveness of a task which numbs the mind. If data are entered in marked text form, the computer can, with some programming effort, do the translating itself on the basis of instructions that replicate the codebook (*postcoding*). Variable tagged entry is especially useful in cases of uneven record length, since it provides considerable flexibility. The alternative of *precoding* more regular information by badly paid assistants requires constant monitoring, through sampling every tenth entry, in order to eliminate systematic errors. Though the routine aspects can often be delegated, the difficult decisions that crop up intermittently require expert judgment. Much categorization rests on qualitative choices which need contextual experience. While military hierarchy facilitates classifying ranks, the assignment of occupations to strata and classes continues to be difficult. In the end, the analytical purpose of the study must guide decisions on which categories to adopt and which source distinctions to preserve. The best practical procedure is to code only for a couple of hours per day in order not to lose control over the process. To produce reliable results, researchers should avoid the popular extremes: Transforming words into numbers mechanically risks deforming evidence dangerously. Elaborating ever new wrinkles in complex schemes tends to prevent actual analysis (see also Morris 1990).

ENTERING THE DATA

After a codebook is developed, the data must be physically entered into the computer in order to be available for analysis. In principle, the fewer steps that intervene between the source and an electronic file, the smaller the chances are for making errors on the way. In practice, data entry is somewhat circumscribed by the location of the document and the availability of technology. If a source cannot be moved next to a terminal or PC, the scholar must transcribe the original entry by typewriter or hand. If a file can be copied or transported, this step can be skipped and the historian will code directly from the original. Cheap copying has now obviated transcription except in rare cases, and the proliferation of computers has simplified the actual data entry. A couple of decades ago, this process was still complicated. First the code numbers had to be written onto coding sheets, one line of which contained 80 spaces. Then the information from these sheets was laboriously punched onto cards which had to be read into the computer in order to be stored on tape (Shorter 1971). A better alternative was entering data via video terminal at the university computing center. Coding from source or transcription directly into CRTs eliminated the intermediary step of coding sheets, but it required learning a text editor as well as frequent saving of information, since capacity was often limited. Moreover, a sudden downtime could wipe out hours of work. Finally, at peak periods there could be stiff competition for access to video terminals, and working conditions in computer centers were sometimes problematic, making it hard to concentrate on prolonged coding.

The spread of microcomputers has further facilitated data entry. Currently most data are entered on PCs and stored on diskettes or hard disks. With instant printout of columns of figures, errors can be corrected quickly. The working environment is also usually more conducive to concentration. Some archives have even begun to permit the use of portables so that manuscript materials can be transcribed or coded directly at the source. Optical scanners speed the entry of standardized text as well. The drastic drop in their prices has made them more widely available than the once-expensive Kurtzweil machines. But scanners recognize only clear print and must be trained to pick up foreign letters, and their input still needs to be formatted and/or coded. While offering many advantages, coding with PCs also has some drawbacks. Originally, the numbers had to be entered with a clumsy text editor, such as EDLIN for IBM machines. Since its formatting characters were incompatible with statistical programs, word-processing software could only be used if the data were saved as an ASCII file. But the leading statistical packages have recognized this difficulty and are now supplying basic editors and data entry programs of their own. Unlike coding sheets, simple PC editors have no visible squares to put figures into, making column alignment sometimes tricky. For small projects, the novice might want to skip a space between each variable so that alignment can be checked visually. For more complex data entry, the researcher should employ a screen formatting program which places clearly labeled "boxes" on the screen to control the location of information in a file. Throughout the coding and data entry, it is important to keep copies of each stage of the process so that the number strings can be traced back to an original wording when errors need to be tracked down and corrected.

Once the data have been entered, they can be *stored electronically*. No longer is the information preserved on cumbersome decks of cards which tended to spill out of their boxes and had to be protected according to the slogan "Don't fold, spindle or mutilate!" On large computers, data are now stored on on-line disks or magnetic tape, while on microcomputers they are usually kept on floppy diskettes or hard disks. Unfortunately, all of these storage media are susceptible to destruction by a variety of bad twists of fate such as accidental (or malicious) erasure, disk head crashes, or tape breakage. Hence it is essential to back up one's data in a different location, preferably on another medium that is unaffected by the hazards of the first. Once a suitable storage place and form has been found, the researcher should carefully consider which versions of the data set should be preserved. Because historians are likely to transform their information during analysis, it is important to store the raw data in original form separately. With subsequent refinement, a more advanced working copy will become the actual workhorse of the analysis and must remain easily accessible. But should something happen, such as a power surge, to wipe out the most recent versions of the data, the scholar must always be able to return to the initial copy and retrace the subsequent steps. Since electronic storage is cheap, it is better to build in some redundancy than to run the risk of an inadvertent keystroke, a slipped power plug, or some other accident obliterating hundreds of hours of intellectual labor. In spite of their vulnerability, however, diskettes, hard disks, and tapes are much more convenient than cards.

ESTABLISHING A SYSTEM FILE

After coding and entering the data, the next step is the creation of a *system file* which can be read and manipulated by statistical software. In order to allow a program package to address the data, the computer does not just need strings of digits but must also have some information on what they represent. As an electronic version of the codebook, a system file consists of short memorable variable names, longer descriptive definitions, formatting information, and the data itself. First, a program such as SAS has to be notified to begin a file:

DATA SOLDIERS;

A data set should have a clear and simple *name*, provided that is has eight or fewer characters and begins with a letter. Then the computer has to be told where the raw data file is located, such as on a PC:

INFILE 'A:MOULTRIE.DAT';

Next, the program requires a description of a raw data record, telling the machine in which columns a particular variable resides:

INPUT ID 1–3 RACE 4 AGE 5–6 SEX 7 RANK 8 . . . ;

This command indicates that the identification number is located on columns 1–3, the variable race in column 4, age in columns 5–6, etc. In SAS such an input statement is written in free format, always listing the data in the same sequence, separated by a blank space. Since words and numbers are treated differently, the computer also has to be told whether the data are alphabetic, signified by a $ sign after the variable, or numerical. Data stored in dBase IV files or created by Lotus 1-2-3 files can also be imported by PROC, DBF, or DIF (see SAS Institute 1985a, 1985b, and 1985c).

To be addressed successfully, variables also have to be named and labeled. Since most programs limit *variable names* to eight characters and exclude statistical keywords, they should be brief, unmistakable, and mnemonic. However, *variable labels* can be longer and more descriptive:

LABELS OCCUPATN = 'SOCIAL CLASS OF JOB';

For the sake of intelligibility, it is also useful to provide labels for the specific values of qualitative variables, especially in long and complex codes. In reading pages of printout, who could recall that 41 of the Moultrie occupational code designates a baker? In SAS this operation is somewhat cumbersome:

IF OCCUPATN = 41 THEN OCCLABEL = 'BAKER';

Only when the values of a variable like age, expressed in numbers such as 21, are immediately understandable by themselves is there no need for special labels. Missing values should either be declared separately so that they are not considered as indicators or left blank so they are excluded from calculations. Fortunately, a system file has to be defined in this elaborate manner only once, since it can then be saved and immediately used the next time.

The result of this laborious transformation process is the *data set*. Instead of confronting an endlessly confusing mass source, the historian can work more easily with a computerized and coded file. Once transferred from the page to an electronic medium, the data can be manipulated by the computer. The information is either formalized according to symbolic tags for textual interrogation or translated into strings of numbers amenable to statistical analysis. Through pre- or postcoding, ambiguous document entries become stylized into firm cases characterized by a uniform number of variables with different values to be investigated. Instead of being magical, this transformation from text to computer code is labor-intensive. Since even scanners require considerable additional work, the majority of a historical project's research effort often goes into making the material machine-readable. It is therefore important to have no illusions about the amount of effort required to prepare a source for computer analysis. But the potential rewards are also considerable. Surpassing the capacity of traditional card files, electronic sorting allows recombination of information, crucial for family reconstitution in demographic research. The speed and complexity of testing hypotheses statistically are equally impressive. In order to make a wise choice, the researcher needs to weigh the evident cost against the likely analytical gain. If the number of cases is at least 50 and the number of variables over 5, their investigation begins to exceed the powers of pencil and pocket calculator. Since historical computing has been getting cheaper, the decision depends more than ever on the significance and complexity of the historical question.

5

Managing a Data Base

O nce the data have been entered into the computer, historians often become impatient for research results. While they can take pride in the successful completion of the preparatory phase, researchers will only reap the full benefits of their labors if they process their information carefully. Excessive haste tends to lead to underinterpretation of the data. All too often the intellectual yield of a lengthy project is disappointing because the scholar assumed that a few keystrokes would magically produce output that would answer all questions. Unfortunately, historical computing is more complicated than that. Between the creation of a data set and its linguistic or statistical analysis intervenes the important stage of data management. A historian has to become familiar with the basic logic and operation of program packages. In order to be reliable, the data in a system file need to be checked and cleaned systematically. Usually the computerized information must be transformed, aggregated, or recomputed for the sake of hypothesis testing. Many projects also involve data from different sources, requiring individual records to be linked from birth, marriage, and death registers or wills and deeds. During these procedures a simple data set may gradually grow into a complex data base. Historians will realize the analytical potential of their data only if they do not view computers just as giant calculators but explore their impressive powers of data management as well.

WORKING WITH PROGRAM PACKAGES

Though their thick manuals may seem forbidding, statistical packages basically have a simple structure. In spite of stylistic differences between SPSS and SAS, such as the use of the period or the semicolon to differentiate steps from each other, the fundamental architecture of the programs is quite similar. First, the leading packages include data definition statements, such as INPUT in SAS, which help define the format of the raw data. A second set of instructions allows data transformation by algebraically computing new variables from existing ones or by recomputing or aggregating particular values. A third group of procedures rearranges cases by selecting subgroups and sorting or merging related files. These commands are essential for tailoring variables to a specific analytical purpose. The relationship between social status and wealth in Fort Moultrie, for example, can more easily be explored when occupation is recoded into 5 classes than if all 82 categories are used:

IF OCCUPATN LT 11 THEN SOCLASS = 1;

Comprising the core of the programs, a fourth set of routines offers a wide variety of descriptive or analytical statistical procedures. These powerful routines, varying from simple frequency counts to complex regression analyses, produce the desired calculation with more speed and less chance of human error than traditional methods. One can compare the age and rank of Fort Moultrie soldiers with:

PROC FREQ;
    TABLES AGE * RANK;

Finally, there is a cluster of output commands such as PROC PRINT, specifying the display or printing of data (Lefkowitz 1985).

Programming with such a package consists of a series of simple steps. Almost every statement begins with a keyword, specifying the activity, followed by detailed instructions on how to perform it. After activating the package, the user only needs to follow a logical progression: (1) A specific file has to be called up by indicating its location, such as on drive C; (2) commands should be issued to tell the program what to do with it, such as PROC FREQ. For instance, printing the frequency distribution of all Fort Moultrie variables requires the following SAS/PC commands:

```
LIBNAME IN 'C:\';
PROC FREQ DATA = IN.MOULTRIE;
RUN;
```

The command menu opens a variety of choices for dealing with a file. Data definition and manipulation commands, such as PROC SORT, instruct the program how to define and transform the data at hand. Procedure commands, such as PROC FREQ, call up a specific statistical routine and include a number of options, such as different sets of statistics, which provide great flexibility in customizing the program for a particular purpose. Operation commands, such as RUN;, tell the package to execute the previous statements. If interactive, the program offers execution messages, signaling what it is doing at any given time. When all turns out well, the desired result will be displayed on screen or printed out. Should something go wrong, the package sends error messages (which can be deciphered with the help of the manual). The mainframe computer also issues a job status code indicating the completion or failure of a task.

Beginning to use a program package is a bit like learning a foreign language through Berlitz tapes. The advantages are obvious: By employing their tongue, one can converse with the natives and get them to do whatever one wants, bypassing an interpreter. Instead of laboriously explaining a problem to an expensive programmer, historians can now directly communicate with the computer. Moreover, they do not have to master all the mysteries of programming and can make do with prepackaged pidgin commands. Through their new skill, scholars gain impressive speed and power of analysis. The disadvantages only emerge through experience: Though greatly simplified, program packages have their own syntax and vocabulary which needs to be learned sufficiently. The data also must be prepared through coding in order to be intelligible for the software. The novice will make mistakes, resulting in miscommunication with the machine. There may be some initial disorientation in the strange and glitzy world of pop-up color screens, menus, and other recently commercialized features. The ability to place an order will occasionally tempt the user to issue instructions for the fun of it, without sufficient awareness of their interpretative implications. Fortunately, most of the drawbacks are only temporary and are remediable by outside help. Computer centers frequently offer introductory short courses in SAS and SPSS; they maintain a sometimes helpful user service that can be consulted about software questions; they also provide file copies of the thick program manuals which can be perused for solutions to statistical problems. Though they should try not to get bogged down, historians would be well advised to learn enough of a package to be comfortable with its use.

CORRECTING ERRORS

Before a data set can be analyzed statistically, the mistakes which have crept in during its production must be located and corrected. Since the results depend largely upon the reliability of the information on which they are based, *data cleaning* is essential for the quality of quantitative research. Even with painstaking effort, repetitive tasks such as transcription from the original source, entering information into the machine, and translating words into codes generate a surprising number of errors. Especially if underpaid student assistants are employed, as much as 10 percent of the data can be faulty due to human fallibility. The simplest mistakes are *mechanical*. In transcribing or entering data, lines may be mixed up, spaces skipped, and keys hit inadvertently. The best remedy for such inaccuracies is a *visual check* of the raw data printout, which can be undertaken even before completing a system file. If variables are divided from one another by a blank space, simply going over column alignment will catch many problems. When marked on the printed form, such errors can be corrected by calling up the data and using a text editor. Most packages can also print out the columns of values with their names or labels for all variables, thereby identifying those cases which have no text and must be mistaken. More difficult to catch are simple typing errors transposing several otherwise legal digits. One might want to run through one-tenth of all data to establish their likely frequency. As long as they do not occur more than once in every 100 cases and have no systematic pattern, they can be ignored (see also Jarausch, Arminger, and Thaller 1985).

Another strategy for catching entry errors is *logical checking* for plausibility. If a case's value for a variable falls outside the borders set up by the coding scheme, it is bound to be wrong. Such numbers or characters represent implausible conditions, such as a third gender, people aged over 100 years, places that do not exist, and the like. This kind of mistake can be controlled quite easily. By checking the frequency distribution for each variable, one can spot the values beyond the codebook boundaries which are patently nonsensical. The computer only needs to be instructed to select all these cases and to print them out, line by line. With SAS for the Moultrie data, this procedure might look as follows:

```
DATA ERRORS;
SET SOLDIERS;
IF SEX GT 2 THEN SEXERR = 1;
IF AGE GT 100 THEN AGEERR = 1;
IF BIRTHPLA GT 50 THEN BIRTHERR = 1;
IF SEXERR = 1 OR AGEERR = 1 OR BIRTHERR = 1;
PROC PRINT;
```

The computer can also check by identifying an improbable result in comparing two variables with each other in crosstabulation. Should a logically empty cell, such as for female officers in the army during 1850, suddenly contain information, there must have been a mistake. The offending entry can be located fairly simply:

```
IF SEX EQ 2 AND RANK GT 0 RANKERR = 1;
```

A careful look at the resulting printout will reveal if there is a pattern to the errors or whether they occur at random. Systematic mistakes can be recoded by computer; if, for example, in SEX many 2's were misentered as 7's, it would be easy to convert them back into 2's. However, random slipups must be corrected individually by a text editor.

More dangerous are *coding errors*, since they tend to distort the data systematically. Such mistakes can occur because information in the source may be invalid, since the census taker might have misunderstood an answer. Here only the traditional canon of her-

meneutic source criticism can help. Coding errors also crop up because of sloppy procedure. An assistant who has to use additional
references, such as a nineteenth-century geographical dictionary, to
classify a variable like the size of a city may not be able to find a
particular town and just guess at a value. Only repeated quality
controls during the actual process can spot this kind of problem.
Finally, there is the danger of inconsistency. Increased practice with
a source often produces additional information which prompts a
different assignment—for instance, moving an occupation to another part of the class scheme. If recorded carefully in the coding
diary, such a change need not be problematic. Prior cases, already
entered, can be called up by computer and corrected collectively, if
they can be separated from others in the same category, or individually, should that prove impossible:

IF ID LT 500 AND OCCUPATN = 41 THEN OCCUPATN = 81;

But if arbitrary changes are not documented, only random *reliability control* will have a chance of success. A small portion of the
entire data set should be recoded, preferably by another researcher,
and the results compared by computer. If errors are less frequent
than 1 percent, there is nothing to worry about. Should mistakes be
systematic, they can be corrected through recoding. Only if they
occur in more than 5 percent of all entries may the entire coding
process have to be repeated from scratch.

MODIFYING THE DATA

The computer's ability to transform data is another essential tool
for historical research. Instead of painfully shuffling index cards, a
researcher can use the sorting and combining capability of program
packages to tailor the variables of the data set in order to describe a
population more accurately or test a particular hypothesis more
effectively. Especially if data are entered in close to source form, the
bewildering variety of variables and values will often need to be
reduced in order to make meaningful interpretative statements. If
one wanted to investigate the relationship of age and rank in the 81

individuals of the Fort Moultrie data, one would need to compare a range of 50 years to 10 military levels. Such a table of 500 cells would be too unwieldy for analysis. If one grouped the ages by decades, the printout would shrink to a more manageable size. This modification requires the creation of a new variable called decade:

IF AGE LT 20 THEN DECADE = 1;
IF AGE GE 20 AND AGE LT 30 THEN DECADE = 2; etc.

Since 50 cells are still cumbersome to deal with, a scholar might want to simplify the matrix further by collapsing ranks into nonsoldiers, enlisted men, noncommissioned, and officers:

IF RANK = 0 THEN MILITARY = 'NONSOLDIER';
IF RANK = 1 THEN MILITARY = 'ENLISTED';
IF RANK = 2 OR RANK = 3 THEN MILITARY = 'NONCOMM';
IF RANK GE 4 AND RANK LE 9 THEN MILITARY =
'OFFICER';

This *recoding* of 10 ranks into 4 military levels reduces the table to an eminently workable 20 cells. Such compression has the great advantage of distributing values more equally, since in a small garrison there will be few officers, which, when separated individually, create statistically problematic empty cells (Jendrek 1985).

Beyond collapsing values, program packages offer other, more complex and powerful data modification routines. In studying race relations in Christ Church Parish, Charleston, one might want to *sort* the cases by computer according to white, mulatto, or black:

PROC   SORT DATA = CHRISTCH;
        BY RACE;
RUN;

If one were particularly interested in comparing the English with the German-speaking foreign-born soldiers in Fort Moultrie, one could simply *select* the nonnatives and ignore the rest during subsequent steps of analysis using a subsetting IF statement:

IF BIRTHPLA GT 30;

Conversely, one might want to delete the blacks:

IF RACE NE 1 THEN DELETE;

Such IF statements are governed by simple Boolean logic and expressed in comparison operators such as less than, greater than, equal to, etc. When studying the social and economic characteristics of New England counties (see appendix A), a historian might want to know the size of the labor force in manufacturing. Instead of recombining the separate variables female workers and male workers by hand, one can simply order the machine to *compute* the total:

TOTLABOR = FEMLABOR + MALLABOR;

Any of the simple arithmetical procedures, such as subtraction, addition, multiplication, or division, apply to recombining variables mathematically. If a data set representing a sample is biased, but the overall distribution of the population from which it was drawn is known, a researcher can also *weight* the cases with a factor to restore the correct proportions.

Modifying data is not an onerous chore but an important analytical opportunity. Clearly, the researcher needs to proceed with caution, especially in aggregating, since much discrete information can be lost by collapsing values or variables. But the converse question must also be posed: Are all distinctions essential for the interpretation? In complex variables such as occupation, the hierarchical structure of the codebook already implies a higher level of analysis. If combination, such as designating all jobs from professional to hotelkeeper as "high white collar," is already built in, the scholar will rarely hesitate to move to the next plane. But even when the coding scheme does not directly reflect larger entities, it may be useful to group values together. Often geographic data such as place of birth is easier to handle when combined into regional clusters (New England, Middle Atlantic, etc.) rather than treated on an individual state level. Fortunately, the computer permits data modification choices to be made empirically. In spite of the attendant aggravation, all variables should initially be checked in their disaggregated form by simple frequency counts or comparisons with each other. Patiently read, the pages of confusing printout will reveal bunching as well as gapping of values. The sensitive historian will base grouping decisions on these discontinuities within the data. Once identified, the clusters and fault lines facilitate informed recombination of surprising boldness. While description needs concrete texture, statistical analysis often requires aggregating variables in order to construct economical models. Data modification allows scholars to move carefully from the specific to the general.

LINKING RECORDS

If essential information resides in more than one source, researchers will need to link records. Many interesting questions about the past can only be answered by bringing together evidence from several documents. If one wanted to find out the wealth of Fort Moultrie soldiers beyond their real estate holdings, one would have to search the Charleston tax lists by name and match their content with the census register. Simple records can be linked by hand during coding. Especially when the length of the lists to be compared is grossly unequal, it is preferable to code the short and circumscribed roster while scanning the more extensive register visually. While investigating student radicalism, it would be easier first to create a computer data set of activists, based on newspaper accounts or police lists. Then one might want to identify the rebels in the university matriculation registers and fill in the remaining details on major, religion, father's profession, and the like (Jarausch 1982). While four-fifths of the entries can usually be matched without difficulty, a significant minority will resist linkage due either to incomplete information or to erroneous record keeping. In order to resolve as many of the problem cases as possible, the historian should proceed by probability, drawing upon as much additional information as possible and excluding logical implausibilities. When birthdate is available, this variable often produces positive identification, since shared birthdays are quite rare. If the additional coding requires more effort than searching visually, records had best be linked by hand.

Larger and more complex linkages should take advantage of the sorting and merging capacity of the computer. When lists are roughly of comparable size and cases can be clearly identified either by name or number, machine matches will be faster and more reliable. If one wanted to investigate the size and justice of the military pension system, one might seek to link the surviving company rosters of the revolutionary war with the rolls of veterans later indemnified by the government. Since both of these populations would be interesting in their own right, they ought to be entered as separate data sets. Matching cases requires (1) sorting by an unmistakable name or unchanged identification number; (2) adding an additional control variable such as birthdate so as to exclude spurious linkages; and (3) carefully listing all irreconcilable entries for later hand matching. Written in SAS, such linking of the data sets, named ROSTER and VETROLL, requires the following steps:

```
PROC SORT DATA = ROSTER;
     BY  NAME   BIRTHDAT;
PROC SORT DATA = VETROLL;
     BY  NAME   BIRTHDAT;
DATA PENSION;
     MERGE  ROSTER (IN = INR)  VETROLL (IN = INV);
     BY NAME  BIRTHDAT;
IF (INR AND NOT INV) OR (INV AND NOT INR)
     THEN PUT _ ALL _ ;
```

While somewhat cumbersome, the above procedure would merge thousands of cases in a revolutionary war roster and veteran support roll quickly and accurately. Moreover, it would also generate a list of nonmatches that could be combined, as far as plausibility might allow, by hand. If the unlinked rest is small and its character does not deviate from the successful mergers, the failed matches can safely be disregarded in further analysis.

The biggest difficulty in linking records is the great variety of spelling in the past. The simple surname Robbins can occur in parish registers as Robins, Robens, or Robbyns, just to suggest a few variants. Since statistical software cannot tolerate ambiguity, names and other attributes, such as occupations, need to be standardized in order to be matched. Family reconstitution projects frequently encounter the problem of having to link individuals or their attributes (birth, marriage, and death) in the same source or between sources. Hence demographers have developed a number of solutions such as SOUNDEX, based on the principle of breaking names down into sound-producing elements and assigning codes to them. Some spelling variations rely on simple shifts of consonants or vowels such as *f* for *ph* or *i* for *y*. Others are more complex deformations of pronunciation based upon local dialect. In complicated linkages of massive numbers of scanner-entered data, large research enterprises such as the Philadelphia urban history project or the Cambridge Population Group have created a scoring system that uses all other available information such as age, birthplace, etc. to establish potential compatibility (Hershberg 1975–76, and K. Schurer in Denley and Hopkin 1987). In additional passes through the material the researcher probes these scores and accepts or discards successive matches of the more recalcitrant entries. Once all plausible identifications have been added to the new composite data set, it is better to desist than to make questionable guesses. When confronted with massive record linkages, historians should not reinvent the wheel but rather start with prior software developed for similar projects and adapt it to meet their particular needs. (For a successful example of transatlantic matching, see Kamphoefner [1987].)

The cumulative effect of data modification and record linkage is the transformation of original data sets into a *data base*. While there is no clear definition of this term, most commentators agree that it involves the storage of data, large in size and daunting in complexity. Though many data bases eventually involve numbers, their basic material generally tends to be stored in words, close to the form of the original source. Due to the limitations of software, the first-generation data bases were largely structured *hierarchically*: They preserved information in formatted files which combined data with imbedded commands so that it could be manipulated through a specific control language. One such example would be the transformation of the Fort Moultrie and Christ Church Parish records into two similar SAS system files based upon the same codebook. More recent efforts have been proceeding *relationally* and store the original wording in open-ended files accessible to different kinds of software. Such an approach would enter the Charleston military and civilian records in source form as separate text files, with variables defined either by location or special markers. Due to their greater needs for storage space, data bases quickly outstrip the memory capacity of first-generation PCs and require voluminous hard disks, laser disks, or mainframe access. But the relational approach allows great freedom in software, starting with commercial products such as dBase IV, passing through historical packages such as KLEIO, and ranging all the way up to programming languages such as PROLOG. The potential to store information in its raw form, amenable to a variety of qualitative and quantitative analyses, has made data bases particularly attractive to historians as a kind of electronic archive (see Denley and Hopkin [1987] as well as Best [1988] and Greenstein [1989] for new examples).

In spite of much enthusiasm, the research promise of data bases still faces considerable problems. By appealing to the collector instinct, this approach is intuitively congenial to scholars accumulating knowledge about the past. The ease of information storage, retrieval, and management facilitates many central tasks of historical research. Moreover, data basing is analytically neutral. Humanists interested in texts can reproduce their original wording in editions, compile dictionaries from them, and analyze their structures linguistically. Historical social scientists fascinated by generalizations and theories can test their hypotheses statistically. However, the rapid proliferation of data bases during the last decade is leading to an information chaos, with hundreds of projects proceeding independently and using incompatible methods. The lack of communication within and between countries has triggered some efforts at standardization which have yet to bear tangible fruit (Thaller 1986 and Genet 1988). During its initial stage, the data-base impulse has generated more procedural discussions about optimal management structure than substantive conclusions expanding historical knowledge. Due to the intellectual effort and expenditure of resources required for the establishment of context-sensitive data bases (Thaller and Müller 1989), some scholars have gotten caught up in the process of refining their electronic files to the detriment of producing substantial results. Recent hardware development and software advances have made data basing one of the most promising historical frontiers. But in the excitement over the great potential for multiple use, secondary analysis, and data libraries, scholars should keep a sense of perspective: Even the most impressive data base will only contribute to understanding the past if its contents are further analyzed in linguistic or statistical form.

6

Data, Information, and Statistics

After laboriously creating a data set, the historian will want to extract meaning from the machine-readable material. While linguistic analysis can reveal textual characteristics, the accurate description of large amounts of numerical information and the testing of hypotheses require statistical analysis. Unfortunately, popular myths complicate the use of statistics unnecessarily. For some technical minds, numbers seem more valid than words because of the precision which they suggest. But researchers find out quickly that the accuracy of figures often is an illusion which depends upon the quality of measurement of the phenomena observed. For some humanistic souls, statistical inference possesses a magical quality, largely because its procedures transcend common sense. However, investigators soon realize that statistical reasoning only involves a more formalized logic which requires the employment of correct procedures. Finally, some neophytes mistakenly claim that their figures "prove" a certain result with finality. Nonetheless, historians rapidly discover that with numbers one can only assess the probability of relationships, making them likely hypotheses rather than definitive truths. To avoid the misperception that statistics always lie, one must understand the peculiarities of numerical reasoning, the principal steps of sampling, the implications of levels of measurement, and the basics of hypothesis testing. Subsequent chapters will proceed from descriptive to inferential statistics, progress from one to several variables, and finish with a glimpse at even more high-powered, recently developed methods.

STATISTICAL REASONING

Statistical analysis can be thought of as a process that distills information from data. A collection of numbers by themselves seldom imparts useful insights. Rather, the features of and relationships within the data can only be understood after careful statistical analysis. As discussed in chapter 2, the information in the data is based on measures of various characteristics taken on a number of entities under investigation. The objects and attributes to be examined are determined by the research problem or question under study. The entities are usually referred to as units of analysis, observations, or simply *cases*. For historians, they might be individuals, counties, marriages, farms, shipments of goods, or congressional votes. The characteristics measured are generally called *variables* because their values vary from case to case. For example, a researcher interested in soldiers in pre–Civil War garrisons in the South might collect data on the troops in a particular area. Each soldier would be a case, while his attributes such as age, rank, birthplace, and marital status would be variables. Such a data set can be visualized as a matrix (like table 6.1), with each row denoting a case and each column corresponding to a variable.

The particular information sought from a set of data depends on the broad research problem which an investigator had in mind when the material was collected. In order to be answered, a larger question must usually be "operationalized" by being broken down into a series of smaller queries which are amenable to statistical analysis. For instance, a scholar's general concern with troop characteristics might translate into several specific steps:

1. What is the typical age of this group of soldiers?
2. Are the officers usually older than the enlisted men?
3. Do a soldier's real estate holdings increase with his age?
4. Does rank also influence the value of a man's landed property?
5. If the value of real estate can be inferred from a soldier's age and rank, does the prediction hold as well for immigrants as for native-born Americans?

Table 6.1 *Characteristics of Soldiers at Fort Moultrie, Charleston Harbor, S.C., 1850*

	Name	Age	Rank	Birth-place	Marital Status	Prior Occupation	$ Real Estate
				Variables			
Cases	Erving, J.	50	Col.	Mass.	M	Officer	2.500
	Luther, R.	35	Cpt.	Penn.	S	Officer	1.500
	Wagner, G.	26	Sgt.	Ga.	M	Soldier	400
	Alger, L.	22	Pvt.	Ireland	S	Laborer	?

Note: A complete listing of this data is contained in appendix A.

None of these questions could be easily answered through a detailed, case-by-case inspection of the Fort Moultrie data, particularly if the number of soldiers ran into the hundreds or thousands. Instead, every query requires general statements about the range of values of one variable or the relationship between the values of several variables that do not unduly distort the detailed information provided by each case.

Such generalizations can be made in the form of summary figures, called *descriptive statistics*, which portray the chief characteristics of the data. For example, a descriptive statistic with which almost everyone is familiar—the average value or, more formally, the mean—may yield a compact but accurate picture of the typical age of Fort Moultrie soldiers. Such statistics sacrifice the detailed information on each value of a variable for every case in favor of a broader but more useful statement regarding the entire set of values. In a sense, descriptive figures provide a feel for the main outlines of the data. More complex procedures can also represent the relationship between variables. When probing the connection between maturity and wealth, one might want to use the correlation coefficient which summarizes the degree of accuracy with which value of real estate could be predicted from age. This measure provides the basis for a generalization about the relationship between these two variables that could not be divined by simply inspecting the data for each soldier. Since they measure aspects of a purported relationship, such *analytical* statistics are crucial for exploring the interconnections between multiple variables. By probing the inter-relationships within the data, statistical analysis helps the investigator see the forest through the trees.

While they are quite useful, descriptive or analytical statistics by themselves are unable to tell whether their generalizations about the data are reliable. This uncertainty stems from the fact that data are either collected or analyzed in a manner that introduces a random component into any statistical calculation. Unfortunately, researchers have no way of knowing from descriptive statistics alone whether they are reliable reflections of what their true values would be if the random error were not present. In historical research, the possibility of random distortion arises from two sources. Most common is *sampling error*, which stems from the collection of only a sample of all possible cases instead of their complete enumeration. The other root of uncertainty is *assumed error*, which derives from the unpredictable influences inherent in the processes that created the data. In experimental design, psychologists and medical researchers must take into account that certain chance elements affect their results because they randomly assign subjects to treatments. In dealing with extant economic information supplied by business or government, econometricians are compelled to make similar assumptions about the likely effects of random factors that might influence their analysis. Since historians rarely experiment with the past, their use of process-produced data encounters problems of randomness similar to those confronting economic research.

Random error introduces much uncertainty into descriptive statistics, since researchers cannot be sure that calculated values correspond to true values. For a random sample of cases, this doubt raises the question whether the value of any descriptive statistic calculated from that data can be expected to be generalizable to the entire population from which the sample was taken. For example, if an age difference of 15 years on the average between officers and enlisted men was found for a random sample of soldiers taken from the complete records for an army, could an investigator be certain that this average difference would hold for the entire army? In addition, if a correlation between age and the probability of being married were found in the same data, how could one be sure that this relationship was not just a result of accidentally selecting a set of cases which contained it and that it really was not present in the army as a whole? For aggregate data, reflecting a whole population, assumed error poses similar problems. In a study of New England counties, a scholar must be certain that individual wealth is a result of the peculiar economic structure of the entire region rather than the outflow of a chance association of income with manufacturing instead of fishing or agriculture in a particular location.

Inferential statistics assist researchers in making inferences about the true values of descriptive statistics contaminated by random error. They can provide answers to problems caused by random distortion in questions like those above and others. Unfortunately, these answers are not definitive. Rather, they have a low probability of being wrong. The reason for this limitation is that statisticians can mathematically calculate the ranges of error possible for descriptive statistics using assumptions about the patterns taken on by random error in particular circumstances. On this basis they assign probability levels to the likelihood that the values obtained from a given set of cases were due simply to the *random error* rather than some true regularity. If this probability is quite low, for example, less than 1 chance in 20 or less than .05, then the investigator's uncertainty about whether or not the value obtained from calculations contaminated by random error is likely to be close to the actual value is substantially reduced. The positive result of such a statistical *significance test* does not mean that one can be absolutely sure that this is the case. Rather, it only suggests that the probability or *P value* that the calculated value of the descriptive statistic is a result of random error due to sampling or other random factors is acceptably low for both the researcher and his or her professional peers. Conversely, the *level of confidence* that this is not the case is high. While inferential statistics can provide excellent guidance on the precision of results, they cannot answer the question of what level of reliability or statistical significance is adequate. A 1 in 20 chance of winning the grand prize in the New York state lottery would be big enough for most people to buy a ticket, whereas the same risk of dying during a medical operation seems unacceptable. Therefore, historians ought not be content merely to describe or even analyze their data but should also test their results inferentially for the sake of reliability.

DRAWING A SAMPLE

Because many sources are too voluminous to be computerized in their entirety, scholars often resort to analyzing a sample rather than the whole population. Though some researchers instinctively doubt the admissibility of such a procedure, there is nothing wrong with selecting a subset if it is done without bias. Impressionistic browsing of the "interesting" deviants that neglects the drab average cases can dangerously distort conclusions. Even a seemingly innocuous procedure such as picking out names beginning with certain letters of the alphabet runs similar risks of misrepresentation, since they tend to cluster according to region, religion, race, and ethnicity. (Only when one wants to link records via names is letter sampling useful by avoiding the necessity of complete enumeration, provided the sample is reweighted to eliminate likely distortion [see Phillips 1979].) Since statistical accuracy changes little after a certain sample size has been reached, however, there is no need to follow the historical impulse of collecting everything and processing all cases. Additional cases yield minimal error reduction, while the effort required to improve results further will increase exponentially. Some social scientists have the opposite tendency of including as few cases as possible, sometimes taking too small a segment of the population and making statements about hundreds of thousands of individuals on the basis of a few hundred. If done correctly, sampling cases is not only legitimate but also necessary in order to save time and effort.

What is involved in drawing a statistically valid sample of a body of historical material? The basic principle of sampling demands that any subset of cases from a larger population must be representative of the entirety. At first blush, the imperative of correspondence between the part and the whole seems simple enough to implement. After browsing through all the material, cannot one just select a group of cases that seem to include a broad spread of values on the variables under study? This common sense approach is misleading, however, since no two researchers are likely to agree on what subset would properly reflect the character of the entire population. Moreover, for voluminous sources, no one could obtain an adequate overall impression of the material to make a reasonable selection possible. Fortunately, statisticians have developed a technique called *simple random sampling* that usually insures representativeness by giving each case in the population an equal probability of being included in any sample. The basic steps involved are easy to understand. First, all potential cases in the population are listed and assigned a unique identification number. Second, a list of nonduplicated, random numbers in the same range as the numbering scheme for the cases, which can be generated by computer or obtained from a printed table of random numbers, is constructed. The number of numbers in this list is equal to the desired sample size. Finally, the cases with identification numbers corresponding to those on the list of random numbers are selected for data collection and analysis. The only limitation of this procedure is the requirement of listing all relevant cases before selection begins.

If the volume of data precludes assigning unique numbers, another technique, called *systematic sampling*, can also produce a random selection of cases. This procedure is particularly useful when cases are recorded in an orderly manner in registers and lists or filed systematically in drawers or alphabetized indexes. To draw a systematic sample one first must establish how many cases are in the population to be sampled. Then one selects a sample size that evenly divides into the total number of cases or comes as close as possible to evenly dividing into it. (The issue of how large samples should be will be discussed below.) The result of this division will be an integer number, called k. From a table of random numbers which may be found in the back of most statistics books, a random number between 1 and k is then selected. Beginning with this chance starting point, the cases for the sample are extracted by thereafter taking every k'th case in the population listing or file. Unless the cases are arranged in some cyclical fashion that synchronizes with the selection interval (k), systematic sampling will provide samples that are at least as representative as simple random samples and, in certain circumstances, more representative (Schaef-

fer, Mendenhall, and Ott 1979, chap. 8). While there are some subtle differences between systematic and simple random samples, for
most practical purposes they are equivalent and the data from them
may be analyzed with the descriptive and inferential statistics produced by statistical software packages (Sudman 1976, chap. 3). So, if
they are unable to sample cumbersome sources in a simple random
fashion, historians can resort to systematic sampling without losing analytical power.

In particularly difficult circumstances, yet other sampling techniques may be required. Often sources relevant to economic, demographic, and social historical problems are spread across many
county seats, churches, or state capitals, making coverage of all
locations complicated. If exhaustive listings or accurate estimates
of the numbers of cases at these sites can be obtained, the cases can
still be extracted randomly or systematically. However, a *cluster
sampling* strategy may prove more practical. For this technique, all
the relevant data sites are listed and a simple random sample of
locations is chosen. Then either simple random or systematic samples of cases are drawn from these sites. The savings in time and
money for cluster sampling are readily apparent, because it also can
be applied to letters of the alphabet and thereby facilitates nominal
record linkage. But efficiency brings severe penalties. If the number
of locations is not large enough, sampling sites may distort the
data, since geographic differences often have considerable implications. Moreover, the inferential statistics produced by most statistical packages for data from such samples are not always accurate.
(See Kalton [1983] and Lee, Forthofer, and Lorimer [1989] for further
details on this issue.) If a researcher is particularly interested in a
subgroup only sparsely represented in a population, he or she may
want to draw a *stratified sample*. For the sake of special analysis,
this technique purposely selects a larger sample of a particular subset than justified by its occurrence in the whole. In investigating
the social plight of mulattoes in Christ Church Parish in Charleston during the 1850s, a scholar would extract all racially mixed
individuals but only pick a small segment of whites. But in order to
make accurate statements about the character of the entire popula-

tion, the correct proportions need to be restored by weighting the undersampled portion.

In addition to choosing an appropriate sampling technique, a scholar also needs to determine an adequate sample size for the problem being considered and the data source at hand. While one can never have more than enough cases, cost and time constraints inevitably place limits on data collection. Selecting a sample size is not always simple, because it depends both on the available resources and on the statistical techniques to be employed. If the purpose of a study is to obtain descriptive statistics such as average age at first marriage or taxes paid, then rather precise formulas can calculate the exact sample size needed to obtain estimates of these quantities within a specified range of error at a given level of statistical significance (see the sampling texts by Schaeffer, Mendenhall, and Ott [1979] or Sudman [1976]). For an estimate of the proportion of married individuals (likely to be .5) in a manuscript census of 15,000 cases with a margin of error of .025 at the 95 percent level of confidence, the necessary sample size would be:

$$n = \frac{Np(1-p)}{(N-1)(E^2/4) + p(1-p)} = \frac{15,000 \times .5 \times .5}{14,999 \times (.000625/4) + .5 \times .5} = 1,446$$

In this formula, n is the sample size, N (population size) = 15,000, E (acceptable error) = .025, and p (likely proportion) = .5. When the permissible margin of error is raised to ± .05 of the true proportion, the appropriate sample size decreases to 390. In other words, doubling the level of accuracy from .05 to .025 requires almost four times the sample size, indicating that the more precise and confident one wishes to be, the more cases are required. However, at the .95 level of confidence, sample sizes in the range of several hundred to 2,000 cases can provide reasonable levels of accuracy for many studies, irrespective of the size of the population.

Many historians are more interested in analyzing relationships among several factors that may influence a certain critical variable than in simply describing their data. Estimating sample sizes for such studies is often more an art than an exact science, because it depends more on the number of variables to be examined than on the size of the population from which the sample is to be taken. Rules of thumb found in statistical texts vary greatly and their recommendations differ from technique to technique. To arrive at a correct size, one should either know the statistical procedures to be used so well that one can come to an intelligent decision about the number of cases which they require or seek the counsel of an experienced statistician. Simpler techniques such as multiple regression may demand only a minimum of 10 or 20 times as many cases as variables. While large studies of 10,000 to 20,000 cases involving 20 variables might be content with 10 percent samples, small populations of around 1,000 cases with two dozen variables might require samples of over 20 percent. Other procedures such as multiple logistic regression may require an even higher ratio of cases to variables in order to avoid the "zero cell problem." Small sample size often produces missing rows and/or columns in crosstabulations of categorical variables, since the number of selected cases does not suffice to include all combinations of categories found in the population. Hence even 30 percent samples might not prove adequate under especially adverse circumstances. When the relevant population is small (under 1,000 cases) and numerous subgroups are to be compared, one might be better off to rule out sampling altogether and to collect data for the whole.

Choosing the correct sample size is further complicated when multiple analyses are anticipated. If a sample is drawn from some large, important source such as the manuscript returns of a federal census and placed in a data archive, the many different scholarly uses cannot be anticipated during sampling and data collection. Since research agendas change, methodological approaches evolve, and statistical methods become more refined, it is impossible to forecast how many variables might be examined or what newly developed statistics might require. In these instances, it seems wise to collect the largest sample of as many variables as resources will permit. In essence, sampling always remains a tenuous compromise between the conflicting imperatives of accuracy (requiring large samples) and effort (limiting the size of selections). Making responsible decisions requires considerable forethought during planning to avoid coming up short during analysis. In order to reconcile the clashing demands of statistical techniques and limited resources, investigators should resort to pilot studies. Extracting one-tenth of the cases of the ultimate sample and analyzing them with the anticipated procedures will yield valuable experience in the effort involved as well as the statistical requirements. It should go without saying that the quality control measures discussed in chapter 5 must also be observed during sampling, since elaborate efforts to calculate a correct sample size can easily be vitiated by inaccurate data collection.

When sampling, a historian finally needs to be aware of the effect of source bias on statistical conclusions. Virtually all historical records are less complete than a scholar might desire. For example, blacks often cannot be found on voter registration lists. Deaths of unbaptized children usually go unrecorded in parish registers. Propertyless people tend not to be listed on property tax roles. Black market deals do not show up in municipal trade figures. Sometimes official statistics on crime or prostitution reflect public policy rather than actual behavior. Due to selective record keeping or subsequent destruction, information on cases that should be in the research population is often incomplete. Samples taken from such problematic sources incorporate their bias, seriously impairing the numbers derived from them. Though statistical analyses based on such selections are not necessarily invalid, their results need to be interpreted with proper qualification. Descriptive or analytical generalizations derived from problematic samples must be examined for the likely effects of bias. Averages or percentages, for example, might be over- or underestimates of the true values, had all the relevant cases been recorded or survived the ravages of time. A relationship found between several variables might be expected to hold for the subgroup in the sample but not for other groups excluded or underrepresented. Though cross-checking of missing values can probe the cases in the sample with incomplete information, supplementary qualitative studies are required to assess the likely distortion of those cases not present at all. Proper use of sampling therefore also requires a conscious confrontation with the problem of source bias.

LEVELS OF MEASUREMENT

As previously noted, data consist of the values of variables for each case or unit of analysis. The range of values that a particular variable may assume and the values assigned to specific cases are determined by a measurement rule which describes the characteristic being measured and the procedure used to assign a value for each case. For many variables, these standards are implicit and well known. For example, for Fort Moultrie soldiers height and weight can be measured using scales such as inches or pounds that are almost universally agreed upon. Similarly, much data collected by historians is measured in units defined by parish priests or customs officials. However, other variables require more careful specification of measurement rules, and the categories employed might be controversial. In the Fort Moultrie study, for example, the investigator might choose to measure the socioeconomic status of soldiers by systematically assigning individuals to categories based on their reported occupations. The values assigned to variables differ in the degree to which they may be treated as real numbers susceptible to the usual range of arithmetic manipulations. There are four general levels of measurement, which are also often called scales of measurement. It is important to know the differences between these categories and to be able to identify which scale each variable in a data set reflects. The descriptive and inferential statistics that are appropriate for answering particular research questions are largely determined by the scale of measurement of the variable or variables involved.

The values of *nominal* scale variables represent a set of exhaustive and mutually exclusive categories of the characteristic or quality being measured. Hence they are also sometimes called *categorical variables*. Such variables in effect derive from simple classification schemes. The only information imparted by such variables is that cases assigned to one category are deemed equivalent with respect to some characteristic being measured and different with respect to that characteristic from cases placed in other categories. Though it is customary to do so, it is not necessary to assign numbers to the categories of such variables, since letters or any other set of unique symbols would do as well. But it is important to remember that any numeric values employed are merely labels applied without regard to their ordering or magnitude. In the Fort Moultrie data, birthplace, occupation, and marital status would be good examples of nominally scaled variables. Other common categorical variables in historical research include sex, religious preference, and province or state.

Ordinal scale variables satisfy the exhaustive and mutually exclusive categorization rule for nominal scale variables. In addition, their categories must be orderable to indicate which cases have more or less of some property. While the numeric values assigned reflect their categorical ranking, they do not indicate the magnitude of any differences between them in the amount of the property. For this reason they are sometimes referred to as ranked or rank-ordered variables. In the data in table 6.1, military rank is clearly an ordinally scaled variable. Other ordinally scaled variables found in historical data include socioeconomic status and bureaucratic position.

Interval scale variables have all the ordinal properties with the addition that the intervals between the ordered categories have equal values. This means that differences between values can be measured by subtraction and that the zero point on such scales is arbitrary. The most familiar illustrations of this measurement type are the Fahrenheit and centigrade scales for temperature. While each has a different zero point with respect to water freezing, it is possible to calculate differences in temperatures in constant units on each scale and to compare these differences. Note that age and value of real estate in the Fort Moultrie data are not interval scale variables because they each have an absolute zero point. There are very few examples of truly intervally scaled variables in historical data except possibly for dates on the Christian or Jewish calendars, which have arbitrary zero points and equal intervals.

The measurement for *ratio* scale variables is even more stringent than for interval variables due to the requirement of an absolute zero point. Thus, not only can differences be compared as ratios, but also ratios of the values themselves. Age and value of real estate in the Fort Moultrie data are examples of ratio scale variables. For most practical statistical purposes the subtle distinction between interval and ratio scales can be ignored and the two types of variables thought of together as *quantitative* or *continuous* variables. Similarly, the difference between categorical and rank-ordered variables is sometimes neglected in practice and both are simply treated as categorical variables.

In order to obtain reliable results, it is imperative that measurement be precise. Most statistical techniques assume accurate, appropriate, and complete measurement of the data from which they are calculated. Generally, statistics do not take errors in measurement, be they random or systematic, into account. Almost every procedure's reliability depends on an assumption about the level of measurement of the variable or variables involved in its calculation. Using a statistic that assumes a quantitative level of measurement on a variable or variables actually measured on an ordinal or nominal scale does not produce reliable information but rather misleading gibberish. Moreover, most statistics do not correct for the fact that some proportion of the values for some variables in a data matrix may be missing or unknown. Because machine-readable data tend to be coded numerically, statistical software calculates statistics on the nonmissing values of variables. Since computers are only uncritical number processors, novices often generate an inappropriate statistical analysis with the press of a few keys. When neglecting to specify the proper level of measurement, it is all too easy to make a statistical silk purse out of a poorly measured sow's ear.

STATISTICAL HYPOTHESIS TESTING

When historians want to explain the causes of certain phenomena, they can apply the logic of inferential statistics to *hypothesis testing*. In order to make it possible to examine a supposition statistically, the hypothesis must be stated clearly and unambiguously as a first step. Though it may seem self-evident, it is often difficult to formulate a number of specific assertions on the basis of a general research question. First, hypotheses must be narrower questions derived from the more general problem to be investigated. Second, hypotheses must be rather precisely stated in order to be translated into mathematical expressions involving the descriptive or analytical statistics used to answer the question that they embody. These formalized statements are often called *statistical models*. The questions based on the Fort Moultrie data above illustrate this process of refinement for a simple investigation of the characteristics of soldiers prior to the Civil War. Because research hypotheses must be amenable to translation into statistical models involving descriptive or analytical statistics, the forms of research hypotheses that can be examined are dictated by the available statistical models. In order to make informed choices, scholars need to be acquainted with the types of statistical models that are useful for examining various research hypotheses.

The second step in hypothesis testing is to formulate the *null hypothesis* for the statistical model. Because only certain types of questions can be answered by statistical tests, the proposition to be examined with an inferential statistic is stated as a null hypothesis to be rejected rather than an affirmative statement to be accepted. The null hypothesis almost always asserts that some descriptive statistic has a value of 0. For example, in order to examine the research hypothesis that the enlisted men at Fort Moultrie had fewer dependents on average than the officers, one would actually test the null hypothesis that there was *no difference* between them. If a value significantly larger than 0 for an inferential statistic allowed the hypothesis of no difference to be rejected, then the opposite conclusion—that there was a difference—would by implication be accepted. The reason for this seemingly nonsensical reversal of the real question under consideration is based on a principle of formal logic—the induction fallacy. In effect, the testing of a hypothesis stands the intuitive process of making correct inferences on its head. In formal logic, valid inferences can result from true conclusions drawn from true assumptions or from true conclusions drawn from false assumptions, but false conclusions can never be drawn from true assumptions. Thus, knowing that a conclusion is true never "proves" that the assumptions leading to it are true. However, knowing that a conclusion is false does allow one to be logically sure that the assumptions cannot be true.

Statisticians develop mathematical models for null hypotheses that can predict the probability of obtaining a particular value for a descriptive statistic based upon many assumptions. Unfortunately, a researcher is rarely in the position to know whether all the premises on which a test is based are in fact true. The mathematical models upon which the tests depend make various unprovable assumptions about the patterns of random error or other factors affecting the variable or variables involved. The only thing the researcher has to work with is the value of the descriptive statistic calculated from the data and the probability of finding that result given by an inferential statistic with a known frequency distribution that is mathematically derived from the model. If the probability of arriving at a particular value of the inferential statistic is high, then the result was likely to be the product of the random factors considered in the statistical model. Therefore, the null hypothesis is accepted but not proven. If the probability of finding a particular value of the inferential statistic is very low, then the result was not likely to be the product of random factors and the null hypothesis is rejected. In this case the research hypothesis receives support, even if it is not conclusively proven.

The probability of an inferential statistic depends not just on its absolute size but on its value relative to the number of *degrees of freedom* for the particular model being employed. Thus, the probability associated with a specific value may be quite high for a model with 1 or 2 degrees of freedom but low for a model with 20 degrees of freedom. While a formal discussion is beyond the scope of this text, degrees of freedom can be briefly defined as the difference between the total number of mathematical variables for a statistical model and the number of independent restrictions placed upon them (see Walker and Lev 1953, p. 90). Most statistical software packages correctly calculate and report both degrees of freedom and probability levels for inferential statistics. But it is important to remember that one must usually know both the value of an inferential statistic and the number of degrees of freedom of the statistical model before the probability level can be determined.

The third step in testing a hypothesis is the choice of a *level of significance* for the probability of obtaining the value of the inferential statistic from the data. If the likelihood is at or below this level, then the null hypothesis must be rejected. Otherwise, it is to be accepted. Choosing this level depends on the problem at hand and on the researcher's need to be certain about falsely rejecting a particular null hypothesis or committing a *Type I* error. A common example of this kind of mistake is a jury's false conviction of a truly innocent man. In this case, a significance level of .05 means that due to random error there is a 5 percent chance of rejecting the null hypothesis even when it is actually true. Nonetheless, for most scholarly purposes a level of .05 with 1 chance of error in 20 is acceptable enough. However, specifying a level of significance for the test of the null hypothesis does not provide a known probability of failing to reject a null hypothesis when it is actually false or committing a *Type II* error. A popular case of such a fallacy is a jury's failure to convict a truly guilty defendant. Again due to random error, there is some chance that any inferential test will not reject a null hypothesis when, in fact, it should be repudiated. In practice, Type II errors are seldom assessed because they are more difficult to calculate and since controlling for Type I error is a conservative strategy which mitigates against *false positive* findings of support for research hypotheses. More detailed treatments of Type I and Type II errors in hypothesis testing may be found in almost any introductory statistics text, such as Mendenhall and Ott (1976) or Blalock (1972).

The fourth step in hypothesis testing is the calculation of the appropriate inferential statistic from the sample data and the comparison of its associated probability level with the level of significance selected in step three. If the likelihood of obtaining the inferential statistic is less than or equal to the level of significance selected, then the null hypothesis is rejected and the research hypothesis receives support from the data.

While the calculation of different inferential statistics can be complicated and cumbersome, most available statistical software removes this burden from the researcher. The leading statistical packages provide all the values of necessary descriptive statistics as well as inferential statistics and their associated probabilities for all types of analyses. Since the computer takes virtually all of the burden of calculating off the researcher's shoulders, the above steps become compressed in practice. Even if the use of these testing routines has become deceptively simple, it is still necessary to know the procedures and models appropriate for particular hypotheses and to understand the reasoning underlying the process of hypothesis testing.

The choice of a particular statistical procedure ultimately depends upon the analytical question and the nature of the data. In order to test a hypothesis, one must be able to translate a general interest into a specific proposition. Not only does the level of measurement play an important role, but the routine selected also has to be appropriate to the number of variables required to resolve the specific problem under investigation. In the Fort Moultrie data, the first question about typical age can be answered by analyzing only one variable. Such issues are addressed with *univariate* statistics, concerned with only a single variable. Questions 2 and 3, comparing the ages of officers and enlisted men or probing the relationship between age and real estate holdings, involve predicting the values of one variable, usually called a dependent variable, from the values of another, usually called an independent or predictor variable. Such puzzles may be solved with *bivariate* statistics, because they require the analysis of two variables. Problems involving additional factors such as rank or distinctions between native-borns and immigrants also require the prediction of a dependent variable, but with more than one independent variable. Resolving such issues demands *multivariate* statistics, because the questions concern the relationship between many variables.

The next four chapters present an introduction to statistics based upon the level of measurement of variables and the number of variables analyzed to answer particular questions. This brief overview for use in quantitative history cannot hope to provide all of the background necessary for the intelligent application of all techniques to the analysis of complex historical questions and data. Rather, what this introduction hopes to provide is a foundation in basic concepts and an intuitive understanding of some of the statistical tools available for extracting information from data. Since most commonly used statistics are reliably calculated by statistical software programs, little emphasis is placed on formulas and calculation. However, the chapters that follow contain references to basic and advanced statistical texts that do cover these important details. You are strongly urged to pursue them to flesh out your understanding of the material presented here. These texts were chosen for their clarity to a mathematically unsophisticated audience. However, understanding of the more advanced techniques will require some commitment to learning basic algebra and matrix algebra. Thus, many of the advanced texts combine tutorials in these areas along with explanations of the advanced statistical models.

7

Statistics for Questions about One Variable

The first step in any statistical analysis is to examine the values of each individual variable. This process is often called performing a *univariate descriptive analysis*. There are good reasons for starting with one variable at a time. First, since virtually all statistical analyses are now accomplished with a computer-based statistical package, an examination of the values of individual variables serves as an important check on the accuracy with which the data were recorded and entered into the statistical program. If impossible and improbable values or too many missing codes for a variable are found, the problem cases should be corrected before proceeding any further, since subsequent calculations will be flawed. Second, many useful research questions can be adequately answered by carefully examining only a single variable. These include:

1. What values from the range of possible values for a variable do the cases in the data take on?
2. What are the most common values for this variable?
3. What is the typical value for this variable?
4. How varied or concentrated are the values of this variable?
5. Are there any impossible or unusually high or low values of this variable?

If, for example, the historian wants to ascertain the average tonnage of freight shipped from a certain seaport during a particular period of time, a univariate analysis of a variable measuring shipments may be all that is required. Third, a knowledge of the values of individual variables is a necessary precondition for any intelligent investigation into the possible relationships among them.

DESCRIPTIVE STATISTICS

UNIVARIATE CATEGORICAL

Categorical variables generally take on a limited number of values, often less than 5 and seldom more than 10. Therefore, a *frequency distribution* is usually employed to examine the values of a categorical variable. A frequency distribution is constructed by simply counting how often each value of a variable appears in the data and representing the result in tabular form. Table 7.1 presents a frequency distribution for the values of the variable occupational category for the complete data set introduced in table 6.1. While there may be some differences among statistical packages in the printed format, most popular programs present frequency distributions with some or all of the column headings shown.

Understanding the structure of table 7.1 will assist in interpreting the computer output from any popular statistical package. The first column of a frequency distribution for a categorical variable usually lists the mnemonic labels for the values of the variable under consideration, since the numbers themselves have little intrinsic meaning. However, if these categorical labels were not supplied at the time the data were read into the statistical program, the initial column would contain just numeric or alphabetic codes. Usually, it also shows some label such as "unknown" for values designated as *missing values* when the data were entered, provided some of the information was unclassifiable or incomplete.

The next column, labeled "Frequency," gives the count of the number of times each distinct value for the variable occurred in the data. For example, in the Fort Moultrie data there were 14 soldiers from unskilled working backgrounds, 6 from semiskilled occupations, 11 from skilled pursuits, etc. The frequencies and, for ordinal-level variables, cumulative frequencies are useful for determining the range of values that a variable takes on as well as the frequency with which each value is found in the data. They can also provide an indication of the most common values of a variable. The value with the highest frequency is called the *mode*. The mode is one measure of the most typical value of a variable. For nominally scaled variables it is the only such measure. Examination of

Table 7.1 *Frequency Distribution for Values of Occupational Category*

Category	Frequency	Percent	Cumulative Frequency	Cumulative Percent
Unskilled	14	31.1	14	31.1
Semiskilled	6	13.3	20	44.4
Skilled	11	24.4	31	68.8
Low white-collar	8	17.8	39	86.7
High white-collar	6	13.3	45	100.0
Unknown	0	0.0	45	100.0

the values and frequencies can also reveal the presence of any impossible or missing values that might have been introduced into the data because of coding or keying errors or because a value was not available in the source.

The column labeled "Cumulative Frequency" gives the tally of the number of times a value and all lower values occurred in the data. For strictly nominal-level variables these frequencies are not very useful, since there is no ordering inherent in the values representing a set of categories, as pointed out in the previous chapter. However, cumulative frequencies can be helpful for ordinal and continuous variables. For example, because the data for occupational category can be interpreted as reflecting an ordinal measure of socioeconomic status, it may be useful to know that 20 soldiers were from either unskilled or semiskilled working backgrounds.

The two columns labeled "Percent" and "Cumulative Percent" express the frequency and cumulative frequency counts in percentage terms. Some statistical programs label them as "Relative Frequency" and "Cumulative Relative Frequency" instead. The "Percent" column gives the percentage of the total count of cases that the number of cases with a particular value represents. The "Cumulative Percent" gives the percentage of the total number of cases, representing the cumulative frequency for a given value. Like cumulative frequencies, cumulative percentages are not useful for nominal-level variables. But relative frequencies are helpful in investigating common values of variables because those values with the highest percentage values will also be the most common in the data. The value with the highest percentage will, in fact, be the mode. For instance, relative frequency can indicate the precise share of military personnel which possessed a certain level of landed property.

A familiar and practical visual device for displaying a frequency distribution of a categorical variable is the *bar chart*. Each bar indicates the value or category of the variable. The length of each bar corresponds to either the frequency or percentage of the value it represents. The vertical axis provides the scale for interpreting how many cases a particular bar denotes. The bar chart in figure 7.1 depicts the frequency distribution of the variable occupational category in table 7.1. It is easy to see that soldiers from unskilled working backgrounds are the most frequent, those from skilled backgrounds the next most frequent, and those from higher white-collar and semiskilled backgrounds the least frequent.

In addition to visually summarizing the range and most common values of categorical variables, bar charts provide a quick impression of how dispersed or concentrated the values of a categorical variable are. If there are a few very tall bars and many short ones, then most cases are concentrated in a small number of categories and are considered to have little *variability*. On the other hand, if many of the bars are similar in height, then there is great variability in the values assumed by the cases. The degree of variability of a categorical variable with i categories can be calculated from the relative frequencies using the following formula:

$$D = 1 - \text{Sum}_i \, (n_i/N)^2 = 1 - \text{Sum}_i \, (P_i)^2$$

Sum_i means sum over the i categories, n_i is the number of cases in the i'th category, N is the total number of cases, and P_i is the proportion of cases in the i'th category which are obtained from the entries in the column of table 7.1 labeled "Percent." Values of D close to 0 indicate that almost all cases are concentrated in just one of the categories and that the distribution has very low variability. Values of D close to 1 indicate that each category has about the same number of cases and that the distribution has high variability. For the Fort Moultrie data, D = .777, which indicates a considerable amount of variability in the working backgrounds of its soldiers.

Figure 7.1 *Bar Chart for Frequency of Occupational Category*

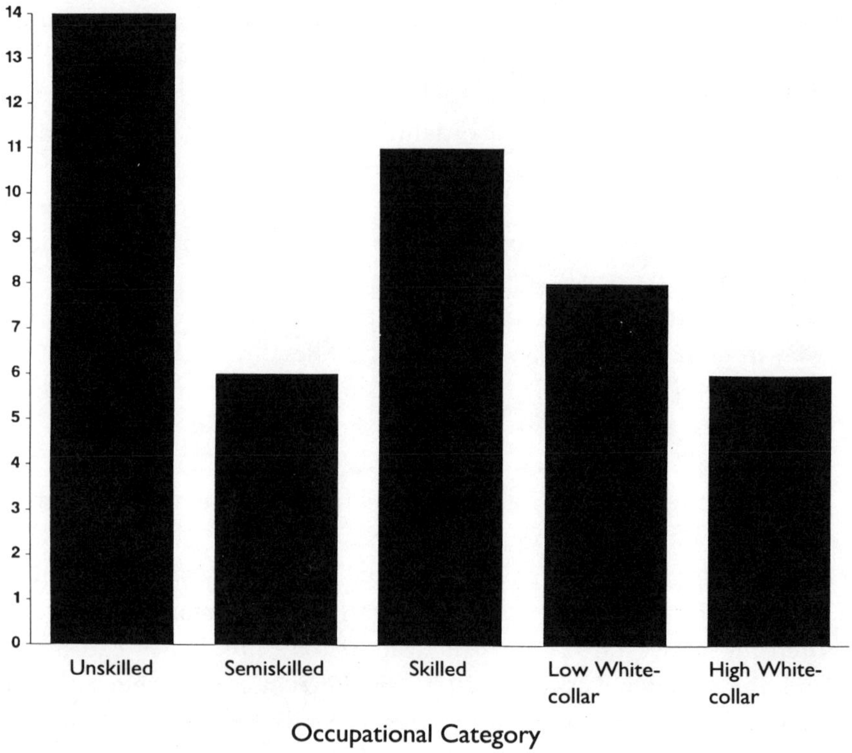

UNIVARIATE CONTINUOUS

In contrast, continuous variables usually take on many values. Sometimes there may be as many unique values as there are cases in the data set. In that instance, a frequency distribution of such a continuous variable would list each value with a corresponding frequency of 1 and be so lengthy that it could no longer summarize the range and central tendency of the values conveniently. Therefore, the frequency distributions for values of continuous variables with many values are often constructed by using categories that encompass ranges of values rather than the simple values themselves. These categories are called *classes* and the ranges of values encompassed by them are referred to as *class intervals*.

Choosing the number of classes to be used in constructing a frequency distribution for a continuous variable involves both formal and judgmental elements. On the one hand, the upper and lower limits for the class values should be related in some intuitive fashion to the way the investigator thinks about the data values. On the other hand, there ought to be a sufficient number of classes to allow the frequency distribution to capture any complexities in the distribution of values. Perhaps the best suggestion on how to combine these considerations has come from D. P. Doane (1976). For distributions with most of the values concentrated in the middle of the range, the ideal number of classes should be the integer closest to $3.3 \times \log(N)$, where N is the number of cases and the logarithm is taken to the base 10. In more irregularly shaped distributions, two or three more classes should be added to the figure derived from the basic formula. In practice, unless they are specified by the data analyst, most statistical software will "choose" a reasonable number of classes based on a rule such as Doane's.

The statistically ideal number of classes should only be used as a starting point from which the actual class intervals are derived. The final selection is guided by judgmental factors such as using whole numbers and class intervals that provide analytical purchase to the researcher. Mechanically lumping all the values of age for Fort Moultrie soldiers into just three categories, such as 20 to 39, 40 to 59, and 60 and over, does not make sense for most analytical purposes because it obliterates interesting distinctions (which may involve the legal age of majority, the constitutional age of holding office, the customary age of promotion to officer, etc.). Instead, grouping age values into smaller 5- or 10-year intervals is usually preferable. For age cohort studies, uneven intervals bordered by certain significant years of birth or maturity may be selected as well. Instead of being intimidated by numerical mumbo-jumbo, historians should understand the statistical reasons for certain procedures but make their choices with discretion, based on their own analytical ends.

The frequency distribution for the classes of a continuous variable is usually graphically depicted in a *histogram*, which may be thought of as a bar chart with many bars. An example of such a histogram for age with 12 classes is shown in figure 7.2. It demonstrates clearly that most of the cases are clustered around the

Figure 7.2 *Histogram for Age*

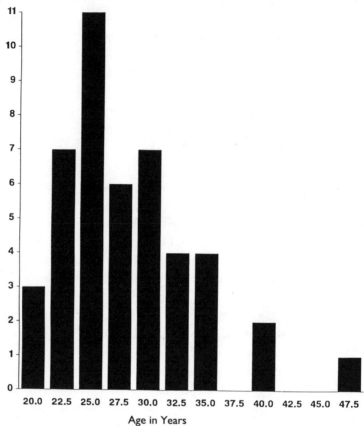

Frequency

Age in Years

modal class with a midpoint of age 25 and that very few of the soldiers at Fort Moultrie were over 40 years old.

Histograms depicting frequency distributions of continuous variables can have many different shapes. However, their contours usually resemble one of several general classifications which are useful for guiding the selection of an appropriate typical value or *measure of central tendency* for a distribution. Figure 7.3 shows some of these profiles in terms of idealized smooth curves rather than bar graphs. This curvilinear approach has two advantages. First, it is easier to represent and remember the shapes using continuous lines. Second, such curves can be constructed from bar graphs for large numbers of values by connecting the midpoints of many bars encompassing extremely narrow class intervals. Distributions constructed in this manner have important uses for inferential statistics which will be discussed later. Figure 7.3a represents a bell-shaped, *symmetrical* curve. Such distributions have approximately the same number and spread of values on either side of a central, modal class interval. The normal curve is an important example of this type. Figures 7.3b and 7.3c show nonsymmetrical or *skewed* distributions that have extended left or right *tails* indicating the presence of a few extremely high or low values. Finally, figure 7.3d illustrates a *bimodal* distribution which has concentrations of values around two peaks. Knowledge of the ideal type of distribution that an actual variable being examined approximates helps determine the choice of a single descriptive statistic to characterize the empirical distribution's typical value.

Often a scholar wishes to select or calculate a number to indicate the typical value or *central tendency* of a variable's distribution of values. For instance, average values of players' performances, budget deficits, or population growth are quoted by everyone from sports fans to newscasters and politicians. Three such measures of central tendency are commonly used in univariate statistical analyses. The most popular is labeled the *mean* and measures the common average value of a set of values. Somewhat less frequent is the *mode*, which simply denotes, as mentioned above, the most frequently occurring value. For frequency distributions of continuous variables using classes, it is the middle value of the most frequent class. Least understood is the *median*, which indicates the value that divides the frequency distribution in half, placing 50 percent of the cases above it and 50 percent below it. Table 7.2 presents a frequency distribution for the age of the soldiers in the Fort Moultrie data. For these figures the median would be approximately 27.5 years of age because, as can be seen from the cumulative percentages, 48.9 percent of the soldiers are 27 years old or younger.

Though such "averages" are readily obtained from any statistical package, their unreflected use sometimes creates problems. While most people routinely quote the mean as the measure of central tendency, this statistic is not always appropriate. In wage negotia-

Figure 7.3 *Ideal Shapes for Frequency Distributions of Continuous Variables*

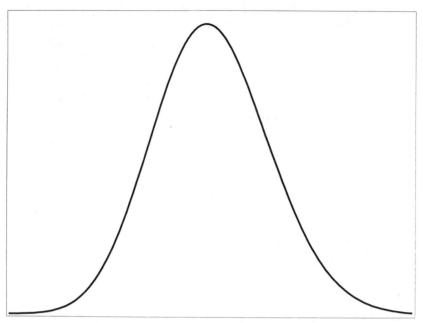

a. Symmetric Distribution

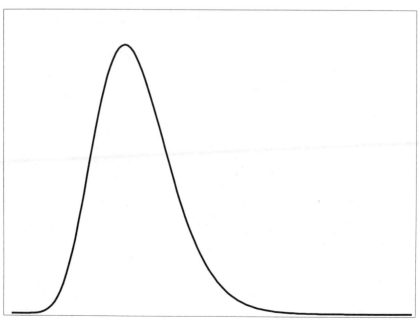

b. Positively Skewed Distribution

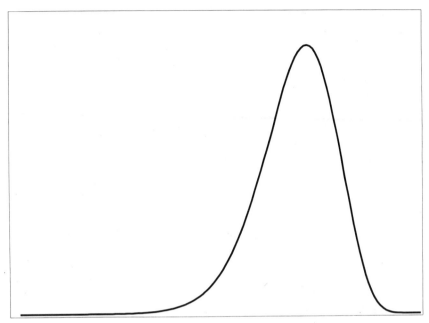

c. Negatively Skewed Distribution

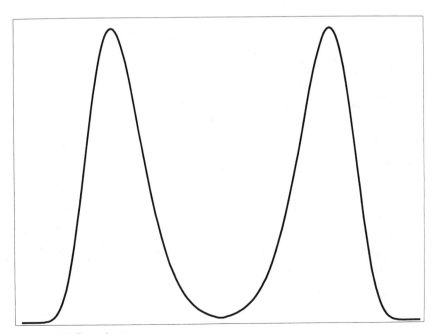

d. Bimodal Distribution

Table 7.2 *Frequency Distribution for Age in Years*

AGE	Frequency	Percent	Cumulative Frequency	Cumulative Percent
19	1	2.2	1	2.2
20	2	4.4	3	6.7
22	2	4.4	5	11.1
23	5	11.1	10	22.2
24	1	2.2	11	24.4
25	6	13.3	17	37.8
26	4	8.9	21	46.7
27	1	2.2	22	48.9
28	5	11.1	27	60.0
29	3	6.7	30	66.7
30	1	2.2	31	68.9
31	3	6.7	34	75.6
32	2	4.4	36	80.0
33	2	4.4	38	84.4
34	2	4.4	40	88.9
35	1	2.2	41	91.1
36	1	2.2	42	93.3
40	2	4.4	44	97.8
50	1	2.2	45	100.0

tions management would be likely to focus on mean pay while union leaders would prefer the median as less affected by a few high salaries. Figure 7.4 shows the values of the three measures of central tendency for the ideal distributions of figure 7.3. For bell-shaped, symmetrical curves (figure 7.4a) the mean, median, and mode have exactly the same value. Therefore, the use of the mean to indicate the "average" value is entirely appropriate for data that approximate a normal distribution. However, in figures 7.4b and 7.4c the mean, median, and mode have quite different values. In practice, the actual amount of the disparity between them is governed by the degree to which the frequency distribution is skewed. Typically, the mean values for these figures are farthest down the value axes in the direction of the skew. Means are quite influenced by the presence of even a small proportion of unusually high or low values. Hence the mean is not a good descriptive statistic for characterizing a variable with a skewed frequency distribution. The median is more appropriate for skewed curves, because it will always be the middle value in a distribution. Finally, examine figure 7.4d. This distribution is difficult to characterize with just one statistic. The mean and median do indicate the most central value but they do not reveal the presence of the high and low modal values. Moreover, there are two modes rather than one. For these reasons it is often best to use the median together with the high and low modal values to describe a bimodal distribution.

The variability or dispersion of continuous variables can be measured in several ways. Once again, the type of frequency distribution of a variable determines the appropriateness of the various measures of dispersion. The simplest measure is the *range*, which is simply the difference between the lowest and highest values of a variable. For the variable age in table 7.2 the range would be 31 (50 − 19). Because the range only deals with the most extreme values of a distribution, it is a rather crude indicator of variability and other measures of dispersion often better characterize the degree of variability of a frequency distribution.

A useful yardstick for both symmetric and nonsymmetric distributions is the *interquartile range*. Understanding this statistic requires a brief digression into the concept of *quartiles* of a distribution. Just as the median value can divide a distribution into two halves, two additional values, called quartiles, can be defined which divide it into quarters. Thus, 50 percent of the cases must lie between the lower quartile value and the upper quartile value. These cases would be the 50 percent that are closest to the median value of the distribution. Moreover, exactly 25 percent of the cases must be found in each of the value ranges demarcated by the three values. The line plot of data in figure 7.5 illustrates where these values would be located for a variable with a nonsymmetrical distribution. The interquartile range is simply the difference between the upper and lower quartile values and, therefore, measures the dispersion of the values of the most typical cases. Examining the distribution for the age of soldiers at Fort Moultrie in table 7.2 reveals that the lower quartile boundary is 25 years of age and the upper quartile boundary is 31 years of age. Therefore, the interquartile range is 6.

If the frequency distribution of a continuous variable looks approximately like a bell or mound, the *variance* and *standard devia-*

Figure 7.4 *Location of Measures of Central Tendency for Some Ideal Distributions*

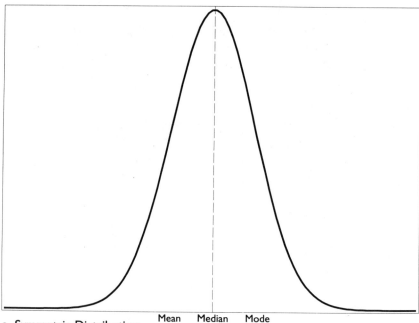

Mean   Median   Mode

a. Symmetric Distribution

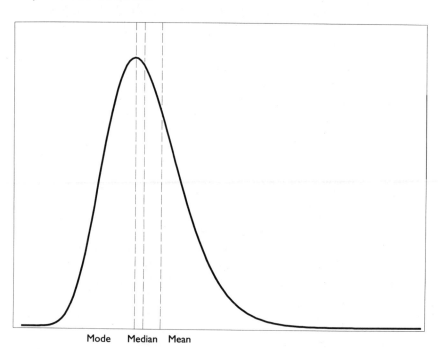

Mode   Median   Mean

b. Positively Skewed Distribution

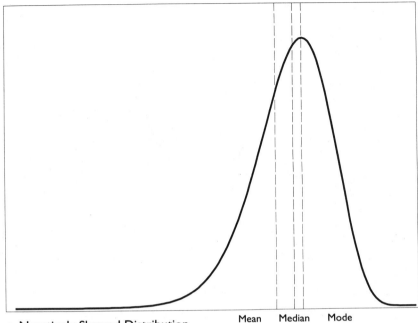

Mean   Median   Mode

c. Negatively Skewed Distribution

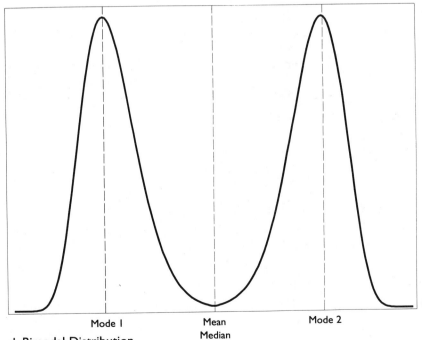

Mode 1   Mean   Mode 2
                         Median

d. Bimodal Distribution

Figure 7.5 *Interquartile Range for a Nonsymmetric Distribution*

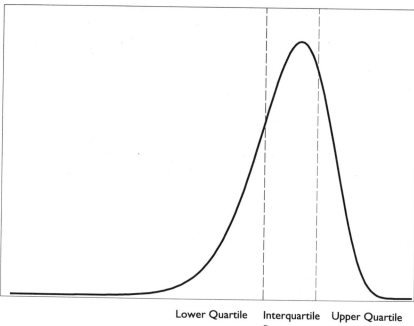

Lower Quartile   Interquartile   Upper Quartile
                 Range

tion provide the best measures of dispersion. The population variance of the distribution of a continuous variable is calculated by
subtracting the mean value of a variable from the value for each
case, squaring those differences, summing the squared differences,
and, finally, dividing that sum by the number of cases. The standard
deviation is obtained by taking the positive square root of the variance. In algebraic terms this process translates into the formulas

$$\text{Variance of X} = \text{Sum}_i(X_i - \text{Mean}_x)^2 / N$$
$$\text{Std. Deviation of X} = \text{Sqrt(Variance of X)}$$

where Sum_i means "sum over the values of X" and Sqrt stands for
"take the positive square root of." The formula for estimating the
variance from a random sample differs from the above only by using
$N-1$ in the denominator instead of N. The computation of this
statistic demonstrates that the variance is really the *mean squared*
deviation of the values of a variable from its mean value, while the
standard deviation is the *mean absolute deviation*. Obviously, the

larger this average deviation is, the greater the variability of the individual values of a variable about its mean value. The variance of age in the Fort Moultrie data is 35.5, while the standard deviation is 5.96. Interestingly enough, the latter value is almost identical with the interquartile range because the frequency distribution for age is approximately mound-shaped.

As a graphic representation of the distribution of a continuous variable, the *box plot* is often more useful than a frequency histogram (Tukey 1977). While it omits data on the absolute frequencies of values or class intervals, this representation neatly summarizes information about the mean, median, interquartile range, and atypical values of a variable. Figure 7.6 shows a box plot for the ages of the soldiers at Fort Moultrie. The horizontal center line indicates the location of the median while the plus sign shows the value of the mean. The bottom and top edges of the box demarcate the quartiles and, therefore, the length of the box represents the interquartile range, which for bell-shaped frequency distributions will be approximately equal to the standard deviation. Rare values that lie at least 1.5 times the interquartile range from the median are plotted with an O, while very atypical values that are more than 3 times removed are plotted with an asterisk. The location of the box, the closeness of the mean and median, and their location within it provide a quick visual check on how ideally bell-shaped the distribution may be. If the box is centered in the range of values represented by the vertical lines, O's, and asterisks while the mean and median are located near its middle, then the distribution is ideally bell-shaped and quite close to normal. If the box is located toward the top or bottom of the range of values and the mean and median are quite separate, then the distribution is skewed.

Figure 7.6 reveals that the box is positioned about in the middle of the range of values. However, while the mean and median are almost at the same point, they are located toward the top of the box in the direction of the single highly atypical value. Thus, this distribution may be characterized as approximately bell-shaped but with a slight skew in the direction of older soldiers.

The larger the variance is relative to a particular mean, the more varied will be the values of the variable and the flatter its distribu-

Figure 7.6 *Box Plot of Age of Soldiers at Fort Moultrie*

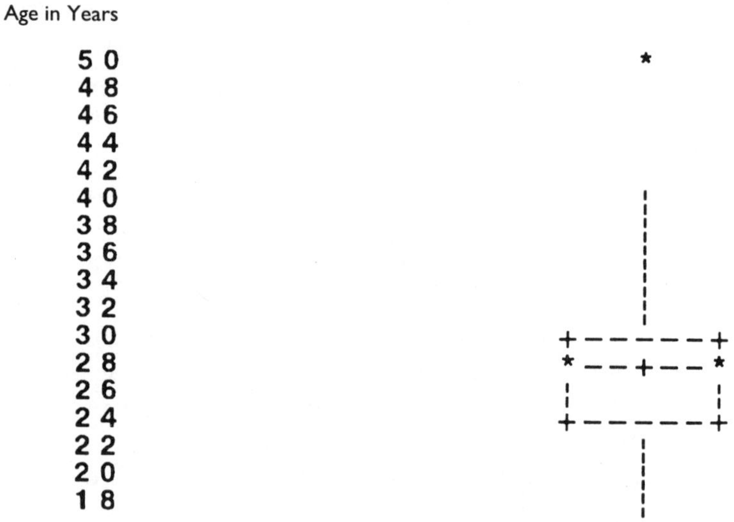

Age in Years

```
 5 0                                              *
 4 8
 4 6
 4 4
 4 2
 4 0                                              ¦
 3 8                                              ¦
 3 6                                              ¦
 3 4                                              ¦
 3 2                                              ¦
 3 0                                   + — — — — +
 2 8                                   * — — + — — *
 2 6                                   ¦         ¦
 2 4                                   + — — — — +
 2 2                                        ¦
 2 0                                        ¦
 1 8                                        ¦
```

tion. However, larger numeric values of a mean of a variable generate greater numeric values of the variance simply because the overall magnitude of all the values of the variable will be large. For this
reason, a useful statistic for comparing the variability of the values
of a continuous variable for two or more groups which have different mean values is the *coefficient of variability*. Because it is calculated by simply dividing the standard deviation by the mean, it en-
ables a researcher to control for the magnitude of the means when
trying to compare the variability of a variable across two or more
groups of cases.

INFERENTIAL STATISTICS

UNIVARIATE CONTINUOUS

Since univariate statistics are simple, their tests are also uncomplicated. One can ask three questions of sample data on a single continuous variable: Does the population mean equal, exceed, or fall
short of a particular value? Such problems are easily solved by
means of a test based on either the standard normal distribution,
sometimes called the Z distribution, or the Student's t distribution.
The choice between the two is dictated by the size of the sample

used for the test. The Student's t distribution is properly used when the sample size is 30 cases or less. Inferential tests for larger sample sizes employ the normal distribution. The hypothesis testing procedure outlined in the preceding chapter requires a series of simple but systematic steps. Suppose that the Fort Moultrie data were a simple random sample from a larger population of soldiers and one wished to find out whether, on the average, soldiers were older or younger than 30 years of age. Since the sample size is rather large for employing the t distribution, the standard normal distribution can be used to test this hypothesis with the following sequence of steps:

Step 1, *research hypothesis*:
The mean age of soldiers is different from 30.

Step 2, *null hypothesis*:
The mean age of soldiers equals 30.

Step 3, *level of significance*:
The probability of falsely rejecting the null hypothesis must be equal to or less than .05. A table of areas under the continuous frequency distribution of the standard normal distribution suggests that a value of Z less than -1.96 or greater than $+1.96$ is required to reject this null hypothesis.

Step 4, *inferential statistic*:
The Z statistic for this hypothesis is calculated from the following formula:

$$Z = \frac{\text{(Sample Mean of X)} - \text{(Hypothesized Population Value)}}{\text{(Sample Standard Deviation of X)} / \text{Sqrt(n)}}$$

where Sqrt stands for "square root of" and n is the number of cases in the sample.

Entering the figures for the Fort Moultrie data translates to

$$Z = \frac{28.3 - 30}{5.96 / \text{Sqrt(45)}} = \frac{-1.7}{.8885} = -1.913$$

This value of Z is not less than -1.96. Thus, we cannot reject the null hypothesis. This result suggests the conclusion that the mean age of the soldiers in the population is not very likely to be much greater or less than 30.

UNIVARIATE CATEGORICAL

Three similar questions can be asked about a simple dichotomous variable: Is the proportion of cases falling into one of the two categories of the variable equal to, greater than, or less than a particular value? A military historian might, for example, wish to find out whether the proportion of officers in the larger population is greater than .10. Again, the hypothesis testing process suggests a four-step sequence for examining this question:

Step 1, *research hypothesis*:
The proportion of officers is greater than .10.

Step 2, *null hypothesis*:
The proportion of officers is less than or equal to .10.

Step 3, *level of significance*:
The probability of falsely rejecting the null hypothesis must be less than or equal to .05. A standard normal distribution table suggests that the Z statistic must exceed a value of $+1.64$ in order to reject the null hypothesis.

Step 4, *inferential statistic*:
For moderate to large samples, questions about values of proportions can be answered with a test based on the normal distribution by calculating a Z statistic as follows:

$$Z = \frac{(P_s - P_h)}{\text{Sqrt}[(P_h \times (1 - P_h)) / \text{Sqrt}(n)]}$$

where P_s is the proportion from the sample data, P_h is the hypothesized proportion, and n is the number of sample cases.

Entering the figures for the Fort Moultrie data results in

$$Z = \frac{.133 - .100}{\text{Sqrt}[(.10 \times (1 - .10)) / \text{Sqrt}(45)]} = \frac{.033}{.0134} = 2.463$$

Because in this case Z is much greater than 1.64 and its corresponding standard normal probability less than .01, the null hypothesis
may be rejected and it is permissible to conclude that the proportion of officers is probably greater than .10.

A comparison of the rejection values in the previous two examples reveals that while both tests used a .05 level of significance,
the Z values employed differed. In the test for age, two values
(−1.96 and +1.96) were used. However, in the test for the proportion of officers a single value of +1.64 was employed. This disparity
stems from the difference of the two null hypotheses with respect
to whether they implied a direction for the deviation of the hypothesized value from the sample value of the mean or proportion. The
null hypothesis about age only implied that the average age was
different from 30, but did not specify its direction. On the other
hand, the null hypothesis for the proportion of officers suggested
that only sample proportions in excess of .10 would contradict it.
Two rejection values were required for the hypothesis about age to
allow for the possibility of unlikely sample values that were greater
than or less than the hypothesized mean. These rejection values
individually were at a .025 level of significance but when combined
gave an overall .05 level of significance for the test. Such tests are
often referred to as *two-tailed tests* because they use areas from
both ends or "tails" of the standard normal distribution and imply
nothing about the direction of any difference between the sample
mean or proportion and the hypothesized mean or proportion. *One-
tailed tests* do predict a direction for this difference and their rejection values encompass the entire area at either the high or low end
of the distribution of the test statistic. The choice of which tail
to use, and of whether to employ a positive or negative rejection
value, is dictated by the direction of the difference predicted by the
research hypothesis. Thus, for the proportion of officers example,
+1.64 is the value of Z that demarcates the upper tail of the stan-

dard normal distribution corresponding to a probability of .05 that such values could come from a population with a proportion of .10 or less. Understanding the difference between one- and two-tailed tests is important and has implications beyond univariate statistics. Further details can be found in every introductory statistics text.

The initial step of analysis should therefore be the close examination of each variable alone. No other procedure allows the researcher to spot coding and data entry mistakes as quickly. Moreover, careful scrutiny of the distribution of values in a single variable can answer many important questions. When historians are searching for reliable descriptions of such attributes as average age, height, weight, or racial composition for a previously unexamined group such as Fort Moultrie soldiers, simple univariate statistics will solve many research problems. Moreover, diligent perusal of one variable at a time will reveal the basic character of its value distribution—information that is essential for analyzing the relationship between several variables. All too often inappropriate summary measures cover up outliers and produce spurious impressions of relationships where none exist or obscure connections generated by a few untypical extreme values. Instead of ignoring univariate statistics as too elementary for serious scrutiny, historians would do well to start humbly by getting a feel for their data before forging ahead into more exciting and complicated modes of analysis.

SOFTWARE NOTES

SAS produces frequency distributions with either PROC FREQ or PROC UNIVARIATE. PROC UNIVARIATE provides bar charts, box plots, and more complete statistics for distributions than PROC FREQ, including quartiles, mean, median, mode, variance, and standard deviation. PROC CHART in SAS will also generate useful bar charts. The FREQUENCIES procedure in SPSS-X and SPSS/PC produces frequency distributions, bar charts, and histograms, as well as quartiles, means, medians, modes, variances, and standard deviations. SPSS/PC's EXAMINE generates statistics similar to SAS's

PROC UNIVARIATE as well as some additional plots and measures of central tendency. Unless labeled as one-tailed tests, the probabilities printed out for univariate inferential statistics by software are two-tailed tests. In order to obtain a one-tailed probability, one simply needs to divide the printed significance level by 2.

8

Statistics for Questions about Two Variables

The most general statistical question that can be asked about two variables is whether or not they are *related* in some way. In other words, can the values of one be used to predict the values of the other for a certain set of cases? If this is possible, the two variables are said to be related or *correlated*, even though the predictions may not be infallible. Perfect correlation implies that every value of one variable may be predicted exactly from the values of the other. Imperfect correlation between variables suggests that knowing a particular value of one variable provides information about the most likely value of the other variable. For example, because it is possible to predict the average weight of a group of persons for each of a range of values of height, body height and weight are said to be highly but not perfectly correlated. In such relationships a few predictions may be exact, but most will be off the mark to some small extent. The *strength of a relationship* between two variables is based upon the amount of error in the predictions. The less such forecasts turn out to be wrong, the stronger the correlation.

One important limitation on statistical analysis, often misunderstood by laymen, is the difference between *correlation* and *causation*. Simply put, showing that two variables covary is not sufficient to prove that one variable actually *causes* another to behave as it does. It is both tempting and wrong to infer cause from covariation. Correlation may be accidental, such as the coincidence between fluctuations of the New York stock market and the monsoon in India, or dependent upon a third variable, such as the drop in the Swedish birthrate and the disappearance of storks, both of which may be attributed to industrialization. However, in many practical situations it is difficult not to think about problems in causal terms, particularly when the temporal ordering of the variables seems apparent as is often the case in historical inquiry. The resolution of this dilemma lies in understanding that causal thinking can be a fruitful heuristic device in examining possible relationships among variables, but that from a statistical point of view all that can ever be established is that two variables either do or do not correlate.

In order to be plausible, causal research hypotheses require that several basic assumptions about the variables involved must be supportable. First, the temporal sequence of the variables should be clear. A change in one variable, often called the *independent* variable, has to precede any change in the other, which is often referred to as the *dependent* variable. Second, the relationship must be asymmetrical in the sense that, at a given point in time, a shift in the independent variable produces a shift in the dependent variable, but not vice versa. Third, the alteration in the dependent variable must not be induced by some third variable that either is affected by the independent variable and in turn produces an effect in the dependent variable or is a common cause of both the independent and dependent variables. While the first assumption is often easily demonstrated, the latter conditions are invariably more difficult to sustain. Nevertheless, in practice, causal research hypotheses are quite commonly used to guide statistical analyses because there are no other paradigms that have comparable heuristic value. For a more complete discussion of the problems involved in causal thinking in quantitative research see Heise (1975).

NOMINAL DEPENDENT VARIABLES

The basic descriptive statistics for measuring the relationship between two nominally scaled variables are developed simply by counting the number of times each combination of attributes for the two variables occurs in the data. This *joint frequency distribution* is often presented in the form of a *contingency table* or *crosstabulation* which shows the count for each combination of attributes and some percentages which are calculated from it. Table

Table 8.1 *Crosstabulation for Variables X and Y*

		Y		
		1	2	*Row Totals*
	1 Freq.	80	20	100
	Pct.	80%	20%	33%
X	2 Freq.	50	50	100
	Pct.	50%	50%	33%
	3 Freq.	20	80	100
	Pct.	20%	80%	33%
	Column Totals	150	150	300
		50%	50%	

8.1 is an example of a simple crosstabulation for an independent variable (X) with three categories and a dependent variable (Y) with two categories.

While at first glance this table may seem confusing as a whole, its individual parts are quite easy to understand. First, the categories of the independent variable (X) are presented at the beginning of each row, while the categories of the dependent variable (Y) are found in the columns. The *dimensions of a table* are described in terms of the number of categories of the row and column variables respectively. Thus, table 8.1 would be called a 3 × 2 or "3 by 2" table, because it has three rows and two columns. Second, a frequency count of the number of cases having a unique combination of X and Y category values appears in the body or *cells* of the table on the line labeled "Freq." in every row. Immediately below them is a percentage which is 100 times the proportion that the frequency above it is of the total number of cases in that row. To simplify computation, in this example the number of cases in each row conveniently adds up to 100. Thus, the percentages are immediately apparent. Finally, the column labeled "Row Totals" and the row labeled "Column Totals" are often referred to as the *marginals* of the table. They are the frequency distributions of the X and Y variables that do not reflect what the degree of relationship between the two variables might be.

The basic measure of relationship between two categorical variables in a crosstabulation with the independent variable as the row variable is the magnitude of the differences in the row proportions compared across a particular column of the table. The larger the differences between these proportions, the stronger the relationship between the variables. If the greatest differences were close to 100 percent, the relationship would be close to perfect. However, if the largest differences in percentages were close to 0, the relationship would be nonexistent. Examining the first column of the table 8.1 reveals that the greatest difference (60 percent) is found between row 1 and row 3. The same is true for the second column. Thus, the relationship between the hypothetical variables in table 8.1 would be described as moderately strong. Instead of the raw, joint frequencies, percentages must be compared in order to standardize comparisons across tables which might have different marginal and grand total numbers of cases. This reasoning becomes clear when the joint frequencies in table 8.1 are doubled. The magnitude of the differences among the numbers in any row would also double. However, the differences in the row percentages for this new table would be exactly the same as those in the original. Independent of sample size, comparing percentages yields a more stable measure of relationship than using the differences among the joint frequencies.

If a crosstabulation is based on a simple random sample, differences in row percentages of the table might be due to chance rather than reflecting "true" distinctions existing in the population. In order to detect whether the disparities observed are greater than what might be expected due to random error, a *Pearson chi-square test* can be used. This inferential statistic compares the joint frequency distribution seen in the table to an *expected joint frequency distribution* that would be found if the two variables had no relationship or, in statistical terms, were *independent*. Hence the null hypothesis asserts that the two variables have no relationship. The expected joint frequency distribution is calculated from the marginal distributions of the two variables by multiplying the row total percentage times the column total number of cases. In other words, if there were no relationship between the variables, one would expect 33 percent of the cases in each column to appear in the first

Table 8.2 *Chi-square Test for Variables X and Y*

			Y	
			1	2
	1	observed	80	20
		expected	50	50
		cell chi-square	18	18
	2	observed	50	50
X		expected	50	50
		cell chi-square	0	0
	3	observed	20	80
		expected	50	50
		cell chi-square	18	18

table chi-square = 18 + 18 + 0 + 0 + 18 + 18 = 72

row, 33 percent in the second row, and 33 percent in the third row. Because all row total percentages are 33 percent and all column frequency totals are 150, all expected values for table 8.1 are 50. For each cell of the table the difference between the expected frequency and the observed frequency is squared and that result divided by the expected frequency. These *cell chi-squares* are then summed to produce the *chi-square for the table*. The observed frequencies, expected values, cell chi-squares, and table chi-square for table 8.1 are presented in table 8.2.

The value of a chi-square that would result in rejecting the null hypothesis at a given level of statistical significance depends on the dimensions of the table. The greater the number of rows and columns in a table, the higher is the minimum level of chi-square necessary to achieve statistical significance. The actual critical value is determined from the level of significance and the *degrees of freedom* for the table. The degrees of freedom are simply the product of the number of rows minus one and the number of columns minus one. Thus, for table 8.1 the proper number of degrees of freedom would be 2 ($[3-1] \times [2-1]$). From a chi-square table available in the appendix of most statistics texts, one would find that the chi-square calculated for the above table would have to be at least 9.2 in order to reject the null hypothesis of no relationship at the .01 level of significance. Since the chi-square value of 72 calculated for this example is well above that value, it is highly unlikely that the relationship observed between X and Y was due to random sampling errors. In practice, most statistical software constructs the crosstabulation and calculates the correct chi-square as well as the lowest possible level of significance for it.

While the calculation of a chi-square test for the relationship between two categorical variables is relatively straightforward, interpreting its results is not always as easy. The problem stems from the dependence of the chi-square test on several assumptions which render it only approximate for tables with cells containing small numbers of cases. The two most important premises are that the underlying data are a product of a simple random sample and that the categories of the variables are exhaustive (i.e., cover all the possible divisions) and mutually exclusive (i.e., a case may only belong to one particular category). These conditions are usually not difficult to fulfill. More vexing, however, is the problem of a small number of cases, since empty or nearly empty cells greatly distort the accuracy of the test. Fortunately, there are some helpful rules of thumb. First, whenever a table has 20 percent or more of its cells with expected frequencies of 5 or less, the probability level associated with the chi-square is likely to be too optimistic about rejecting the null hypothesis. Second, if this situation occurs and the table's dimensions are 2 × 2, Fisher's exact test should be substituted, since it always yields a precise level of significance. Third, if the table is larger than 2 × 2, the rows or columns with the low expected values may be combined with others to eliminate the problem. Often one has to settle for grosser categorizations in order to produce a valid chi-square test. Sometimes such *collapsing of categories* does not make substantive sense, however, and the researcher is simply forced to conclude that the data do not allow a valid test of the independence hypothesis.

While "eyeballing" percentage differences in a table and calculating chi-square tests gives a rough idea, it is an inconvenient way to gauge the strength of relationship between two categorical variables. In the first place, chi-square is not a good measure because its value can vary with the number of cases in the table and some of its derivatives, like the contingency coefficient, have no consistent maximum limit. Thus, it is hard to tell whether a large value results from a strong relationship or a weak relationship for a large number of cases. Differences in percentages also cause difficulty because of the numbers of pairs of percentages that need to be examined and because there is no one number with known upper and lower bounds that conveys where the relationship lies on a continuum ranging from no association to perfect association. To measure the strength of a relationship between two categorical variables more conveniently, statisticians have constructed several measures which may range between 0 for no relation and 1 for perfect association. Some are based on the table chi-square while others involve the *proportional reduction in error*, or "PRE." The latter simply indicates the reduction in mistaken prediction of values of the dependent variable due to knowing the values of the independent variable. Generally PRE measures are preferred over those that are chi-square based, because the latter do not always have a fixed maximum value of 1 for all possible table dimensions and are difficult to interpret. Unfortunately, the most commonly used PRE measure has a blind spot that the best chi-square measure does not. Thus, the best rule of thumb is to examine both.

One chi-square based measure that always has a maximum value of 1 for perfect association is Cramer's V, which essentially corrects the chi-square for the sample size and dimensions of the table. It is useful when the most commonly used PRE measure—Goodman and Kruskal's asymmetric lambda—equals 0. Lambda measures the proportion of reduction in the errors that result from using the independent variable's categories to estimate the correct category of the dependent variable as opposed to using only the modal category of the dependent variable. Unfortunately, it can equal 0 both when there is no relationship between the two variables and when there is a relationship but the modal categories of the dependent variable are the same for all categories of the independent variable. Tables 8.3a through 8.3d illustrate a variety of ideal relationships between two categorical variables and the values of chi-square, Cramer's V, and lambda for each table. Notice especially the 0 values for lambda in tables 8.3c and 8.3d and the lack of relationship

Table 8.3 *Bivariate Nominal Measures of Association for Some Example Tables*

Table 8.3a *Perfect Prediction*

	A	B	C
A	100	0	0
B	0	0	100
C	0	100	0

chi-square = 600, Cramer's V = 1, lambda = 1

Table 8.3b *Imperfect Prediction*

	A	B	C
A	50	0	0
B	50	50	100
C	0	50	0

chi-square = 225, Cramer's V = .61, lambda = .50

Table 8.3c *No Relationship*

	A	B	C
A	33	33	33
B	34	34	34
C	33	33	33

chi-square = 0, Cramer's V = 0, lambda = 0

Table 8.3d *Relationship with Same Modal Category*

	A	B	C
A	25	50	0
B	25	0	50
C	50	50	50

chi-square = 100, Cramer's V = .41, lambda = 0

between the variables in table 8.3c, while Cramer's V detects an association in table 8.3d.

Examining the relationship between birthplace and work experience for the Fort Moultrie data provides an example of a bivariate analysis for two categorical variables. An immigration scholar might want to find out whether being a native-born soldier as opposed to being born abroad had any relationship with whether prior work experience was of a blue-collar or white-collar nature. The null hypothesis, of course, asserts that there was no relationship. Table 8.4 presents a crosstabulation of birthplace by occupational category collapsed into the groups just mentioned. An examination of the row percentages shows that a higher proportion of foreign-born soldiers came from blue-collar backgrounds (77.8 percent) than American-born soldiers (55.6 percent). The low values for Cramer's V and lambda show that the association is not particularly close. Moreover, the nonsignificant (P > .10) chi-squares indicate that the observed relationship is not strong enough to reject the null hypothesis that what is seen in the table might be the result of random factors.

ORDINAL DEPENDENT VARIABLES

While the relationship between two ordinal variables can also be summarized by a crosstabulation, statistics which include information about their order are more appropriate. Because such variables have ordered categories, these statistics can measure not only the strength but also the direction of a relationship. A *positive relationship* indicates that the ordinal value of the dependent variable either increases or remains the same when the ordinal value of the independent variable increases. A *negative relationship* suggests that the dependent variable either decreases or does not change as the independent variable increases. Statistics summarizing both the direction and strength of a bivariate relationship have a range of values beginning at − 1 (perfect negative relationship), increasing to 0 (no relationship), and continuing on through + 1 (perfect positive relationship).

Table 8.4 *Birthplace and Prior Occupation of Fort Moultrie Soldiers*

		Prior Occupation		
		Blue-collar	White-collar	Total
Birthplace	Foreign-born	21	6	27
		77.78%	22.22%	100%
	Native-born	10	8	18
		55.56%	44.44%	100%
	Total	31	14	45
		68.89%	31.11%	100%

Statistic	DF	Value	Prob.
chi-square	1	2.488	0.115
Fisher's exact test			.106
Cramer's V		0.235	
lambda		0.000	

Two of the most commonly used measures of association for ordinal variables are gamma and Stuart's tau c, sometimes also called Kendall's tau c or Kendall and Stuart's tau c. Both have a range of −1 to +1, and their significance tests are relatively straightforward. Since many statistical packages calculate their standard errors but not their significance levels, it is important to know the formula for hand calculating the significance levels given the standard errors:

$$Z = \frac{\text{Estimate} - \text{Hypothesized Value}}{\text{Standard Error}}$$

where "Estimate" is the value of either gamma or tau c and "Standard Error" is the standard deviation of the distribution of the statistic for repeated random samples under the null hypothesis. The "Hypothesized Value" is the value one wishes to test the estimate against. Since the most common test is for a null hypothesis of no relationship, it is usually 0 and therefore can be ignored. Because Z has a normal probability distribution, its value may be compared to a table of areas under the normal curve to determine the probability of error in rejecting the null hypothesis that the gamma or tau c statistic is different from the "Hypothesized Value." In practice, the most important points on this curve are the two-tailed .05 and .01 levels of significance, which have corresponding Z values of 1.96 and 2.57. Thus, if the Z calculated for either a gamma or tau c is greater than 1.96, the level of significance is at least .05, and if it is greater than 2.57, the significance is at least .01.

In spite of their usefulness, gamma and tau c do have some problems that need to be considered when interpreting them. First, the significance test outlined above only applies to simple random sampling of cases and is accurate for samples of 50 or more cases. Second, gamma has a tendency to approach 1 or -1 for several patterns of relationship for which tau c gives values close to 0. Because it does not correct for ties in ranks, gamma tends to inflate considerably if tables with larger numbers of rows and columns are collapsed into smaller tables. Third, neither statistic can detect a curvilinear relationship between two ordinal variables. In such a configuration the dependent variable's values either increase and then decrease or decrease and then increase as the independent variable increases. Such patterns will yield significant chi-square statistics but insignificant gamma and tau c statistics. In order to deal with these problems, one should never try to interpret either statistic without examining the other and should always scrutinize a crosstabulation of the variables they were based upon. Tables 8.5a through 8.5f show a variety of idealized patterns of relationship that could be found between two ordinal variables, along with values of chi-square, gamma, and tau c. For tables 8.5a, b, c, and e, gamma has a value of $+1$ or -1, while tau c takes on other values for tables 8.5c and 8.5e, which intuitively show less than perfect relationships. For tables 8.5d and 8.5f, gamma and tau c are 0, but in table 8.5d the reason is a curvilinear relationship rather than none at all, as in table 8.5f. Moreover, the chi-square for table 8.5d is quite large, indicating some not necessarily linear relationship,

Table 8.5 *Bivariate Ordinal Measures of Relationship for Some Example Tables*

Table 8.5a *Perfect Positive Relationship*

	Low	Medium	High
Low	100	0	0
Medium	0	100	0
High	0	0	100

chi-square = 600, gamma = +1, tau c = +1

Table 8.5b *Perfect Negative Relationship*

	Low	Medium	High
Low	0	0	100
Medium	0	100	0
High	100	0	0

chi-square = 600, gamma = −1, tau c = −1

Table 8.5c *Imperfect Positive Relationship*

	Low	Medium	High
Low	50	0	0
Medium	50	50	0
High	0	50	100

chi-square = 250, gamma = +1, tau c = +.75

Table 8.5d *Curvilinear Relationship*

	Low	Medium	High
Low	50	0	50
Medium	50	50	50
High	0	50	0

chi-square = 150, gamma = 0, tau c = 0

Table 8.5 *continued*

Table 8.5e *Imperfect Negative Relationship*

	Low	Medium	High
Low	0	50	100
Medium	50	50	0
High	50	0	0

chi-square = 250, gamma = −1, tau c = −.75

Table 8.5f *No Relationship*

	Low	Medium	High
Low	33	33	33
Medium	34	34	34
High	33	33	33

chi-square = 0, gamma = 0, tau c = 0

while for table 8.5f it appropriately indicates no relationship of any kind.

If a crosstabulation of two ordinal variables yields a large number of cells with frequencies of either 1 or 0, Spearman's rank order correlation coefficient (r_s) is preferred for measuring the degree of association between them. It is based on the notion that if two ranked variables are highly related, the differences between the ranks of the independent and dependent variables should be quite small, and if they are unrelated, the disparities between the rankings will be rather large. Spearman's r_s ranges from −1 for perfect negative relationships through 0 for nonexistent relationships up to +1 for perfect positive relationships. Computational details need not be belabored because this statistic is also calculated by most software.

For an example of two ordinally measured variables, one might want to study the relationship between the social status of civilian job and military rank of the soldiers at Fort Moultrie. Because occupational category has 5 levels and army rank has 9, the crosstabulation is too large to be presented here. But table 8.6 shows the

Table 8.6 *Tests for Relationship between Occupational Category and Military Rank*

Statistic	Value	Std. Error	Z	P <
gamma	.963	.030	32.1	.0001
tau c	.511	.093	5.5	.0001
r_s	.743	.070	10.6	.0001

values for gamma, tau c, and r_s derived from it. While the values of the gamma and r_s statistics are quite high, that of tau c is moderate. The disparity in these figures does not mean that one is correct and the others are not but that each statistic measures the degree of association differently (see Siegel and Castellan 1988, chap. 9, for further explanation). Nonetheless, all of these measures and their associated very low probability values clearly indicate that there is a moderate to strong relationship between civilian job status and military rank, depending on which measure is employed.

The choice of statistics for testing for a relationship between one nominal variable and one ordinal variable depends on which variable is considered to be dependent and which independent. When the dependent variable is nominal and the independent variable is ordinal, the ordinal variable is usually treated as though it were nominally scaled and the statistics discussed for the relationship between two nominal scale variables are employed. However, when the dependent variable is ordinal and the independent variable is merely categorical, statistics based on rankings of the observations are used, because they incorporate information about the ordering of the observations on the dependent variable. These measures are based on the observation that an increase in the between-category difference in rank sums of dependent variables indicates a closer relationship. Ties in ranking are broken by assigning average rank scores.

While many statistics measure and test the relationship between a nominal independent variable and an ordinal dependent variable, the two most powerful are the Mann-Whitney U, also called the Wilcoxon test, and the Kruskal-Wallis H statistic. The Wilcoxon test applies only to situations where the independent variable is *dichotomous* (i.e., has only 2 categories). The Kruskal-Wallis statistic may be used when the independent variable is either dichotomous or *polytomous* (i.e., has 3 or more categories). Assuming that the observations are products of a simple random sample of the groups represented by the independent variable and that the number of observations is greater than 10, the Wilcoxon test uses the normal distribution Z as the inferential statistic for testing the null hypothesis of "no relationship" between the variables. For 3 or more groups with at least 5 cases in each group, the Kruskal-Wallis H has a chi-square distribution with k − 1 degrees of freedom where k is the number of categories of the independent variable. Because these measures are calculated by most software, their computational details are not presented here. For their limitations and problems of interpretation, see the standard texts on rank statistics (such as Siegel and Castellan [1988]).

Testing for a relationship between marital status and rank in Fort Moultrie exemplifies a bivariate analysis of a categorical independent variable and an ordinal dependent variable. The null hypothesis asserts that there is no difference in the rank of married and unmarried soldiers. However, as table 8.7 shows, the mean rank scores for the two groups differ by approximately 14, with the married group having the higher mean. This finding suggests that higher ranking soldiers were more likely to be married. If this group of soldiers were a random sample, the hypothesis of no relationship in the population would be rejected, because both the Wilcoxon and Kruskal-Wallis tests are very significant with probability levels of .0008 and .0007 respectively.

CONTINUOUS DEPENDENT VARIABLES

Because the data points for continuous variables may be treated as true numeric values, the easiest way to visualize any bivariate relationship among them is to plot their values on an X-Y grid. Such a *scatterplot* gives a picture of their joint frequency distribution. By

Table 8.7 *Wilcoxon Scores for Military Rank by Marital Status*

MARITAL	N	Sum of Scores	Expected under H_0	Std. Dev. under H_0	Mean Score
Married	7	247.50	161.0	25.53	35.35
Single	38	787.50	874.0	25.53	20.72

Average scores were used for ties.

Wilcoxon 2-Sample Test (Normal Approximation)
S = 247.500   Z = 3.36741   Prob > |Z| = 0.0008
Kruskal-Wallis test (chi-square approximation)
CHISQ = 11.472   DF = 1   Prob > CHISQ = 0.0007

convention, the values of the dependent variable are arrayed on the Y axis and the values of the independent variable are placed on the X axis. A great variety of patterns is possible. Figures 8.1a through 8.1d show some idealized configurations. In figures 8.1a and b the cloud of points trends upward and downward in an orderly band, indicating an imperfect but discernible *linear* relationship between the two variables. In a perfect association, of course, all the points would lie on a single line. The relationship in 8.1a is positive, because increases in X tend to be associated with increases in Y. When increases in X tend to be associated with decreases in Y, the relationship is negative (as in 8.1b). In contrast, no trend is apparent in figure 8.1c. The values of Y rest in a horizontal cloud that parallels the X axis. However, the *curvilinear* band of points in figure 8.1d indicates that Y tends to rise for lower values of X, reaches a peak at the midrange of X, and trends downward for high values of X.

The simplest association between two quantitative variables to describe statistically is a *linear* or straight-line relationship (figures 8.1a and b). In algebraic terms, a perfect straight-line relationship between an X and a Y can always be expressed as Y = a + bX, where b is the slope of the line expressed as the ratio of the amount of change in the value of Y for a unit change in X and a is the point on the Y axis that the line crosses when X equals 0. By convention a multiplication sign is not used to indicate that b and X are multiplied. *Least squares regression* can find the "best" fit for a set of X

Figure 8.1 *Scatterplots of Possible Relationships between Two Continuous Variables*

Y

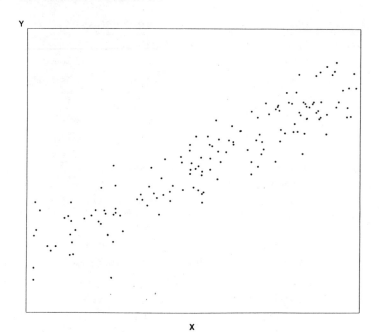

X

a. Positive Linear Relationship

Y

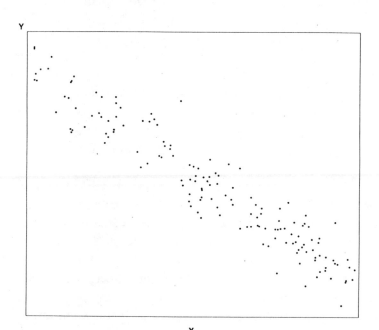

X

b. Negative Linear Relationship

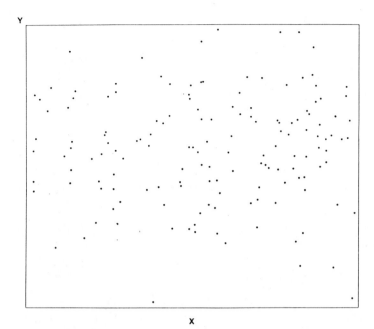

c. No Relationship

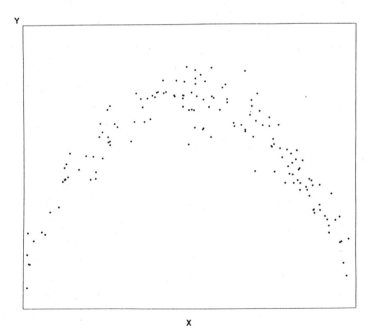

d. Curvilinear Relationship

and Y data points by plotting a line to the points that minimizes the sum of the squared errors in prediction of the values of Y from the values of X. In other words, this line drawn on the scatterplot minimizes the sum of the vertical distances between the plotted points and the line itself. Often it is called the *least squares* regression line and can be described by the formula

$$Y_i = a + bX_i + E_i$$

where a and b are defined as before, the subscript i indicates the i'th observation, ranging from 1 to the number of cases (N), and E_i is the error difference between the Y_i'th value predicted by the equation and the actual Y_i'th value observed in the data. It might be useful to visualize the least squares regression line as a connection between the points that are the average values of Y in the population for each of the values of X.

Several descriptive statistics must be examined in order to interpret any least squares regression line. Most important is Pearson's *product moment correlation coefficient*, often referred to simply as r. Like measures of association for ordinal variables, r may vary between − 1 and + 1, with 0 indicating no relationship. The sign of r indicates whether an association is positive or negative. The magnitude of r measures the strength of the relationship between the two variables. The closer r is to − 1 or + 1, the better the least squares line fits the data and, therefore, the smaller the size of the errors in predicting the values of one from the other using the regression equation for that line. Figures 8.2a and b illustrate this point by showing two plots that have the same best fitting regression line for a population but different values of r due to the difference in the amount of scatter of the data points about that line. The greater the average distance of the points from the line, the lower the value of r. Thus, the value of r for figure 8.2a is greater than that for figure 8.2b.

The significance test for r examines the null hypothesis that there is no linear relationship at all between the independent and dependent variables by assuming that the correlation is equal to 0. More important than the complicated details of the numerical calculation is an understanding of the logic of the test. Simply

Figure 8.2 *Two Scatterplots for Relationships with Different Strengths*

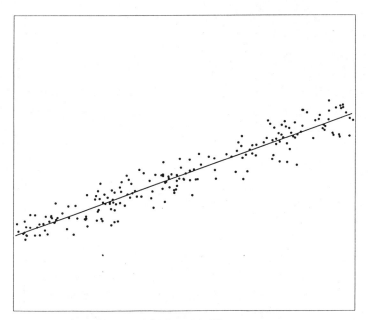

a. Scatterplot of Y versus X for r = .90

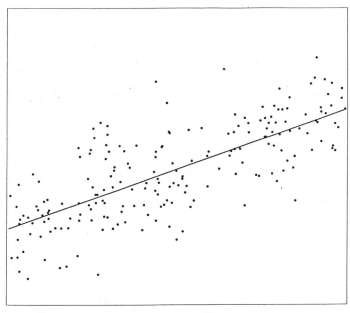

b. Scatterplot of Y versus X for r = .75

put, it compares the sum of the squared errors in prediction (i.e., Sum[Yobserved$_i$ − Ypredicted$_i$]^2) when just the mean of the dependent variable (Y) is used as the best estimate for the dependent variable with the sum of the squared errors in prediction when those values are generated from the estimated regression equation. Fortuitously, the formula for the significance test of this comparison can be reduced to a simple expression using the square of the value of r:

$$F_{1,N-2 \, df} = r^2 / \{[1-r^2] \times [N-2]\}$$

In this formula, r^2 is the proportion of the total squared error about the mean of Y that is reduced by knowing the relationship between X and Y derived from the estimate of the regression equation which is called the *explained sum of squares*; $1-r^2$ is the proportion of the total squared error about the mean that is not accounted for by the estimated regression which is referred to as the *error sum of squares*. Clearly, if the proportion of squared error in predicting the values of the dependent variable about the regression line is small relative to the proportion explained by the regression equation, knowledge of the values of the independent variable improves the prediction of the values of the dependent variable and, hence, they must be linearly correlated to some degree greater than 0. This F statistic and its associated minimum probability need to be checked before turning to other measures such as regression *coefficients* or *parameters* which estimate the constant term a and the slope of the regression line b. However, for two variables the significance test of the correlation coefficient already answers the question about the existence of a relationship.

Like their categorical and ordinal cousins, correlation coefficients must be interpreted carefully with an eye toward the assumptions that underlie them. The most important premise holds that the relationship between the two variables is in fact linear. If it is not, the correlation coefficient will not be a true measure of the strength of the association and the regression coefficients will describe a straight line that does not fit the data very well. Nonlinearity is best detected by examining a plot or scattergram of the data points on an X-Y grid before running the regression analysis. If curvilinearity is detected, various mathematical transformations of the independent variable, such as squaring it, may be employed in order to "bend" a regression line through a nonlinear pattern of data. Daniel and Wood (1980) provide an excellent discussion of such methods. Several other assumptions must also be met for correct estimates of regression coefficients and accurate significance tests. The independent variable must be measured without error. The expected mean value of the errors in prediction must be 0, be normally distributed, and not be related in any fashion to the values of the independent variable. This is another way of saying that there must be no other variables associated with both the independent and dependent variables. The variance or spread of the errors about the regression line must be identical for all values of the independent variable. This is often called the *homoscedasticity assumption*.

Some of these premises can be checked by examining the errors in prediction for a particular regression model. Often collectively called the *residuals*, these errors are simply the set of differences between the predicted values and the actual values of the dependent variable noted previously. Plotting the distribution of the residuals for the cases can reveal suspiciously high or low values, called *outliers*, which might bias the estimates of r and b. Comparing the residuals with the predicted values for Y can help diagnose violations of the linearity, normality of error, and equality of variances assumptions. Detailed treatment of these plots and other so-called *regression diagnostics* is beyond the scope of this presentation. However, they are important tools for evaluating and interpreting any regression analysis, and scholars who often use these statistics are urged to pursue the topic further in the SPSS-X *User's Guide* discussion of SPSS-X's regression procedure and in other texts such as Belsley, Kuh, and Welsch (1980). Hence historians would do well to start with a visual examination of the scatterplots and to employ regression diagnostics before putting too much faith into summary coefficients.

The relationship between age and value of real estate for the soldiers at Fort Moultrie offers a fine example of a bivariate regression analysis. Common sense suggests that the older a soldier was, the more likely he would be to have accumulated property. Conversely, the null hypothesis asserts that there is no relationship between these variables. Figure 8.3 presents a plot that suggests a relationship more complicated than that described by a simple regression line. In close examination the scatterplot reveals a two-tier relationship, with one group of points rising quite rapidly with age while another cluster of data hardly moves at all. One interpretation of this finding might be that many soldiers between 19 and 30 had gathered no real property, but that for those who did obtain landed possessions, the value increased with their age. Table 8.8 gives the test of significance for the correlation between these variables. However, the r^2 of .45 indicates that a single regression line accounts for a good percentage of the total variance in real estate value, and its significance test in the row labeled "Model" suggests that if this were a sample, the hypothesis of no relationship could be rejected with less than 1 chance in 10,000 of being incorrect.

A CONTINUOUS DEPENDENT AND A CATEGORICAL INDEPENDENT VARIABLE

When the dependent variable is quantitative and the independent variable is only categorical, their joint frequency distribution is a bit more difficult to picture. However, it can still be visualized with box plots, like those presented in figures 8.4a and 8.4b. The categories of the independent variable (X) have been arrayed on the horizontal axis, while the values of Y are on the vertical axis. As explained in the previous chapter, the values of Y within the interquartile range lie inside the boxes and more extreme values are plotted on the vertical lines extending from them. Moreover, the ordering of the categories of X on the X axis is arbitrary because they have no inherent ranking. However, any order would do, because what is really important is the difference in the mean levels of Y, denoted by " + ," across the categories of X, irrespective of any ordering. Thus, similar to percentages for crosstabulations, the greater the differences in the means of Y across the categories of X, the greater the strength of the relationship between X and Y. If there is no association between X and Y, all of the category means

Figure 8.3 *Scatterplot of Value of Real Estate versus Soldier's Age*

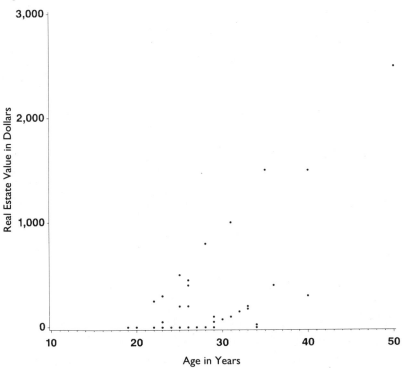

lie on approximately the same value of Y, as in figure 8.4a. In contrast, a strong relationship reveals a pattern of differences in the means of Y for the categories of X, such as the pattern shown in figure 8.4b.

The most common statistic for measuring the relationship between a quantitative dependent variable and a nominally scaled independent variable is an extension of the Pearsonian r for two quantitative variables, called *eta*. In the simplest case, when X has only two categories, eta is r for the least squares regression of Y on a categorical X variable, with the categories of X coded as a *dummy variable* with a pattern of zeros and ones that indicate which category of the X variable a particular case belongs to. The value 1 is assigned to cases in one group and the value 0 is given to the cases in the other. For categorical variables with more than two categories, the number of dummy variables is one less than the number

Table 8.8 *Relationship between Value of Real Estate and Age*

Dependent Variable: REAL   Value of Real Estate

Analysis of Variance

Source	DF	Sum of Squares	Mean Square	F Value	Prob>F
Model	1	4833770.94	4833770.94	35.337	0.0001
Error	43	5881979.06	136790.21		
C Total	44	10715750.00			

Root MSE	369.85161	R-square	0.4511	
Dep Mean	255.00000	Adj R-sq	0.4383	
C.V.	145.03985			

Parameter Estimates

Variable	DF	Parameter Estimate	Standard Error	T for H_0: Parameter = 0	Prob>$|T|$
INTERCEP	1	−1317.048	270.140	−4.875	0.0001
AGE	1	55.614	9.355	5.945	0.0001

of categories and the regression estimation becomes more complicated. However, the interpretation of the measures of relationship
is identical. In practice and in most statistical software, this procedure is usually called the *one-way analysis of variance* or one-way
ANOVA and the measure of relationship is referred to either as eta
or as *multiple R*. The interpretation of these statistics is basically
similar to a Pearsonian r in the range 0 to + 1. However, neither eta
or multiple R can have a negative sign because relationships in this
context cannot be said to have a direction and only the positive
range of values is employed. Thus, the closer the value of either of
these statistics comes to 1, the greater the differences between the
means of Y for the categories of X and, hence, the stronger the
relationship between the two variables.

The significance test for both eta and multiple R checks the null
hypothesis that there is no relationship between the two variables.
In other words, it asserts that all the means of Y within the categories of X are not different from the overall or *grand mean* of Y. The
test uses the F distribution which compares the sum of squared
errors for the regression model of the dummy variable or variables

Figure 8.4 *Two Examples of Relationships between Quantitative Dependent and Categorical Independent Variables*

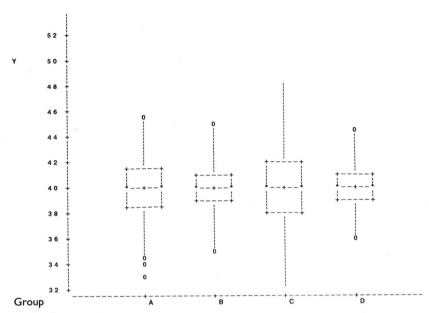

a. No Relationship

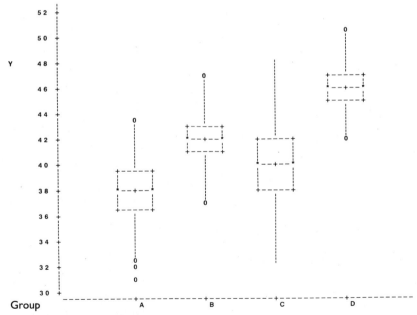

b. Relationship

with the sum of squared errors for a model based on only the grand mean of Y, using exactly the same method as outlined above in the discussion of regression for quantitative variables. Most statistical packages calculate the appropriate value for F, the degrees of freedom, and the lowest level of significance for that F and degrees of freedom but present them in an analysis of variance table in a row labeled as either "Model" or "Between Groups" sum of squares.

Interpreting an analysis of variance requires understanding some of the inferential assumptions and additional steps to clarify exactly which of the group means is significantly different from the other. Several premises have implications for the degree of confidence that may be placed in the accuracy of the F test. First, the categories of the independent variable are assumed to be exhaustive and mutually exclusive. Second, the population variances for each of the groups are presumed to be equal. Third, the prediction errors for the group means are supposed to be normally distributed and have an expected value or mean of 0. Finally, the mistakes in forecasting are expected to be unrelated to the independent variable. If all these assumptions hold, the F test and its associated significance level are accurate. If these premises fail to apply, the consequences are unclear. Some statisticians consider the technique *robust* and useful, since it holds up well under breaches of the second and third assumptions and corrections can be made for violating the first and last premises. Others are more concerned about the effects of violating the last two and particularly the second assumptions. In practice, if there is any reason to suspect that the first premise of exhaustiveness is being violated, one should use an F test for a "random effects" rather than for a "fixed effects" ANOVA. If the categories represent measurements of the same cases at different points in time, a "repeated measures" model ought to be employed. If it is possible that assumptions two and three might not be true, the cases should be rank ordered, based on the continuous values of the dependent variable, in order to perform a Kruskal-Wallis H test, because this procedure makes no assumptions about the distributions of the values of the dependent variable within the groups of the independent variable. For further

Table 8.9 *Real Estate Holdings of Fort Moultrie Officers and Soldiers*

Dependent Variable: REAL   Value of Real Estate

Source	DF	Sum of Squares	Mean Square	F Value	Prob>F
Model	1	7560173.077	7560173.077	103.02	0.0001
Error	43	3155576.923	73385.510		
Corrected Total	44	10715750.000			

R-square	C.V.	Root MSE	REAL Mean
0.705520	106.2344	270.8976	255.000000

Level of CRANK	N	Mean	SD
Enlisted	39	94.23	131.35
Officers	6	1300.00	707.11

details on these and more sophisticated ANOVA techniques, consult Kirk (1982) and Wilcox (1987, chaps. 8–11).

As an example of relating a categorical independent variable and a continuous dependent variable, one can examine whether Fort Moultrie officers owned more real property than enlisted men. The results of an analysis of variance for this question are presented in table 8.9. It comes as no surprise to find that the mean real estate value of $1,300 for officers is much greater than the mean property value of about $94 for enlisted men. This difference is so great that, assuming this was a sample, the null hypothesis of no difference is rejected with a probability of being wrong of only .0001. However, the large disparity in the group standard deviations (131 versus 707) would indicate that the homoscedasticity assumption is probably not satisfied and therefore the probability level for the test of significance of the difference between the means may not be strictly accurate. Nevertheless, the means are so far apart and the probability level so low that it is plausible to conclude that the population means are in fact different.

A CONTINUOUS INDEPENDENT AND A CATEGORICAL DEPENDENT VARIABLE

As shown above, the basic regression model for a continuous dependent variable may be used when the independent variable is either continuous or categorical. It may also be employed with some modifications in cases where the dependent variable is categorical. Adjustments are needed because the statistical properties of categorical dependent variables automatically violate the homoscedasticity and other assumptions required by the classical least squares regression technique. Aldrich and Nelson (1984) provide further details on this point. While several statistical models are appropriate for this situation, the technique most often used to modify the classical model for categorical dependent variables is *logistic regression*. In order to understand this procedure, one might want to start with a simple dichotomous dependent variable and give one category a score of 1 and the other a score of 0. In practice, the category of interest, such as voting Democratic in an election, is usually assigned the score of 1 while the category merely employed for comparison is assigned the score of 0. Imagine that the data consist of a random sample of ten voters for which vote and age are known, as shown in table 8.10. The sum of the dependent variable (5) is the number of persons voting Democratic, and its mean (.5) is the proportion of persons in the sample that voted Democratic. Thus, the mean of a dichotomous variable scored 0 and 1 can be thought of as an estimate of the overall probability of an observation scoring 1 in the population from which the sample was taken, irrespective of the values of any other variable.

The probability of scoring 1 might also be related to another variable. For example, it could be hypothesized that older people are more conservative in their political philosophy and, therefore, more likely to vote Republican. In other words, the probability of a result (i.e., scoring 1) might be conditional upon the values of another variable. For a variety of mathematical reasons too involved to pursue here, logistic regression tries to predict not the conditional probabilities of an outcome but a mathematical transformation of those probabilities called logits. They are defined as

$$\text{Log}_n[P(Y_i = 1 | X_i = v) / [1 - P(Y_i = 1 | X_i = v)]]$$

Table 8.10 *Example Relationship between Age and Voting Democratic*

Observation	Y *Voted Democratic*[*]	X *Age*
1	1	25
2	1	28
3	1	32
4	1	36
5	1	50
6	0	27
7	0	38
8	0	42
9	0	45
10	0	62

Sum of Y = 5
Mean of Y = .5

[*] 1 = voted Democratic in last election; 0 = voted Republican.

where Log_n stands for "take the natural logarithm of" and $P(Y_i = 1 | X_i = v)$ is the probability of the dependent variable for the i'th observation being 1, when the independent variable X has some particular value v. Though this equation seems complicated, it is readily understandable if one realizes that the ratio of the numerator to the denominator is the more familiar betting odds of the dependent variable being 1. For example, if the probability (P) of an outcome were .75, then the likelihood of it not happening $(1 - P)$ would be .25 and, therefore, the odds of it occurring would be 3:1 or 3 (i.e., .75/.25). A conditional logit is simply the natural logarithm of the odds of the dependent variable being equal to 1 for some particular value of the independent variable.

Logistic regression uses logits in a manner similar to a continuous dependent variable in least squares regression. Thus, the general form of a bivariate logistic regression equation is

$$\text{Log}_n[P(Y_i = 1 | X_i = v) \, / \, [1 - P(Y_i = 1 | X_i = v)]] = a + bX_i$$

where a is the intercept, b is the slope of the "best fitting line" for the logits, and X is the independent variable. While logits might seem to be a rather abstract quantity to predict, they do have the advantage that estimates of a and b and their associated significance tests are mathematically obtainable by *maximum likelihood estimation*. By using a little algebra it is possible to translate the results of a logistic regression back into either odds or probabilities. The odds for an outcome being 1 can be obtained by taking the antilogarithm of both sides of the above expression, so that

$$\text{Odds}(Y_i = 1 | X_i = v) = P(Y_i = 1 | X_i = v) / [1 - P(Y_i = 1 | X_i = v)] = e^{(a + bX_i)}$$

or 2.71828 raised to the power given by the value of $a + bX_i$. While the product bX_i adds a quantity for predicting logits, it multiplies the odds, since they are being predicted on a logarithmic scale. Solving for P in the expression for the odds produces

$$P(Y_i = 1 | X_i = v) = e^{(a + bX_i)} / [1 + e^{(a + bX_i)}]$$

so it is possible for any value of X to predict the most likely value of either a logit, odds ratio, or probability from the estimates of a and b provided by logistic regression. (Strictly speaking, it is only possible to predict probabilities for data in which the outcome is not known at the time of observing the independent variable.)

Unfortunately, there is no generally accepted measure of the strength of the relationship between the variables in a logistic regression. Since most computer programs fail to include one, no straightforward analogue to r or multiple R can be presented here. However, there are two tests of significance that resemble the test for r which assess whether the logits for each case predicted by a logistic regression model fit the observed data. The first, given by most software for logit models, is the likelihood ratio chi-square test of the fit of the logistic regression model to the observed pattern of 1's and 0's in the data. Since the larger this chi-square is, the poorer the fit, one hopes to obtain a low and therefore nonsignificant likelihood ratio chi-square. Conversely, probability levels in the range of .7 to .99 are indications that the model fits the data well.

The second significance test is based on the difference between a chi-square for the fit of the values predicted by the logistic regres-

sion equation to the data and a chi-square for the fit of the unconditional logit to the data. Just as in the test for the difference of r from
0, the errors for the two predictive models are compared to see if
the mistakes from a logistic regression are significantly smaller
than those from a model based on unconditional probability, using
only the intercept as an independent variable. Because the difference in the two chi-squares is itself a chi-square, a statistically significant chi-square for this test means that the improvement in
prediction for the logistic regression model is more than might be
expected by chance. To determine the effect of the independent
variable, it is important to examine the magnitude and direction of
the estimate of b in the logistic regression equation. Just as in least
squares regression, a positive sign indicates that increases in the
value of the dependent variable are associated with increases in the
independent variable and a negative sign implies the opposite. Coefficient values can be interpreted as odds multipliers. Since a logit
model is additive and adding logarithms is equivalent to multiplying numbers, taking the antilog of the b will give the expected mul-
tiplier of the odds for a one-unit increase of the independent variable. The effect of changes in X on the probability of Y must be
assessed by calculating a separate probability for each value of X
and then comparing them.

When the dependent variable is polytomous, calculations get
more complicated, but the logic is just an extension of a dichotomous variable. If there are more than 2 categories, more potential
odds and, therefore, more logits are possible. In general, if Y has C
categories, then Y has $C-1$ possible logits which compare the
probability of being in one of the $C-1$ categories with the probability of being in the C'th. Thus, for Y with 4 categories there
would be 3 logits:

$$L_{i1} = Log_n[P(Y_i = 1) / P(Y_i = 4)]$$
$$L_{i2} = Log_n[P(Y_i = 2) / P(Y_i = 4)]$$
$$L_{i3} = Log_n[P(Y_i = 3) / P(Y_i = 4)]$$

As a consequence, $j = C-1$ logistic regression equations, each
with a different a and b, are needed to estimate the relationship
between X and Y. They can be represented by the following:

$$L_{i1} = a_1 + b_1 X_i$$
$$L_{i2} = a_2 + b_2 X_i$$
$$\vdots \quad \vdots \quad \vdots$$
$$L_{ij} = a_j + b_j X_i$$

Though j equations are needed, the significance test for whether the variables are related, outlined above, still follows the same logic. It is only extended by calculating the two subtracted chi-squares for testing the fit of the set of equations to the data rather than just one equation. In addition, it is possible that the independent variable is related to some of the logits but not others. In other words, it might predict voting Republican as opposed to Democratic but not independent as opposed to Democratic. Logistic regression software for polytomous dependent variables will also calculate a 1 degree of freedom chi-square test for the significance of the difference of each b_j from 0. If the chi-square for the b_j for a particular equation is significant, then the independent variable is helpful in predicting that particular association.

Predicting from the value of real property whether a soldier is an officer or an enlisted man offers a simple example of the use of logistic regression. Table 8.11 presents the results of such a regression for the military at Fort Moultrie. Since the likelihood ratio chi-square test of fit is nonsignificant ($P > .30$), this model can be considered to fit the data, though not as well as one might like. Because the coefficient for value of real property is statistically significant ($P < .003$), this variable does seem to be able to predict whether a soldier is an officer or not. Since the program employed for this analysis compared the probability of being an enlisted man with that of being an officer, high values for value of real property were related to low probabilities of being an enlisted man. Therefore, the sign of the coefficient for property value is negative.

A CONTINUOUS INDEPENDENT AND AN ORDINAL DEPENDENT VARIABLE

When the dependent variable is ordinal and the independent variable continuous, the logistic regression model may be extended by

Table 8.11 *Logistic Regression of Rank on Value of Real Property*

Maximum Likelihood Analysis of Variance

Source	DF	Chi-square	Prob
Intercept	1	8.67	0.0032
Value of real property	1	8.93	0.0028
Likelihood ratio chi-square	15	16.85	0.3278

Analysis of Maximum Likelihood Estimates

Effect	Parameter	Estimate	Standard Error	Chi-square	Prob
Intercept	1	3.8227	1.2981	8.67	0.0032
Value of real property	2	−0.7311	0.2446	8.93	0.0028

using an *ordered response model.* This form of logistic regression is closely related to logistic regression for polytomous dependent variables in that more than one regression equation is required to estimate the relationship between X and Y. Rather than each equation having j different estimates for a_j and b_j, the technique assumes that there is only one estimate for b, but j estimates for a. In the general case, the equations would be

$$L_i(Y>1) = a_1 + b_1 X_i$$
$$L_i(Y>2) = a_2 + b_1 X_1$$
$$\vdots \qquad \vdots \quad \vdots$$
$$L_i(Y>j) = a_j + b_1 X_i$$

This formula implies that each of the $j = C-1$ logits is based on the probability that the value of Y is greater than or equal to the j'th ordinal value of the dependent variable and that the a_j's are the quantities that reflect the order. While the form of the ordered response model is different from that for the polytomous model, the logic of testing for the null hypothesis that the two variables are unrelated is identical. The same chi-square test of the goodness of fit of the logits predicted by the model to the data may be used in this instance. The reader may wish to consult Maddala (1983) for a complete discussion of this approach.

Bivariate statistics are essential for historical research, since they probe relationships between variables. It is crucial to understand their basic principles, since more complex techniques build upon their assumptions and procedures. In large and sometimes bewildering data sets, the accurate description of a connection between two attributes can provide important insights. In many cases, the association between a pair of core variables such as ethnicity and party vote already tells a great deal of the story. But when historians intend to explain more complex relationships and make causal statements about the influence of one factor upon another, they must go on to testing such hypotheses inferentially. Since descriptive appearances can be deceiving due to random error, conclusions may rest upon mere coincidence unless the impact of chance is systematically excluded. In spite of their simplicity and power, however, bivariate statistics are still quite limited because they can only examine one relationship at a time. To untangle the confused web of historical interrelationships requires more potent techniques which can weigh the relative influence of many variables simultaneously.

SOFTWARE NOTES

The chi-square, Cramer's V, lambda, gamma, and tau c statistics are produced by PROC FREQ in SAS and the CROSSTABS procedure in SPSS-X and SPSS/PC. Spearman's r_s is calculated by PROC CORR in SAS and the NONPAR CORR procedure in SPSS-X.

The Mann-Whitney and Kruskal-Wallis statistics as well as many other useful measures for ordinal dependent variables may be found in PROC NPAR1WAY in SAS or the NPAR TESTS procedure in SPSS-X and SPSS/PC. The Cochran-Mantel-Haenszel statistic labeled "ROW MEAN SCORES DIFFER" in SAS's PROC FREQ is equivalent to a Kruskal-Wallis test for simple row by column tables when SCORES = RANK is specified as an option on the TABLES statement.

Common statistical routines for performing regression analysis are SAS's PROC REG and SPSS's REGRESSION procedure. SAS's PROC PLOT and SPSS-X's and SPSS/PC's PLOT are useful for plotting data. SPSS's REGRESSION procedure provides helpful residual plots while SAS's PROC REG produces most sophisticated regression diagnostics found in Belsley, Kuh, and Welsch (1980).

Analysis of variance may be performed with PROC GLM in SAS or the ONEWAY or MANOVA procedures in SPSS-X and SPSS/PC. TYPE I sums of squares in PROC GLM correspond to the SEQUENTIAL sums of squares in SPSS MANOVA. TYPE III sums of squares in PROC GLM correspond to UNIQUE sums of squares in SPSS MANOVA. For cases involving only one categorical independent variable, these distinctions may be ignored.

Logistic regression analysis for dichotomous dependent variables may be performed by using PROC CATMOD and PROC LOGIST in SAS version 5, PROC PROBIT or PROC LOGISTIC in SAS version 6, or by requesting the MODEL = LOGIT subcommand of the PROBIT procedure in SPSS-X or the LOGISTIC REGRESSION procedure in SPSS/PC. Care should be taken when using the PROBIT procedure in SPSS-X for ungrouped data, because the standard errors which it produces for the coefficients of continuous independent variables are incorrect. The ordered logit model is estimated by PROC LOGIST in SAS version 5.18 and PROC PROBIT or PROC LOGISTIC in SAS version 6 for any polytomous dependent variable.

9

Statistics for Questions about Many Variables

As might be expected, the number and type of possible relationships among variables becomes quite complex when questions are asked about a dependent variable and two or more independent variables. There are, however, four basic issues which apply to many analytical situations:

1. *Can the values of two or more variables be used to predict the likely values of another variable?* For instance, in trying to explain the overwhelming success of the Republican party in southern New England during the 1860 presidential election, a historian would systematically examine which of the chief social and economic characteristics of the region, such as urbanization or industrialization, were associated with the Lincoln vote. Therefore, this first query simply restates the problem of whether or not two variables are related in the sense discussed in the previous chapter. When more than one variable may be used to forecast a dependent variable, it is possible to improve predictions of the values of the dependent variable by merely adding the predictive power of all the independent variables together rather than using just one of them. Statistics that accomplish this task are often called *linear additive models*. In most situations additional independent variables must be reasonably well correlated with the dependent variable in order to improve prediction significantly. Moreover, they should not be highly intercorrelated among themselves so as not to be redundant. Otherwise, using any one of them would provide about as much unique information for predicting the dependent variable as employing all of them. The sole exception to this general rule involves so-called *suppressor variables* which actually improve the overall accuracy of the prediction. They are independent variables, unre-

lated to a dependent variable but related to other independent variables, that suppress irrelevant noise in the relationship between the other independent variables and the dependent variable (see Pedhazur 1982, pp. 104–5).

2. *Does a particular independent variable improve the accuracy of the predictions of a dependent variable beyond the level reached by one or more of the other independent variables?* For instance, if urban population and degree of manufacturing were important factors in predicting the success of the Republican party in the 1860 election in New England, a scholar might want to probe additional hypotheses, such as the effect of farm cash value, to establish the pattern of Lincoln's rural support. The second question occurs in one form or another in many substantive investigations. It arises most often when a researcher believes that a factor not yet considered by the existing literature plays a role in predicting an important outcome. Because this new variable may be correlated to some degree with other variables already deemed important, the scholar must test its ability to improve the prediction of the dependent variable over and above the accuracy level of the prior variables rather than simply show a bivariate relationship between the new variable and the dependent variable. This is usually done by comparing the errors from two statistical prediction models, one that includes the variable in question and the established variables and another that includes just the previous variables. This *nested model* strategy is used in many different statistical techniques and will be addressed in greater detail for each particular procedure discussed.

3. *Are an independent and dependent variable causally related after the effects of one or more of the other variables are statistically controlled?* For instance, in the New England electoral study one might want to find out whether the relationship between factors such as urbanity or manufacturing and Republican vote remains the same or changes if one also takes the share of foreign born or geographic location into account. Hence the third problem is an extension of the second, but it requires more elaboration because researchers confronting this question usually make explicit or implicit causal assumptions. Scholars are generally interested not just in *predicting* a dependent variable but also in *explaining*

how the independent variables relate to the dependent variable by employing some hypothesized pattern of linear causal relationships. Because the independent variables are usually intercorrelated, the potential causal effect of any variable must be compared with the impact of the others, controlled or "held constant" in a statistical rather than an experimental sense. Instead of experimentally manipulating the levels of independent variables by random assignment of cases into treatment groups with known levels of the independent variables, investigators must use the values found in their archival data to control the levels of independent variables mathematically.

Since other authors have covered causal analysis extensively, it is only necessary to discuss the basic principle for a simple three variable situation. (For further details, see Blalock [1964]; Duncan [1975]; Heise [1975]; Pedhazur [1982]; and Rosenburg [1968].) Suppose a researcher had data on three continuous variables, called W, X, and Y, for a random sample of cases. Assume also that each pair of variables was correlated and the object was both to predict Y and to explain how W and X relate to it in a causal sense. By positing that Y in fact occurs after W and X, one would already establish some hypothesized causal order. Though not so easily made in practice, this helpful assumption tells little about the way in which W and X might be causally related to Y and to each other.

Figure 9.1 presents three possibilities in the form of simple diagrams, also called *causal models*. The direction of a single-headed arrow indicates a hypothesized effect of one variable on another, and a double-headed arrow means a simple correlation between variables with no hypothesized causal relationship. These diagrams demonstrate clearly why choosing one variable as dependent only simplifies the number of possible causal interrelationships among three variables but fails to leave one clear alternative. While all the models posit that both W and X have direct effects on Y, they differ markedly with respect to what they hypothesize about the relationship between W and X. They might be simply correlated, as shown in figure 9.1a. Alternatively, W might be a cause of X (fig. 9.1b) or X might be a cause of W (fig. 9.1c). The correct model cannot be determined by merely examining the correlations, because all the mod-

Figure 9.1 *Alternative Three Variable Causal Diagrams for Two Variables Directly Causing a Third*

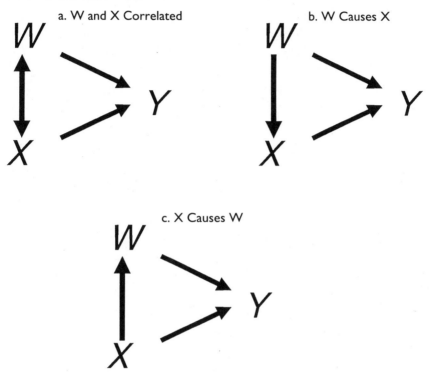

els imply that each pair of variables would be correlated. To make matters worse, if one tested for the incremental predictive effect of both variables on Y with the nested model strategy discussed above and found such impact for both variables, there still would be no way to tell statistically which of the three models was the correct one.

Causal paths for certain models can be untangled by statistically controlling the relationship between two variables for the effects of another. Four such models are diagrammed in figure 9.2. The first two (figs. 9.2a and b) are examples of *spurious relationships* in which the correlation between two variables is not due to a causal influence of one on the other but rather derives from a single common cause responsible for their covariation. The final two (figs. 9.2c and d) are examples of causal chains in which the observed correlation between the first and last variables does not stem from any direct effect flowing from the first to the last but rather from a causal path through a third intermediate variable. Statistical tests for all of these models involve controlling the observed relationship between the two variables, hypothesized as truly unrelated, for the effects of the third common cause or intermediate variable. If the controlled association turns out not to be significantly different from zero, then the analysis supports either a spurious association or an intermediate variable model. Unfortunately, when all three variables are intercorrelated there is no statistical way to choose between the two models. Hence affirmative results of statistical tests of causal models do not necessarily prove the correctness of the model. They merely fail to eliminate that particular model from consideration as one of a set of possible explanations that are consistent with the observed data. Therefore, the researcher must choose the causal model to be tested carefully based on theoretical or substantive knowledge of the problem at hand.

4. *Is the relationship between a set of independent variables and a dependent variable different for distinct groupings of cases?* For instance, the relationship between urban population, manufacturing, and Republican vote might turn out to be rather different for counties with a certain type of economic activity, such as fishing and cotton weaving or leather and woollen goods. The fourth question often occurs when an investigator suspects that the relationship between certain independent variables and a dependent variable might differ for distinct clusters of cases. While applicable to situations where all the variables are ordered or categorical, this issue is most easily illustrated by examining the case in which the relationship between two continuous variables might be affected by a third categorical variable. For example, suppose a scholar obtained sample data on the relationship between years of education and income for black and white males from 1900 to 1930. It is reasonable to hypothesize that during this period racial discrimination constricted the opportunities of blacks to earn as much as their white counterparts regardless of their level of education. How would one go about investigating this question?

The answer requires controlling the relationship between educa-

Figure 9.2 *Four Variable Causal Models for Spurious and Chain Relationships*

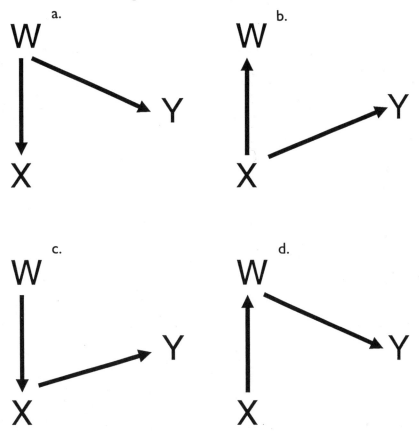

tion and income for the third variable—race. One could accomplish this end by plotting the data points for blacks and whites on separate X-Y graphs and also running separate bivariate regression equations for them. The result might show that the bivariate regression lines for the two groups differed markedly and appeared like those in figure 9.3. Not only does the regression line for the data points for whites have a higher intercept than the line for blacks, but it also slopes upward more steeply. This finding would lend substantial support to the discrimination hypothesis by revealing not only that black incomes were generally lower than white earnings but also that increased levels of education improved wages for whites at

Figure 9.3 *Plot of Hypothetical Relationship between Income and Education for Whites and Blacks*

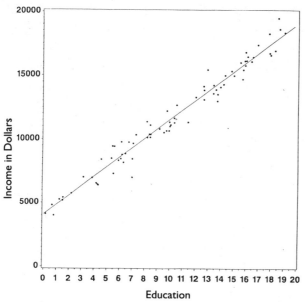

a. Whites

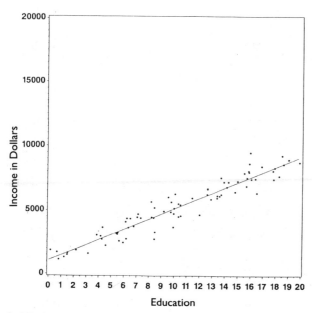

b. Blacks

a rate greater than for blacks. Thus, the relationship between education and income, as measured by the intercepts and slopes of the regression lines, differs for blacks and whites. Such patterns are often referred to as *interactions* because a third variable, in this case race, interacts with or modifies the relationship between an independent and dependent variable.

This simple interaction is called a *one-way interaction*, because only one variable modifies the relationship between two others. However, it is certainly possible, though not common, to have two-, three-, or, for that matter, multi-way interactions among groups of variables. For example, when adding consideration of gender to the above example and plotting the data, one might find four different intercepts and four distinct linear relationships between income and education. These would show that all blacks had lower intercepts than whites but also would indicate that the slopes for females of each race were less steep than those of the males. This result would imply that there is a two-way interaction of race and gender on the relationship between income and education. While these more complicated models are often more plausible and interesting than linear, additive explanations, they are also more difficult to estimate and test.

SINGLE CONTINUOUS DEPENDENT VARIABLES

In questions about many independent variables, techniques for continuous dependent variables are the easiest to grasp initially. In developing a prediction equation for a continuous dependent variable from several continuous independent variables, the most useful method is an extension of bivariate regression called *multiple regression*. If all independent variables are categorical, the procedure employed is termed *analysis of variance*. When some independent variables are continuous and some are categorical, the technique applied is referred to as *analysis of covariance*. While many statistical texts treat these methods as distinct, it is possible to show that the latter procedures are special cases of multiple regression (see Pedhazur [1982] for details). Therefore, this discussion will focus on multiple regression as a paradigmatic approach to examining the four research questions stated at the beginning of this chapter.

When all independent variables are continuous, a multiple regression equation is a straightforward extension of the bivariate procedure. The general form of a bivariate regression equation is

$$Y_i = a + bX_i + E_i \qquad\qquad 9.1$$

where the subscript i symbolically indicates the values of Y, X, and E for the i'th case of a total of N cases, a is the intercept, b is the slope of the least squares regression line, and E is the residual or error term (i.e., the difference between the Y value predicted from applying a and b to the data for the i'th case and the actual value of Y for the i'th case). A multiple regression equation simply extends this equation to include more independent variables, producing the following general form:

$$Y_i = a + b_1 X_{i1} + b_2 X_{i2} + \ldots + b_j X_{ij} + E_i \qquad\qquad 9.2$$

The i subscript again indicates that each of the N cases may have different values of Y and the various X's. The j subscript for the X's indicate that they are different variables labeled X_1, X_2, etc. The ellipses merely mean that the number of X's can, in theory, be quite large. Instead of a single independent variable called X, multiple regression employs two or more independent variables labeled X_1, X_2, etc., and each independent variable has a corresponding b labeled b_1, b_2, etc. Rather than describing a simple, straight line relating Y with a single X, multiple regression models can be thought of as representing a best fitting plane in a multidimensional data space that provides the best least squares prediction of the values of Y from the values of all the X's.

The same assumptions as in bivariate regression must be used to calculate unique values of the b's from the known values of Y and the X's for each case through the least squares method. In addition, the number of cases has to be greater than the number of independent variables in order for the values of the b_j's to be unique. In practice, good estimates require that the cases be much more numerous than variables. Solving for the b_j's by the least squares method produces the unique values of the b_j's that minimize the errors in prediction (i.e., the E_i's). The interpretation of the b_j's is similar to the meaning of b in the bivariate regression equation with an additional qualifier. The value of a b_j is the expected, linear increase in the value of Y associated with a one-unit increase in the value of the corresponding X_j, while the values of all the other X_j's in the equation are controlled by being held constant.

For multiple regression with continuous independent variables the X_j values are simply those found in the data, because they are recorded in their natural units such as dollars, weight in tons, or area in acres. But when the X_j's are categorical, such as gender, race, native-born versus foreign-born, party affiliation, or region, the proper numerical values for these variables are not intuitively apparent. They may be transformed into *dummy variables*, using a pattern of ones and zeros to represent the divisions of the variable. If the variable has only two classes like gender, a single, dummy X variable is created by assigning a numeric value of 1 for the cases in one group while giving a value of 0 for all cases in the other group. Usually the 0 group serves as a baseline for comparison with members of the group of interest. If a scholar were interested in comparing females with males, the males would be assigned a value of 0 and the females a value of 1. Another popular alternative is *mean deviation coding*, which creates variables coded with a pattern of 1's, 0's, and -1's to represent categorical variables (see Cohen and Cohen 1983). In practice, these coding assignments can easily be programmed with the data transformation statements available in statistical software, and most analysis of variance routines perform this task automatically.

The procedure for dummy coding becomes more complicated for variables that have more than two categories because two or more variables must be created to represent all the categories. The logic for creating these dummy variables is as follows:

1. Pick one category as the baseline for comparison.
2. Create $k - 1$ dummy variables, where $k - 1$ is the number of classes or categories left after deducting the comparison category.

3. Choose one of the dummy variables to represent each one of the remaining categories.

4. For each case, assign the dummy variable that represents the case category a value of 1 and assign 0's to all the other dummy variables for that case.

A scholar might want, for example, to create dummy variables to represent three broad categories of religious affiliation of individuals—Protestant, Catholic, and Jewish. If interested in comparing Catholics and Jews to Protestants, one would need to create two (i.e., k = 3 − 1) dummy X variables to represent this single categorical religious affiliation variable. The patterns of coding of the dummy variables for each type of individual would be:

Individual's Religion	Catholic Dummy Variable	Jewish Dummy Variable
Catholic	1	0
Jewish	0	1
Protestant	0	0

It is possible to use only two dummy variables, because three distinct code patterns (0,1; 1,0; 0,0) may be created with two such variables. The three religions can therefore be represented by these distinct patterns and do not require three dummy variables.

Either dummy or continuous X variables or their combinations may be used in multiple regression models to explore the four issues outlined above. The first question concerning simple prediction of a dependent variable by a group of independent variables is most easily answered by examining the *multiple R* for the prediction equation, given by every multiple regression and analysis of variance program. Like its bivariate cousin, Pearson's r, the multiple R is an indicator of the strength of the relationship between the set of independent variables and the dependent variable. However, because it summarizes the relationship of several independent variables, some of which may be positively and some negatively related to the dependent variable, it is restricted in value to the range between 0 and 1. The nearer the value of the multiple R statistic for a given model approaches 1, the tighter the model *fits* the observed data by coming closer to predicting the observed values of Y. Like a simple r, the square of the multiple R, also referred to as *R squared*, R^2, or the *coefficient of determination*, gives the proportion of the total variance of the dependent variable accounted for by the regression equation and forms the basis for a test of significance for its difference from zero.

The F test for the statistical significance of R tests the null hypothesis that R = 0 or that there is no relationship between any of the independent variables and the dependent variable. Like the significance test for Pearson's r, the F test of significance for a multiple R compares the sum of squared errors for a predictive model based only on the mean of Y with those from the model under consideration. The calculation formula is

$$F_{(K, N-K-1 \text{ d.f.})} = [R_2 / K] / [(1 - R_2) / (N - K - 1)] \qquad 9.3$$

where K is the number of independent variables exclusive of the intercept and N is the number of cases. Since K and N determine the correct degrees of freedom for calculating the probability level, the F test must always be evaluated relative to these latter two values. In practice, this probability is routinely displayed by virtually every statistical software package.

Interpreting the results of this test is a bit more difficult than evaluating the significance of r. Even if the probability value for a particular multiple R is in the range of statistical significance, such as below .05, this does not mean that all of the independent variables have a statistically significant relationship with the dependent variable. Technically, the test of the significance of a multiple R only scrutinizes the null hypothesis that none of the b_j's is different from 0 (i.e., $b_1 = b_2 = \ldots = b_j = 0$). In other words, the null hypothesis implies that *none* of the X_j's are linearly related to the dependent variable. Thus, a significant R only means that at least one, but possibly more than one, variable is significantly related to the dependent variable, controlling for the effects of the other variables. A significant R cannot indicate which particular variables have an impact on the dependent variable. To determine which factors are relevant after the other variables are statistically held constant, one must examine the significance tests for the individual b_j

coefficients. This can be accomplished by dividing each coefficient with its associated standard error and comparing the value obtained with the t distribution with 1 degree of freedom. The result gives the probability of falsely rejecting the null hypothesis that the b_j for the regression model is equal to 0. During computerized processing, some multiple regression routines in statistical packages report an F statistic and corresponding level of significance instead of a t. This is an acceptable alternative for because $F = t^2$ testing the likely difference of multiple regression coefficients from 0.

The interpretation given to a statistically significant b_j helps answer the second and third questions raised at the beginning of this chapter. If a multiple regression coefficient is significant, then the inclusion of its corresponding variable in the multiple regression equation improves the accuracy of prediction of the dependent variable over and above that made by the other independent variables alone. In other words, controlling for or partialling out the effects of the other variables, it makes an additional contribution to the prediction of the values of the dependent variable. For this reason these coefficients are sometimes referred to as *partial regression coefficients*. The magnitude of the contribution, however, cannot be judged from the coefficient itself but must be assessed by comparing the multiple R of a regression model which includes the variable in question and the other independent variables with the R from a nested model that includes *only* the other independent variables. The signed difference in these two R's, often called the *semipartial R*, is a measure of both the improvement in prediction provided by a particular independent variable and the direction of the controlled relationship between it and the dependent variable.

A test of significance based on the semi-partial R squared can also determine whether an additional set of independent variables will improve the prediction of a dependent variable. If the R squared for the multiple regression equation including the full set of variables is called RSQ_f and the one for the nested equation including only the base or restricted set is termed RSQ_r, then an F test for the significance of the contribution of the additional variables is:

$$F_{(K_f-K_r, \, N-K_f-1 \text{ d.f.})} =$$
$$[(RSQ_f - RSQ_r) / (K_f - K_r)] / [(1 - RSQ_f) / (N - K_f - 1)] \qquad 9.4$$

where K_f is the number of independent variables in the full regression equation and K_r is the number of predictor variables in the restricted model.

When the dependent variable is hypothesized to be causally determined by some of the independent variables, a significant or nonsignificant b_j coefficient has important implications for any hypothesized causal model. If the spuriousness model (in figure 9.2a) is assumed, then a significant coefficient (b_1) for X in the regression $Y = a + b_1 X + b_2 W$ would indicate that X and Y were not unrelated after W is controlled and that the hypothesized model cannot be correct. Similarly, if causal connections were hypothesized between W and X, X and Y, and W and Y and the coefficient for W (b_2) were not significant in the above equation, then the suspected relationship between W and Y would not be reasonable. For more information on the tests of significance for regression coefficients and the logic of causal analysis, refer to the texts cited above.

Often analysts wish to compare the causal impact of two or more independent variables rather than their effect on predicting the dependent variable. In addition, they may want to construct causal *path models* of the relationships under investigation (see Heise 1975). While it is tempting simply to use the magnitude of the relevant b_j's from estimated regression equations for these purposes, such comparisons are not warranted because each of the corresponding X_j's is usually measured in different units. For instance, while X_1 could be indicated in units of hundreds of dollars, X_2 might be given in dollars. Even if X_1 had exactly the same causal impact as X_2, the difference in measurement units would create a b_1 with approximately 1/100 the strength of b_2. Standardized regression coefficients, sometimes called *Beta coefficients*, may be used to remove the effect of different units of measurement by adjusting unstandardized coefficients as follows:

$$b_j^* = b_j \times \frac{S_j}{S_y} \qquad 9.5$$

where b_j^* is the standardized coefficient, S_j is the standard deviation of X_j, and S_y is the standard deviation of Y. The b_j^*'s are comparable in the sense that they are measures of the increase in expected standard deviation units of the dependent variable resulting from a one standard deviation unit increase in an independent variable. While comparisons among standardized coefficients are appropriate for a particular sample of data, they are generally inadvisable across samples because the standard deviations used in adjusting the raw b_j coefficients are sample specific. (See also Kim and Ferrer [1981].)

Tests of statistical significance for unstandardized coefficients can also provide solutions to problems involving variable interactions such as question four above. An explanatory model for the example about race, education, and income that includes an interaction between race and education can be formulated in the following regression equation:

$$\text{Income} = a + b_1\text{Education} + b_2\text{Race} + b_3(\text{Race} \times \text{Education}) \qquad 9.6$$

where the i subscripts have been omitted for simplicity. In this regression model, a is the intercept, the b_j's are coefficients, the variable names are used instead of X's for readability, and the $\times$ indicates multiplication. The values of education for the cases would be coded in raw years, while those for race would be dummy coded using 0's for whites and 1's for blacks. In addition to including education and race, this model has a product term (Race $\times$ Education) with a coefficient (b_3). This term would be constructed with a statistical package by creating a new variable with values that were the product of the race and education values for each case.

The significance test for b_3 from the multiple regression equation above can answer the question of whether the relationship between education and income for whites is different from that for blacks. Literally, b_3 is the adjustment to the white slope relating education and income (b_1) necessary to show the corresponding relationship for blacks (see Long and Miethe 1988). For this example, the adjustment would be expected to be negative because of discrimination. The null hypothesis posits that the slopes for blacks and whites are equal (i.e., $b_3 = 0$). Therefore, a statistically significant b_3 rejects that hypothesis and provides support for the alternative conclusion that they are different.

This logic for testing a single, one-way interaction can be extended to multiple and higher order interactions. To include further one-way interactions only requires adding independent variables and appropriate product terms to the equation. If an additional interaction between gender and education were hypothesized for the previous example, a dummy coded gender variable and a product term for gender and education would need to be added to the above regression model so as to estimate the R and b_j's for the following:

$$\text{Income} = a + b_1\text{Education} + b_2\text{Race} + b_3\text{ Gender} +$$
$$b_4(\text{Race} \times \text{Education}) + b_5(\text{Gender} \times \text{Education}) \qquad 9.7$$

Moreover, if a two-way interaction were hypothesized between race and gender on the relationship between education and income as discussed previously, then the regression model to be estimated would be

$$\text{Income} = a + b_1\text{Education} + b_2\text{Race} + b_3\text{Gender} +$$
$$b_4(\text{Race} \times \text{Education}) + b_5(\text{Gender} \times \text{Education}) +$$
$$b_6(\text{Race} \times \text{Gender} \times \text{Education}) \qquad 9.8$$

This model includes not only the two-way interaction term (Race × Gender × Education) but also both of the possible one-way interactions and all of the individual variables. Such a model is *hierarchical* in the sense that all of the simpler components of any higher order interaction are also included in it. When estimating and testing multiple regression models involving interactions, it is customary to insure that these models are hierarchical. This principle also extends to categorical and ordinal dependent variables.

Just as the regression models for variable interactions are difficult to specify, the logic of the order of significance tests for them becomes more intricate. Basically the testing procedure for hypothesized interactions follows the hierarchy of the model by successively trying to eliminate each level of interaction beginning with the highest. In the last model above (9.8), one would first test to see whether the two-way interaction for gender and race on education was statistically significant after all the other individual variables and one-way interactions had been controlled. In essence, this is simply asking question two for this interaction. The t or F test for b_6 would provide an answer. A statistically significant b_6 would suggest that there probably is a two-way interaction of race and gender on the relationship between education and income and that the regression model should not be further simplified by dropping this interaction out of the prediction model. However, a nonsignificant b_6 would indicate that the two-way interaction was not likely to be present, so that one could move on to test for other potentially simpler relationships.

In order to test for the elimination of the two one-way interactions, one would need to compare the R^2 for model 9.7 with the R^2 for a model that included just the individual race, gender, and education variables. For this problem, the test of the difference of two R^2's given earlier in this chapter (9.4) proves useful. If the results were statistically significant, then one could examine the significance of the coefficients of each interaction term (b_4 and b_5) to determine if either one or both were responsible for the significant improvement in the prediction. On the other hand, nonsignificant one-way interactions would indicate that there was no difference between blacks and whites or males and females in the partial regression coefficient relating years of education and income. However, if the gender and race variables were each individually significant, this result would suggest that while the relationship between education and income was the same for all groups, they each had different intercepts.

Since this discussion of multiple regression only provides a brief overview, a few notes of caution are in order. First, the validity of conclusions based on this technique depends upon the degree to which its underlying assumptions are met. Clearly, the reliability of the coefficient estimates and the predicted values of the dependent variable are contingent on the premise that the relationship between each independent variable and the dependent variable is linear, that the independent variables are measured without error, that no independent variables are omitted, and that the variances of the errors are constant across the range of values of X_j's. As much as

possible, a researcher should use the regression diagnostics mentioned in chapter 8 to check for the potential violation of assumptions before deriving any final conclusions from a particular multiple regression model. Secondly, some coefficient estimates and
their significance tests can be quite unreliable when the independent variables are highly intercorrelated—a condition called *multicollinearity*. For further information on its detection, implications,
and correction, see Belsley, Kuh, and Welsch (1980).

As an illustration of multiple regression, a scholar might want to
probe how well the value of real estate owned by the soldiers at Fort
Moultrie can be predicted by their military rank and age. One
would expect that officers would generally be wealthier than enlisted men and that older soldiers would be more likely to have
accumulated real estate than younger men. This hypothesis requires a multiple regression model predicting value of real estate
held from two independent variables, soldiers' age and rank, coded
as a dummy variable with a value of 1 for officers and 0 for enlisted
men. The computer output for this model, edited slightly for ap-
pearance, appears in table 9.1a. Notice that it is divided into two
main sections labeled "Analysis of Variance" and "Parameter Estimates." The first part gives the R squared measure of fit of the
model just to the right of the label "R-square." For this example, it
is a respectable .82, meaning that the multiple R is just over .90 (R
= Square Root[R^2]). The value of the F test for the significance of
the difference of this value of R from 0 is given on the right of
the row of figures labeled "Model" under the column heading "F
Value." The degrees of freedom, found under the column labeled
"DF," are 2 for the model and 42 for the error or unexplained variance. The probability of finding this high an R value by chance
appears under the heading "Prob>F" and is .0001. Since it is highly
unlikely that this result occurred because of the effects of random
error, one can safely reject the null hypothesis that R = 0 for this
model and conclude that rank and age together are good predictors
of the value of real estate owned by soldiers at Fort Moultrie.

An examination of the second section of 9.1a reveals what relationship rank and age have to the value of real estate held. The
multiple regression coefficient estimates are found under the col-

umn labeled "Parameter Estimate," because parameters are simply
another name given to coefficients. Rounding off these coefficients
to one decimal place indicates that the estimated multiple regression equation for this model is

$$\text{REAL} = -755.4 + 969.6\,\text{RANKDUM} + 31.2\,\text{AGE} + E$$

where REAL, RANKDUM, and AGE are convenient labels for value
of real estate, the rank dummy variable, and soldier's age and E is
the error term. A quick glance down the column labeled "Prob>|T|"
shows that the T tests for the difference of both coefficients of the
independent variables from 0 are highly significant, suggesting that
each variable has a relationship with the dependent variable when
the other is controlled. Each factor, therefore, makes an independent contribution to predicting the value of real estate held. Examining the value of the estimated b for RANKDUM shows that, controlling for age, on average officers have about $970 more property
than enlisted men. The b for age indicates that regardless of rank,
each year of age results in an expected increase of about $31.20 in
the value of real estate held. Since both coefficient estimates could
be off by as much as twice their standard errors, one should not rely
too strongly on the apparent precision of these figures. Nonetheless, these results do provide a reasonable idea of how age and rank
might have helped determine the accumulation of property among
these soldiers.

To refine the above model, one would need to include an interaction term. Since officers were generally recruited from a higher social stratum than most enlisted men and were better paid, it seems
reasonable to hypothesize that officers accumulated real property
faster than enlisted men. Stating this hunch in multiple regression
terms is to surmise that the partial slope for the relationship between value of real property and age was greater for officers than
enlisted men. This hypothesis may be tested by adding a multiplicative term (RANKAGE) to the previous model in order to find out
whether the sign is positive or not and to test its significance. The
edited computer output for this model is shown in table 9.1b.

It is striking that the value of R^2 (.94) is higher for this model,
indicating that the prediction is improved by adding the interaction

Table 9.1a *Multiple Regression of Value of Real Estate on Age and Rank*

Dependent Variable: REAL   Value of Real Estate

Analysis of Variance

Source	DF	Sum of Squares	Mean Square	F Value	Prob>F
Model	2	8788523.9497	4394261.9748	95.764	0.0001
Error	42	1927226.0503	45886.33453		
Root MSE		214.21096	R-square	0.8202	

Parameter Estimates

Variable	DF	Parameter Estimate	Standard Error	T for H0: Parameter = 0	Prob>|T|
INTERCEP	1	−755.360	167.750	−4.503	0.0001
RANKDUM	1	969.594	104.441	9.284	0.0001
AGE	1	31.170	6.024	5.174	0.0001

Table 9.1b *Multiple Regression of Value of Real Estate on Age, Rank, and Their Interaction*

Dependent Variable: REAL   Value of Real Estate

Analysis of Variance

Source	DF	Sum of Squares	Mean Square	F Value	Prob>F
Model	3	10052506.405	3350835.4684	207.140	0.0001
Error	41	663243.59498	16176.67305		
Root MSE		127.18755	R-square	0.9381	
Dep Mean		255.00000	Adj R-sq	0.9336	
C.V.		49.87747			

Parameter Estimates

Variable	DF	Parameter Estimate	Standard Error	T for H0: Parameter = 0	Prob>|T|
INTERCEP	1	− 153.091	120.676	−1.269	0.2117
RANKDUM	1	−1208.741	254.115	−4.757	0.0001
AGE	1	9.073	4.363	2.079	0.0439
RANKAGE	1	67.342	7.618	8.839	0.0001

term. As might be expected, the F test for the fit of the model is highly significant (p < .0001). The coefficient for the multiplicative, interaction variable (RANKAGE) is also highly significant and its sign is positive. These two facts lend support to the hypothesis that officers accumulated property faster than enlisted men. Comparing the coefficients for AGE and RANKAGE shows that enlisted men accumulated real property at a rate of about $9 per year while the officers gained wealth more quickly at about $76 ($9 + $67). While the figures might not be entirely reliable as precise estimators of this difference, they do indicate that the disparity between officers and enlisted men was substantial.

SINGLE CATEGORICAL DEPENDENT VARIABLES

When the dependent variable is categorical and the independent variables are continuous, nominal, or a mixture of the two, multiple logistic regression may be used to determine if there is a relationship between them. As in the previous chapter, this technique for variables with unordered categories becomes transparent when considering a simple dichotomous dependent variable. Similar to multiple regression, the general form of the multiple logistic regression equation is an extension of the bivariate equation:

$$\text{Log}_n\left[P(Y_i = 1 | X_i = V_i) / [1 - P(Y_i = 1 | X_i = V_i)]\right] = $$
$$a + b_1 X_{i1} + b_2 X_{i2} + \ldots + b_j X_{ij} \qquad 9.9$$

The left side of the equation is almost the same as the expression for the logit found in chapter 8. However, for multiple logistic regression, the X_i refers to the fact that there are now up to K independent variables represented by the subscript j with a corresponding set of V_i distinct values for each of the i cases. At the same time, the probability of Y taking on a value of 1 for any case is conditional on the values of all the X's rather than just a single X. The right side is identical to the general form of the multiple regression equation (equation 9.2).

As in the bivariate case, the above equation may be reexpressed in terms of either the odds or probabilities of Y being equal to 1. The general expression for the odds is:

$$\text{Odds}(Y_i = 1 | X_i = V_i) =$$
$$P(Y_i = 1 | X_i = V_i) / [1 - P(Y_i = 1 | X_i = V_i)] \qquad 9.10$$
$$= e^{(a + b_1 X_{i1} + b_2 X_{i2} + \ldots b_j X_{ij})}$$

The expression for probabilities is:

$$P(Y_i = 1 | X_i = V_i) = \frac{e^{(a + b_1 X_{i1} + b_2 X_{i2} + \ldots b_j X_{ij})}}{1 + e^{(a + b_1 X_{i1} + b_2 X_{i2} + \ldots b_j X_{ij})}} \qquad 9.11$$

Thus, for multiple logistic regression the logits, odds, and probabilities are each determined by all of the X's rather than just a single X.

Estimates of the b_j's and tests of fit for a multiple logistic regression model may be obtained by the maximum likelihood method, using statistical software. As in bivariate logistic regression, no generally accepted measure of the strength of the relationship between the X's and the categorical dependent variable exists. However, both the likelihood ratio chi-square and the chi-square test of improvement of the multiple logistic model over a model with only an intercept may be performed. Often the latter must be accomplished by using a logistic regression computer program to obtain the chi-square for each model separately and then manually subtracting the chi-square for the multiple logistic model from that for the intercept-only model in order to obtain the difference chi-square. The degrees of freedom for this test are equal to the number of independent variables in the multiple logistic regression equation. Keep in mind that for the simple likelihood ratio test, a nonsignificant chi-square is an indicator of an acceptable model, while for the difference chi-square test a significant chi-square means that the model improves the prediction of the dependent variable above simply using the mean logit. It is also important to remember that, especially for smaller samples, the difference chi-square test is more reliable.

If a multiple logistic regression model for a set of data passes either or both of the above tests of fit, then one is likely to be able to predict values of one variable from several others. In other words, the answer to question one at the beginning of the chapter is probably yes. However, as was the case with multiple regression, this result does not reveal anything about the relationships of any of the individual independent variables to the categorical dependent variable. Thus, answers for questions two and three about these relations may be found by examining the individual coefficients and their associated tests of significance. Most logistic regression programs will report the coefficient estimates along with their respective standard errors and either a t or chi-square test of the difference of each coefficient from 0. If either of these tests for a coefficient associated with a particular independent variable is statistically significant, then one can say with reasonable confidence that including that variable in the equation improves prediction, even when the effects of the other variables are controlled. In such cases, the answer to question two would be yes. In addition, if the variable in question was part of a simple causal model that hypothesized a link between it and the dependent variable, the presence of such a connection could not be refuted by this test.

The interpretation of the effect of a statistically significant coefficient in a multiple logistic regression model depends on whether it is given in terms of logits, odds, or probabilities. Strictly speaking, an estimated b_j is the expected increase in the logit for Y equalling 1 for a one-unit increase in the level of the corresponding X_j, when all the other X_j's are controlled by being held at some constant values. In this sense, a logistic regression coefficient is no different than a conventional multiple regression coefficient. However, logits are rather abstract quantities that are not readily grasped, while odds and probabilities are more easily understood. Hence explaining the effect of a particular independent variable in these terms has more intuitive appeal. It is relatively uncomplicated to determine the effect of a variable on the odds of Y equalling one, given the estimate of its coefficient in a logistic regression model. Simply taking the antilog of the b_j of interest (i.e., raising e = 2.71828 to the b_j power) indicates the expected amount of multiplication of the odds if the corresponding X_j were raised one unit, controlling for the impact of the other independent variables. This operation can easily be performed on most scientific hand calculators with an EXP key. Coefficient values greater than 0 would yield odds multipliers greater than 1, meaning that an increase in the corresponding X increases the odds of Y equalling 1. Values less than 0 would yield fractional odds multipliers, suggesting that an increase in X would be expected to decrease those odds.

Unfortunately, equation 9.11 above, relating the coefficients to probabilities, is not linear in form. In fact, the graph plotting the values of any X against the probabilities for those values is shaped like an elongated S. In contrast to calculating the effects on odds, it is impossible to calculate an effect of a unit increase in a particular X on the probability of Y being one that does not depend on the particular values of all the independent variables. Instead, one must assess any such increase with the values of the independent variables set at some determined levels—often their means or modes. Thus, researchers desiring to interpret coefficients in probability terms often calculate several example probabilities of interest for carefully chosen values of the X_j's using equation 9.11 and then compare these probabilities.

Questions about interactions in multiple logistic regression models may be addressed with methods that parallel the techniques of multiple regression. Interaction variables are created as products of single variables and tests for the significance of their coefficients have the same interpretation and logical ordering. The major difference lies in the fact that the tests of significance for interaction terms in multiple logistic regression models use differences in likelihood ratio chi-squares for full and restricted models. Thus, these tests have the general form

$$G^2_{diff} = G^2_r - G^2_{f2} \qquad\qquad 9.12$$

where G^2_{diff} is the chi-square for the difference between the full and restricted models, G^2_r is the chi-square for the simpler or restricted model, and G^2_{f2} is the chi-square for the more complicated interaction model. The degrees of freedom for such tests are simply the difference in the number of variables in the two models.

Readers aware of developments in the analysis of categorical independent and dependent variables may well wonder why the topic of log-linear models has not yet been broached. The formal answer is that as long as a researcher is interested in predicting a dummy coded dependent variable from a set of dummy coded independent variables, the logistic model can be algebraically derived from a log-linear model and the coefficients of the logit model shown to be merely twice the value of the appropriate log-linear model (Swafford 1980). In this case the two techniques are, in fact, equivalent. Since logit models are more easily understood as extensions of conventional multiple regression models, this introduction opted to discuss them rather than the more mathematically complex log-linear models. For further information, consult the discussions in Everitt (1977), Fienberg (1980), and Everitt and Dunn (1983).

As mentioned in chapter 8, when a categorical dependent variable has more than 2 categories, the number of logits for which there need to be separate prediction equations increases to $C-1$, where C is the number of categories of the dependent variable. If Y has 4 categories, then there are 3 possible logits. If one used category 4 as the basis for comparison, one would have

$$
\begin{aligned}
L_{i1} &= \text{Log}_n[P(Y_i = 1) \,/\, P(Y_i = 4)] \\
L_{i2} &= \text{Log}_n[P(Y_i = 2) \,/\, P(Y_i = 4)] \\
L_{i3} &= \text{Log}_n[P(Y_i = 3) \,/\, P(Y_i = 4)]
\end{aligned}
\qquad 9.13
$$

By extending the bivariate equations to include more than one X, the general form of multiple logistic regression for a polychotomous Y becomes

$$
\begin{aligned}
L_{i1} &= a_1 + b_{11}X_{i1} + b_{21}X_{i2} + \ldots + b_{j1}X_{ij} \\
L_{i2} &= a_2 + b_{12}X_{i1} + b_{22}X_{i2} + \ldots + b_{j2}X_{ij} \\
&\;\;\vdots \qquad \vdots \qquad \vdots \qquad \vdots \qquad\qquad \vdots \\
L_{ik} &= a_k + b_{1k}X_{ij} + b_{2k}X_{i2} + \ldots + b_{jk}X_{ij}
\end{aligned}
\qquad 9.14
$$

where the i subscript indicates the case, the j subscript the independent variable, and k the particular logit being predicted.

Programs that estimate the coefficients of this type of model report likelihood ratio chi-squares for the fit of all the equations, taken together, to test whether any of the b_{jk}'s are greater than 0. They also produce separate chi-squares for the significance of the predictive effect of each X across all the equations. Considering the complexity of using this type of logistic regression, this is still the most useful technique for studying controlled associations between independent variables and this type of dependent variable. Finally, chi-square tests for the significance of individual b_{jk}'s for each equation are reported so as to test for the effect of a particular X_j on a particular logit. One may also perform nested model chi-square tests by using the fit chi-squares from separate models to check the significance of the association of a group of independent variables, some or all of which might be interaction variables, with all of the logits.

As an example of a multiple logistic regression analysis, a historian might try to see if there is a difference between native-born and foreign-born soldiers in the probability of being married. Since it is logical to assume up to a point that the older the men were, the more likely they were to be married, one needs to control for age. The researcher would have to estimate a multiple logistic regression model with marital status as the dependent variable and age and a dummy variable for being foreign- or native-born as independent variables. The results of such an analysis for the Fort Moultrie data are presented in table 9.2. Similar to multiple regression, the computer output is divided into two sections of "Goodness-of-Fit" and "Parameter Estimates." Replacing the "Analysis of Variance" heading, the fit section contains both a Pearson and likelihood ratio chi-square test of the fit of the logistic regression model to the data, but it lacks a difference chi-square test. The marked nonsignificance of the likelihood ratio test means that one can probably be sure that this model does provide a reasonable fit. In order to check, a difference chi-square test may be calculated using the likelihood ratio chi-square for a model with just an intercept term. Obtained from another output not presented here, the result was 38.90. Thus, the test of the difference would be

$$G_{\text{diff}}^2 = G_r^2 - G_f^2 = 38.90 - 33.69 = 5.21$$

which is a chi-square with 2 degrees of freedom, because the full logistic regression model has two independent variables. Since this value is not statistically significant at the .05 level, a scholar is left somewhat unsure about whether these two variables actually improve prediction of the logits for marital status. For the sake of argument, however, it might be useful to proceed as if they did.

As in multiple regression, the second section of table 9.2 presents

Table 9.2 *Multiple Logistic Regression of Marital Status on Age and Birthplace*

Dependent Variable: MARITAL   Marital Status

		Goodness-of-Fit Tests	
Statistic	Value	DF	Prob>Chi-sq
Pearson Chi-square	47.9640	41	0.2113
L.R. Chi-square	33.6873	41	0.7842

		Parameter Estimates				
Variable	DF	Estimate	Std Err	Chi-square	Pr>Chi	Label/ Value
INTERCPT	1	−6.172	2.258	7.469	0.0063	Intercept
AGE	1	0.156	0.074	4.454	0.0348	Age in Years
BIRTHDUM	1	−0.452	0.947	0.228	0.6329	Foreign Born

parameter estimates. An examination of the multiple logistic regression coefficients and their test of significance reveals why the
results of the test of fit are ambiguous. On the basis of these estimates, one can construct the prediction equation, which is

$$\text{Log}_n(P_{married}) / (1 - P_{married}) = -6.172 + .156\ \text{AGE} + .452\ \text{BIRTHDUM}$$

However, a review of the significance tests under the heading
"Pr>Chi" shows that while the coefficient for age is likely to be
different from 0, that for the foreign-born dummy variable
(BIRTHDUM) is not. This result suggests that the hypothesis about
a difference between native- and foreign-born soldiers in propensity
to be married is not supported. The disagreement in the two chi-
square tests of fit was probably due to the fact that age does seem to
have a relationship to marital status while place of birth does not.

SINGLE ORDINAL DEPENDENT VARIABLES

The ordered response, logistic regression technique presented in
chapter 8 may also be extended to cases in which there are two or
more independent variables. In this instance, these variables may
also be continuous, categorical, or a mixture of the two. The basic
form of the regression equations for this technique is

$$L_i(Y>1) = a_1 + b_1X_{i1} + b_2X_{i2} + \ldots + b_jX_{ij}$$

9.15

$$L_i(Y>2) = a_2 + b_1X_{i2} + b_2X_{i2} + \ldots + b_jX_{ij}$$

$$L_i(Y>j) = a_k + b_1X_{i2} + b_2X_{i2} + \ldots + b_jX_{ij}$$

This formula is simply an extension of the bivariate procedure for an ordered dependent variable with C categories. Therefore, there are $k = C-1$ equations, each with a separate intercept (i.e., a_1, $a_2, \ldots, a_k$). Statistical software for this model will give estimates of the a_k's and b_j's as well as likelihood ratio chi-square tests of the goodness of fit of the estimated model to the data. The methods for significance testing to answer the four basic questions at the beginning of the chapter are the same as for the multiple logistic regression model. But it is important to remember that only the intercepts and not the b_j's differ from equation to equation for the ordered response model due to the ordered structure of the dependent variable.

To illustrate the use of ordered multiple logistic regression, one might want to consider whether the former occupations of Fort Moultrie soldiers can be predicted from the value of their property and civil status. Marital state may be dummy coded with 1 indicating being married. The former occupations may be divided into three basic categories—unskilled laborers, skilled craftsmen, and white-collar professions—with corresponding ordered values of 1, 2, and 3. This model is therefore expected to have two equations with common b_j's for real property and marital status but two different intercepts or a_k's. Table 9.3 presents the edited output for the estimated, ordered logit model for these data.

The likelihood ratio chi-square has a very nonsignificant probability of close to .80 associated with it. This result suggests that the fit of the model to the data is acceptable and that at least one of the independent variables is probably associated with occupational rank. The parameter estimates show the two intercepts (a_1 and a_2) for the prediction equations, labeled as INTERCPT and INTER.2. The common slopes for value of real estate holdings and the marital status dummy variable appear in the rows labeled REAL and MARDUM. An examination of the significance levels of the chi-

Table 9.3 *Ordered Dependent Variable Multiple Logistic Regression of Occupational Status on Real Property and Marital Status*

Dependent Variable: OCCUPCAT   *Occupational Category*

Weighted Frequency Counts for the
Ordered Response Categories

Level	Count
1	20
2	11
3	14

Goodness-of-Fit-Tests

Statistic	Value	DF	Prob>Chi-sq
Pearson Chi-square	31.7382	38	0.7531
L.R. Chi-square	30.6122	38	0.7972

Parameter Estimates

Variable	DF	Estimate	Std Err	Chi-square	Pr>Chi	Label/ Value
INTERCPT	1	0.823	1.132	0.52854	0.4672	Intercept
INTER.2	1	1.778	0.501			
REAL	1	−0.010	0.003	9.26309	0.0023	Real Estate
MARDUM	1	0.058	1.061	0.00299	0.9564	Married

squares associated with these estimates reveals that, controlling for marital status, real estate value is related to occupational status (p < .0023) but marital status has no relationship, once the value of property has been taken into account (p < .9564). The paradoxical negative coefficient for real estate is explained by the software's use of ordered logits that compare lower values to higher ones rather than vice versa. This slope can be interpreted to mean that the higher the value of a soldier's property, the *less* likely he is to be an unskilled laborer—which is simply a restatement of the positive relationship between real estate and job status.

Though increasingly complex, statistical techniques for testing the relationship between more than two variables are invaluable tools for the historian. Since they come closer to the complexity of relationships found in the often bewildering data about the past, multivariate techniques can help overcome the objection against a kind of quantitative reductionism that simplifies reality excessively. However, in order to reap the full benefits of these more demanding procedures, historians have to make a larger effort to understand their basic logic and limitations. In earlier days when many of these statistics were still calculated by hand, one could be reasonably sure that users knew their basic structure. In the age of canned computer software, it has become all too easy to order up an impressive array of figures without really comprehending its implications fully. The result is sometimes a kind of numerical mumbo-jumbo that reflects the confusion of the author and fails to enlighten the reader. Not every historian has to become an accomplished statistician, but any scholar employing such procedures should be able to understand their assumptions sufficiently to make intelligent choices. If in doubt, one can always turn to one of the leading statistical texts or, better yet, consult a friendly and competent colleague. While a neophyte will not find working with multivariate statistics easy, the potential benefits of these more powerful techniques are so great that the extra effort to master them is well worthwhile.

SOFTWARE NOTES

Multiple regression analysis may be performed with the REGRESSION procedure in SPSS-X and SPSS/PC or with the PROC REG procedure in SAS. Both the SPSS and SAS routines have useful regression diagnostics as optional output. Analyses of variance, covariance, and repeated measures analyses may be accomplished with the MANOVA procedure in SPSS-X and SPSS/PC or with PROC GLM in SAS.

Multiple logistic regression models for cross-classified, categorical, independent variables can be fit to data using SPSS-X's PROBIT procedure. However, this routine does not produce appropriate tests of fit and significance tests of coefficients for continuous predictor variables. SPSS/PC's new LOGISTIC REGRESSION routine provides accurate estimates of these quantities and has an impressive array of diagnostics. SAS also has a number of routines for logit models. PROC CATMOD is most convenient for models in which the dependent variables are polychotomous or the dependent variables are dichotomous and the independent variables are categorical. PROC CATMOD may also be used for models where the independent variables are all continuous. However, if the dependent variable is dichotomous and the independent variables are mostly continuous, either version 5.18's PROC LOGIST or version 6's PROC PROBIT or PROC LOGISTIC is more useful.

Apparently, SPSS has no routines for estimating ordered logit models. Either the LOGIST, LOGISTIC, or PROBIT procedure in SAS may be used to estimate these models. It is important to remember that the LOGIST procedure compares higher ordered values with lower ordered values while the LOGISTIC and PROBIT procedures do the opposite.

10

Advanced Techniques

The univariate, bivariate, and multivariate statistics presented in the preceding chapters provide a foundation for most basic analytical tasks of quantitative history. However, more complex questions about the past necessarily call for more complicated analytical techniques. When addressing more elaborate hypotheses, even a neophyte quantifier will encounter such statistical buzzwords as "time series analysis," "factor analysis," "cluster analysis," "LISREL," and the like, half in awe of their potential power and half in frustration with their difficulty. Since these procedures are too mathematically demanding to be fully presented in an introductory text, this chapter will endeavor to provide a brief overview of the chief approaches. Many of these advanced techniques are extensions of the multiple regression model presented above, while some also address new questions about data that have not been covered up to this point. Experienced quantifiers especially need to have an intuitive understanding of these techniques in order to read the literature more critically and to make informed decisions about which of the procedures might offer solutions to problems in their own research. The subsequent exposition will restrict itself to discussing basic principles and typical applications in order to whet the appetite. More substantial fare can be found in Everitt and Dunn's thorough review of many of these procedures (1983).

EXTENSIONS OF MULTIPLE REGRESSION MODELS

Many extensions of multiple regression seek to adapt that powerful technique to a variety of problems and types of data for which the standard linear model is not suitable. Some of these adaptations simply involve *nonlinear* forms of the hypothesized equation, relating the dependent variable Y to the independent X_j's. For example, the Cobb-Douglas production function used by economic historians relates capital and other inputs in a multiplicative equation to estimate outputs. Through some algebraic manipulations this underlying nonlinear form is transformed into a linear, multiple regression model which is then estimated in the manner detailed in the previous chapter. For example, one may hypothesize that the true model relating a Y to several X's is

$$Y = e^{(a + b_1X_1 + b_2X_2 + b_3X_3)}$$
10.1

which is nonlinear in form. However, by taking the logarithm to the base e of both sides of the equation, the formula becomes

$$\text{Log}(Y) = a + b_1X_1 + b_2X_2 + b_3X_3$$
10.2

which may be estimated as an ordinary linear regression equation. This algebraic transformation exactly parallels the procedure for moving from the nonlinear model for the odds to the linear model for the logits in multiple logistic regression. There are many common nonlinear equation forms explored by economists that may be particularly applicable to economic history. (For more detail see the texts by Kmenta [1986] and Desai [1976].)

More complicated techniques are also required to handle dependent variables that are not truly continuous. In addition to logit models, there are other possible regression models for these dependent variables that require special estimation techniques. If the dependent variable is dichotomous and the independent variables are categorical and their crosstabulation has large cell sizes, a modification of ordinary least squares called weighted least squares can be used to estimate a linear probability regression model for which the dependent variable is the actual probability of the event occurring rather than some less intuitive transformation of it like the logit. If the underlying distributions of all the variables may be assumed to be normal, a condition called multivariate normality, then a procedure called a probit model may be used which also treats the dependent variable as a proportion. Sometimes values of the dependent variable are continuous but are chopped off at some high or low end because the very high or low values could not be sampled. This condition may apply in investigating the transmission of wealth through inheritance or the distribution of income when there are incomplete records for bequests or missing information for the poor. (For a lucid example of Counter-Reformation wills in Lyon, see Hoffmann [1984].) Such censored dependent variables require a tobit estimation technique to obtain valid estimators of the b_j's. (The linear probability and probit models are presented in Aldrich and Nelson [1984]. The tobit estimator is covered in Kmenta [1986]. An advanced discussion of these and other regression models that deal with complicated dependent variables is Maddala [1983].)

Somewhat surprisingly for an introduction to quantitative methods in history, all the techniques explored in this volume thus far have not mentioned data that include time as a factor. The reason for this omission is that most material is essentially *cross-sectional* in nature. Even when a few years are compared, the data represent a slice through the values of the variables at a given moment rather than being longitudinal observations of the same variables at many different points in time. Especially in economic history, scholars often confront long *time series* of prices, incomes, production, and the like and are intent on analyzing their general trend and interrelations. In order to bring out the underlying thrust of development in studying business cycles, the momentary deviations need to be "filtered out" and a smoothed curve produced through some kind of "moving average." In modeling time series, regression analysis of longitudinal data includes past values of the dependent variable as independent variable or variables. The simplest hypothesized form of these regression equations can be

$$Y_t = a + b_1 Y_{t-1} + b_{j+1} X_1 + \ldots + b_{j+k} X_k \qquad 10.3$$

where the $t-1$ subscript indicates that the Y_{t-1} independent variable is the value of Y from one time period before the Y value at time t. Although these *autoregressive* regressions violate the critical assumption about the independence of the errors and the data points, econometricians have developed techniques for dealing with longitudinal regression models. (They are reviewed in Ostrom [1978] and Gujarati [1988].) If the data contain observations for many time periods, perhaps 50 or more, on one or more variables, then Box-Jenkins time series techniques may be employed to analyze the behavior of either one or several variables across time. These procedures are, however, quite difficult to master. (Perhaps their simplest review is in McCleary and Hay [1980] or Stier [1989].)

A special class of regression techniques called *event history models* may be used when the dependent variable measured over time indicates the persistence and then change of state of the cases. Originally developed to predict hazard functions for survival studies in cancer and other medical research, they can be useful for studying any historical phenomenon which involves the passage of time and then a change in some important characteristic of the cases. One demographic example would be a study of the factors determining first marriage for women. Another case from social history might be the number of years of apprenticeship served before promotion to master craftsman. For the simplest of such models the independent variables are assumed not to vary across time, although more complex techniques can allow for this temporal variation. It is also possible to compare the relative rates of change for relevant groups of cases. (An introduction to these kinds of procedures is provided by Allison [1989] and Everitt and Dunn [1983, chap. 10].)

MULTIEQUATION REGRESSION MODELS

Most historical phenomena are so complicated that any single equation will fall short of representing the possible relationships among the many complex factors involved. At the very least, it seems reasonable to assume that certain variables "cause" changes in others and that these latter variables, in turn, affect yet more variables. Thus, a variable at the beginning of the process might have a direct or indirect effect or both on a variable occurring later in the process. A diagram of an idealized, simple process of this type could look like figure 10.1. The subscripts on the X's in this figure give the hypothesized causal ordering of the variables. Notice that there are four variables which are directly "caused" by other variables (X_5, X_6, X_7, X_8). They are referred to as *endogenous vari-*

Figure 10.1 *Causal Diagram with Exogenous and Endogenous Variables*

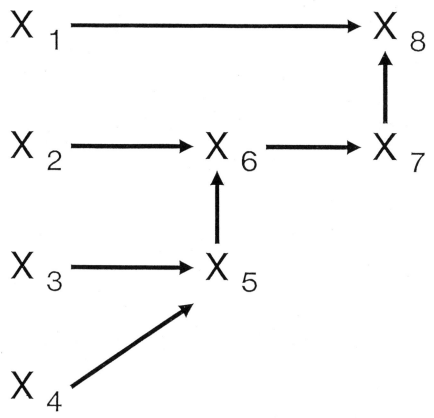

ables. The causative variables that have no explicit causes themselves (X_1, X_2, X_3, X_4) are referred to as *exogenous variables*.

A historical example of such a conceptual problem might be the analysis of the causes of the German hyperinflation between 1918 and 1923, in which negative factors potentiated one another (Holtfrerich 1986). Hypothesized models for causal relationships such as these may be estimated and tested with systems of multiple regression equations rather than just a single equation. Essentially this involves estimating a regression equation for each dependent or endogenous variable. The independent variables for the equation for a particular endogenous variable are those that have a direct causal arrow connected to that endogenous variable.

Ordinary multiple regression may be used to estimate these equations, provided several critical assumptions are met. Space does not permit going over all of them, but one very necessary assumption is that the causal system must be *recursive*. No reverse or reciprocal causation may be hypothesized. (An arrow running from X_8 back to X_6 would render this example nonrecursive.) Thus, for the system in figure 10.1 one would estimate the following equations:

$$X_5 = a_5 + b_{53}X_3 + b_{54}X_4 \qquad X_7 = a_7 + b_{76}X_6 \qquad 10.4$$

$$X_6 = a_6 + b_{62}X_2 + b_{65}X_5 \qquad X_8 = a_8 + b_{81}X_1 + b_{87}X_7$$

where the first subscript for each b gives the dependent variable with which the coefficient is associated, while the second gives the subscript of the particular causal X. If more advanced econometric estimation techniques are employed, the recursiveness assumption may be relaxed. (The texts by Heise [1975], Gujarati [1988], and Kmenta [1986] are primarily devoted to explaining multiequation systems for continuous dependent variables.) More complex techniques are required if any of the endogenous variables is categorical. While multiequation regression models for causal hypotheses cannot encompass all of the complexity inherent in historical phenomena, they can offer a formal framework for attempting to deal with it.

LATENT VARIABLE MEASUREMENT

Up to this point the presentation has assumed either explicitly or implicitly that the measurement of the variables for each of the statistical techniques discussed has been perfect. Another premise required each variable to be unique and to measure a single aspect of any problem that might be investigated. However, while both of these assumptions are sustainable in many situations, there are some factors for which a single variable is unlikely to be an accurate measurement of the characteristic it purports to represent. This is especially true if the variable is not easily susceptible to direct observation but is reflected in a number of imperfect but observable indicator variables. The classic example of these so-called *latent variables* is the psychological concept of intelligence. No single question on an intelligence test purports to measure intelligence precisely. Rather the questions are indicators of intelligence, and a score for the latent variable "IQ" is derived from the answers to dozens of questions. The problem, of course, is how such scores can be developed.

If the indicator variables for a latent variable are continuous, *factor analysis* may be used to detect and measure the latent variables in a group of intercorrelated indicators. For instance, the investigation of the sources of social protest in nineteenth-century central Europe confronts complex interactions among broad factors such as industrialization, urbanization, labor organization, and the like. In order to test conflicting hypotheses, the researcher needs a strategy to clarify the relationships among indicators of these factors by eliminating irrelevant variables and isolating potentially causative connections (Tilly and Hohorst 1975). To accomplish this goal, the indicator variables must be correlated to some degree because the underlying theory for factor analysis assumes that each score on each indicator variable has two components: a common or systematic element associated with the underlying latent variable and a random or unique aspect that is not related to the underlying latent variable. Thus, if each case's score for the latent variable is at a certain level, the corresponding indicator variables should all be at levels that reflect the underlying score plus or minus some random error, and therefore the indicator variables should covary. A factor analysis attempts to form the best linear, additive combination of the indicator variables by solving for the *factor score coefficients* in a factor score which looks very similar to a multiple regression equation:

$$F = b_1 X_1 + b_2 X_2 + \ldots + b_j X_j \qquad\qquad 10.5$$

The major difference is that the value of F for each case is determined by the factor score coefficients, found by the factor analysis procedure, and is not directly observed like the Y in multiple regression.

It is also possible that a set of indicator variables may relate not just to a single underlying, latent variable but to two or more of them. In the simplest situation, one unique subset of indicator variables relates most clearly to one latent variable and another subset is associated with another latent variable. In this case the coefficients for the unrelated subset of variables for a given latent variable are close to 0 and therefore do not affect the factor scores for that latent variable. *Exploratory factor analysis* can help determine both the number of latent variables and the strength of the relationship of each of the indicator variables with the factors. These *factor loadings* are simply the Pearsonian correlations of the values of the indicator variables with the latent variable factor score or scores. Moreover, these loadings can be displayed on graphs whose axes represent the factors to allow researchers to view a spatial representation of the factor structure. If a strong theory exists relating the indicator variables to particular latent variables, *confirmatory factor analysis* may be used to test its propositions. (Everitt and Dunn [1983, chap. 11] provide a good overview of both of these methods, while Kim [1978] gives a more detailed introduction to exploratory methods and Long [1983] as well as Horan and Hargis [1989] offer the same for confirmatory methods.) Latent-class analysis is a method for determining latent variables underlying categorically or ordinally measured indicator variables. (It is reviewed in the article by Shockey [1988].)

The concepts of latent variables and multiequation models may be combined in a powerful but somewhat complex technique which is referred to by a variety of names. Some call this procedure *covariance structure analysis* or *latent variable structural equation modeling*. Others use the designation of the computer software that implements the techniques. Hence the terms LISREL method or EQS technique are also popular. Whatever name is used, the essence of the method is to estimate the regression coefficients of a system of linear equations composed of latent exogenous and endogenous variables that are, in turn, products of a confirmatory factor model for their respective indicator variables. In other words, there may be several latent variables such as X, Y, and Z for which there are no direct measures but several correlated indicators, such

Figure 10.2 *Causal Diagram of a Multiequation Model with Latent Variables*

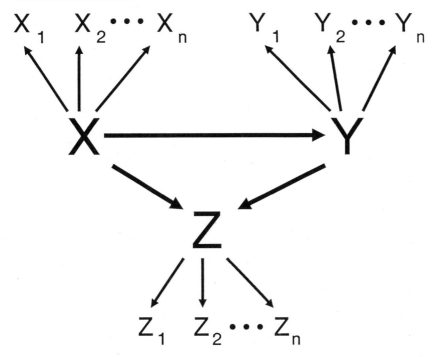

as x_1 to x_n, y_1 to y_n, and z_1 to z_n (see figure 10.2). This technique forms scores for each of the latent variables from the indicators through a confirmatory factor analysis and then performs a regression to estimate the coefficients of the structural equation. (Everitt [1984] provides an introduction to this technique. In-depth discussions requiring considerable background in multiple regression may be found in Hayduk [1987] and Bollen [1989].)

Though this procedure sounds quite complex, it can be made transparent by describing a simple bivariate model. (See the article of Horan and Hargis [1989] for details.) A study of the economy of Georgia counties investigated the relationship between agricultural production and manufacturing functions. These rather broad, but important, concepts have no single satisfactory measure. However, each variable could be broken down into several indicators, such as value of farm products per square mile and number of farms per

square mile for agriculture or number of manufacturing establish-
ments per capita and wages earned in manufacturing per capita for
manufacturing. By using these indicators in a latent variable model,
it was possible to estimate the relationship between an agricultural
latent variable and a manufacturing latent variable. The result indicated that while the relationship between agricultural production
and manufacturing was negative, as had been hypothesized, the
strength of this relationship was not as great as expected.

GROUPING SIMILAR CASES

All of the previously discussed techniques involve statistical procedures that seek to answer questions about variables and summarize
information contained in cases to do so. However, some research
problems wish to solve problems regarding the degree of similarity
of cases with respect to the values of some relevant set of variables.
For example, a historian might wish to classify New England counties into groups depending on the relative mix of various industrial,
commercial, and agricultural outputs in order to improve the explanation of the Republican electoral success in 1860. Or a demogra-
pher might want to classify households into a few groupings based
on the numbers of core family members (spouse, children), relatives
(aunts, uncles), boarders (unrelated people), or servants residing in
the house (Bacher 1989). Two sets of techniques address these questions. If one is interested in simply developing a classification
scheme for the observations based on similar profiles of the values
of variables, which would allow assignment of cases to one of a
reasonably small number of homogeneous classes, then a *cluster
analysis* of the data may be carried out. If one has a matrix of measures of similarities between cases and wishes to plot those cases in
a graphic space that reveals their similarities and differences, then a
multidimensional scaling technique is called for.

Cluster analysis seeks to group cases into clusters that are as
nearly homogeneous as possible with respect to the pattern of the
mean values of a set of continuous variables. To see what this implies, it is easiest to start with a discussion of the somewhat idealized data in table 10.1. Note that the first two cases have values of

Table 10.1 *Example Data for a Stylized Cluster Analysis*

Case	X1	X2	X3
1	5	4	9
2	4	5	8
3	8	2	8
4	7	3	9
5	9	1	7
6	3	5	4

either 4 or 5 for X1 and X2 and that the values for X3 are both high. The next three cases exhibit another pattern, having higher values for X1 and X3 and low values for X2. The sixth case does not seem to match either configuration because it has intermediate level values on all three variables. Thus, in order to obtain a simple classification to represent these six cases, one could claim that cases 1 and 2 belong together in a group or cluster, as do cases 3, 4, and 5. Case 6, however, probably needs to be placed in a class by itself.

As one might imagine, if the ranges of values of the variables were quite different and the number of variables and cases increased, this task could no longer be performed by simple inspection. Cluster analytic techniques provide methods for solving such problems through mathematical measures of similarities between variable value profiles and computer algorithms for searching out the most similar pairs or clusters from among all possible pairwise comparisons of cases. The details of the many possible measures of similarity and the methods for building clusters from cases are beyond the scope of this brief treatment of the topic. (A basic introduction to cluster analysis may be found in Everitt and Dunn [1983], and a more thorough exposition in Everitt [1980].)

Multidimensional scaling (MDS) methods may be used to plot cases on a two-dimensional or greater graphic space, also called a *Euclidean space*. These methods provide information about the possible underlying dimensions in the data that make the cases similar or different from one another. These procedures have the potential for offering more insights than a simple clustering of cases into relatively homogeneous groupings. Moreover, these techniques can be applied to continuous, ordinal, and categorically measured variables. They differ among themselves on the basis of the assumptions made about the form of the data matrix being ana- lyzed. However, the basic task which these routines seek to accom- plish is to array the cases as points in a space of some set number of dimensions, very often two or three, such that the distances be- tween the points in this contrived space correspond well to the observed measures of the similarities between the cases. (An over- view of basic MDS techniques is presented in Everitt and Dunn [1983] and in Schiffman, Reynolds, and Young [1981].)

Sometimes researchers also wish to see whether a set of variables can predict membership in a grouping of cases for which the groups are known a priori. For example, a historian might want to find out if a set of social background variables determines the composition of two strata of a governing elite such as the SS in Nazi Germany (see Ziegler 1989). Widely used for this purpose, the technique of *discriminant function analysis* attempts to build a prediction equa- tion which estimates a value for each case, called a discriminant score. Cases with higher values can be assigned into one of the groups, while cases with low scores clearly belong into the other. However, cases with intermediate values cannot be easily classified based on the discriminant function coefficient and the values of the variables (Klecka 1980). The chief drawback of this procedure is its requirement of strong assumptions about the normality of the pre- dictor variables and the relationship among them in the two groups, which often cannot be sustained (Press and Wilson 1978). For most applications, a preferable alternative is logistic regression using group memberships as a categorical dependent variable, since it will usually produce equally correct results even when the assump- tions behind discriminant function analysis can be met. (See also Harrell and Lee [1985].)

Though the application of these advanced techniques is more com- plicated, the above procedures offer an impressive array of ap- proaches to quite complicated historical questions. Their only re- quirement is the formalization of analysis to such a degree that the argumentation can be expressed in explicit models consisting of hypotheses which link measurable variables. For historians used to the intentional ambiguity of verbal discourse, this process of statistical stylization may seem like an undue reduction of reality. For social scientists habituated to confusing diagrams and complex formulas, the gain in conceptual clarity and empirical falsifiability seems irrefutable. Fortunately, statistical program packages have taken most of the labor out of the arduous calculations involved. But greater accessibility has also increased the risks of misuse. If imperfectly understood, such advanced statistical techniques can be misapplied and their underlying assumptions violated. Moreover, once conquered through further training, the complex procedures seem to exert such a fascination that they are frequently invoked when a simpler method would suffice. To avoid these pitfalls, historians who are just learning to use advanced tools would do well to collaborate with experienced statisticians. If the former learn the basic principles of the techniques and the latter inform themselves about the substantive question at issue, their interaction will produce impressive results.

SOFTWARE NOTES

The linearized form of many nonlinear regression models may be estimated with standard regression software such as REGRESSION in SPSS-X and SPSS/PC or PROC REG in SAS. Time series regression models can be handled with procedures in SAS's "Econometrics and Time Series" collection of programs as well as a specialty package endearingly called RATS (Regression Analysis of Time Series). Box-Jenkins time series procedures may be found in SPSS-X's procedure bearing that name, SAS's ETS AUTOREG and ARIMA techniques, and RATS. Many event history regression models are conveniently produced with PROC LIFEREG in SAS.

Multiequation models may be estimated with the procedures in SAS's ETS series of programs, especially SYSLIN. Both SPSS-X and SAS have exploratory factor analysis routines. Two specialty programs, LISREL and EQS, are popular for confirmatory factor analysis and multiequation, latent variable models. SAS's newly released PROC CALIS also may be employed for these models.

Cluster analysis may be performed with the CLUSTER routine in

SPSS-X and SPSS/PC as well as with PROC CLUSTER in SAS. The ALSCAL subprogram in SPSS-X and PROC ALSCAL in SAS offer various forms of multidimensional scaling. Much of this software is quite complex and assumes that the user is highly proficient in the statistical techniques which its routines implement.

11

Interpretation and Theory Formation

The most important—but also often neglected—step in quantitative research is interpretation. Confronted with growing mountains of computer printout, scholars begin to wonder, What is this output supposed to mean? Instead of being automatic and self-evident, making sense out of descriptive tables and analytical statistics is a difficult process, fraught with pitfalls and frustrations. Unfortunately, time is usually running short at this point of the investigation and the student is exhausted from the data gathering and statistical manipulation just when the greatest concentration and intelligence are essential. The disappointing consequence of underestimating this final research stage is the underinterpretation of laboriously accumulated material which fails to explore the potential meaning of the data fully. Textbooks and short courses usually offer little if any help, since they are preoccupied with the mechanics of the procedures and fail to give advice on dealing with their results (see Shorter 1971; Dollar and Jensen 1971; and Floud 1979). Yet statistics never speak for themselves, not even with a voice synthesizer. Figures must be checked for technical correctness, probed for their meaning, and related to the historical hypothesis to be tested. Often measures seem to point in contradictory directions and appear to allow conflicting conclusions. In short, numbers must be interpreted.

THE NEED FOR ANALYTICAL CONTROL

Since quantitative research techniques tend to be more complicated than qualitative procedures, it is imperative to maintain analytical control. Especially in large research projects (such as the Philadelphia urban history project, directed by Ted Hershberg [1981]), the actual work is often done by underpaid assistants who pile up mountains of data, sometimes with little regard for the overall purpose. This necessary division of labor runs the risk of creating "data cemeteries," storing much valuable information with scant prospect of ever having its peace disturbed by analysis (since the project director is usually busy securing follow-up funding rather than writing up collaborators' results). But even in individual projects scholars tend to work on hundreds or thousands of entries rather than a handful or a dozen, thereby losing touch with each singular case. For all their convenience, data banks invite manipulating information rather than producing conclusions from the evidence. Against the double temptation of getting lost in detail or of merely skimming the surface, periodic efforts to run simple descriptive statistics can help to maintain the "feel" of the data and to suggest analytical possibilities. Both in collaborative and individual research it is vital to keep the interpretative aims clearly in mind during all stages of the research process.

Analytical control is especially important and difficult during the statistical phase of a project. Researchers tend to encounter several common problems with analytical statistics: Some are so attracted by the beauty of a procedure and the power of the computer that they produce numbers for their own sake with little regard for their measurement prerequisites or ultimate meaning. Others who are slightly more sophisticated but lack a hypothesis go on extensive fishing expeditions where they run every variable by every other one in search of "significant" relationships—which may not make any analytical sense afterwards. The SPSS keyword ALL for the statistics procedure is especially pernicious. More ambitious yet, others employ statistical overkill, resorting to linear modeling, factor analysis, or some other high-powered procedure when a modest correlation coefficient would have sufficed. Their counterparts trust only simple procedures which they can calculate by hand, often unnecessarily forgoing exciting analytical possibilities of more complex approaches. One could go on and on listing abuses of statistics. A general remedy for such mistakes is easier to formulate than to apply: The statistical procedure employed must be *appropriate* to the hypothesis to be tested. Not only should it be technically correct (level of measurement, empty cells, and so on), but it also ought to conform logically to the interpretative purpose for which it is chosen.

The interpretation of the printout also tends to produce particular problems. For instance, what is a scholar to do when the statistics do not yield the desired result? Sometimes a relationship which has been an implicit guiding assumption turns out not to be statistically significant. This unexpected result confronts the investigator with a particularly frustrating dilemma: One can either check the entire research process for mistakes which might have weakened an existing connection, try to transform the data into more appropriate categories, attempt to employ different statistical procedures, and so on, or one must abandon the initial hypothesis. In fortunate cases, this procedure will suggest other possibilities. But sometimes the data are too imperfect or the hypotheses not specified correctly enough to allow any conclusion. Instead of "cooking" the statistics, the researcher would be better advised to present the results as disproving the original hypothesis. At the other extreme, it is important to remember that a demonstration of statistical relationship is no proof of a causal connection. Enough cases of high but spurious correlations are known to suggest that a statistical relationship must also be substantively plausible before serving as an explanation. Strictly speaking, statistics can never "explain" anything anyway; they can only test hypotheses for their agreement with the data.

One often overlooked part of analytical control is a constructive relationship to qualitative evidence and scholarly literature. Due to the large amount of labor that goes into putting together a formalized data set and into its statistical analysis, scholars sometimes neglect to draw sufficiently upon textual sources or ignore prior academic debate and so come to grief by approaching their problem too narrowly. There is a widespread fascination with the decimal places behind the period and a mistaken belief in the "objectivity" of numbers, many of which are themselves the product of qualitative decisions. Sometimes statistics substantiate explanations of only a fraction of the variance. While it is preferable to have hard evidence for even one-third of the difference to having none at all, this result still leaves two-thirds of an effect to be explained with other means. It is, therefore, essential to draw upon the scholarly literature of a given field. Interpretations become meaningful only in connection with an ongoing discourse. Hypotheses can be drawn from the existing discussions, and views can be rejected or modified. Failing to engage the qualitative debate on a problem raises the danger of a quantitative antiquarianism, preoccupied with piling up numbers and tables without any broader intellectual implication. Both textual evidence and secondary literature are, therefore, essential in animating otherwise often inanimate statistics (Jarausch 1990).

A final aspect of analytical control is the intelligible presentation of research results. Since dumping raw computer printout into tables sows confusion, the plausibility of quantitative argumentation depends upon attractive *table design*. Who has not become bogged down in a morass of undigested numbers in small print and skipped potentially important information out of frustration with its inaccessibility? Several rules of thumb can help make statistics easier to digest. Tables in the text must be clear and concise. They require unmistakable identifiers, headings, and labels. Their content should be as compressed and to the analytical point as possible, dropping all interesting but extraneous information. Giving both numbers and percents is unnecessary as long as the marginals provide the totals to recompute figures. Strange terms need to be explained immediately below and not in a faraway footnote. Similarly, the sources also should be briefly listed, since credibility depends upon them. In contrast, tables in the appendix must be as complete as possible. They ought to list the information in a disaggregated form, since their primary function is documentation. While text tables should advance a specific argument, appendix tables serve as a numerical form of primary evidence for secondary analysis by other scholars. Descriptive figures may suffice for simple illustration, but causative explanation requires the presentation of inferential statistics and significance tests. Finally, much numerical information can be conveyed graphically, often rendering complex relationships intuitively intelligible. Well designed maps, charts, and graphs not only faithfully reproduce data but summarize massive information and suggest central tendencies in order to make a conceptual point. Used economically and with integrity, visual display is therefore not a luxury but an important tool of analysis and communication (see also Tufte 1983).

QUANTIFICATION AND THEORY

Appearances to the contrary notwithstanding, theories are an essential part of historical research. Even traditional narrative accounts implicitly contain generalizations, often masked by references to "common sense." In analytical history which transcends the historicist tradition, concepts guide research explicitly. Schooled in the Weberian tradition, Jürgen Kocka (1982) defines theories as "an explicit and consistent set of related concepts, which can be used to structure and explain historical data, but cannot solely be derived from the study of sources." This definition suggests that there are many different levels of theories, ranging from the limited and concrete to the general and abstract. For instance, they can be as simple as "socialization theory," dealing with the social learning of children, or as complex as "modernization theory," describing the fundamental transformation of entire societies over centuries. Theories provide an explanatory framework for historians and offer the context in which the specific events discussed make sense. While it has recently been fashionable to call for more theory in history, it is not at all clear what this would imply: What can theories offer to quantitative historians, and how do quantifiers use them?

While theories have some advantages for all historians, they are especially important for quantifiers. A catalogue of their potential contributions might include the following:

1. Theories can suggest questions to be investigated and clarify historical problems.
2. They can also provide criteria for periodization and indicate suitable time frames for investigation.
3. They can help formulate hypotheses for relations among factors or variables.

4. They can supply causal explanations for certain developments and thereby aid interpretation.
5. They can facilitate comparisons between cases through
   establishing standards of comparability.

Though all of these potential contributions of theory are relevant
for quantitative historians, enabling hypothesis formulation, sup-
porting explanations, and aiding comparisons are especially important. As stated repeatedly, the analytical use of statistics requires
hypotheses to be tested. Moreover, single hypotheses need to fit
into a broader interpretative context. At the same time, local case
studies are of general interest only when they can be related to
broader theoretical issues. For quantitative historians, theories are
therefore essential, since they dictate the direction of the analysis
and endow the statistical results with wider meaning (Horan 1987).

Although they possess strong affinities, quantitative and theoretical history are by no means identical. To be sure, both have the
same opponents in the historicists or narrative historians. Both
have the same limitations, since they deal with structures and
trends rather than events or individuals. Both borrow more or less
eclectically from the neighboring social sciences. Both utilize more
precise concepts and pose clearer causal questions than traditional
approaches. Yet there are numerous nonquantitative theoretical
historians, especially those concerned with grand theories like Oswald Spengler, Arnold Toynbee, or Immanuel Wallerstein. Moreover, quantifiers themselves are divided on the question of identity
of theory and quantification. Hermeneutic historians emphasize
the multiplicity of qualitative and quantitative factors which pro-
hibit a "narrowing" of the explanation to the latter alone (Stone
1977). In contrast, historical social scientists want to transform history into a hard behavioral science, firmly grounded in analytical
theory and based upon falsifiable and cumulative results (Kousser
1980 and Clubb 1985). Nonetheless, both sides agree that the formalized research process well-nigh predestines quantification to
theory formation. In quantitative work, theories, whether sweeping
or limited, should play a decisive role in formulating the question,
selecting the sources, choosing statistical procedures, and interpret-

ing the results. They must be the red thread running through the entire process and guiding its course. In contrast to arguing by the seat of one's pants, quantitative reasoning demands stringent and explicit theories. (See also Kocka [1984] and Possekel [1990].)

Recent emphasis on texture over abstraction has identified limits of theorizing without being able to supplant the need for generalization. Postmodernist preferences for softer and experiential approaches to the past have revalidated culture and *mentalité* as central dimensions of understanding the past. Fresh attention to experience, feelings, small units, and everyday life has opened exciting new vistas to historical empathy. But some such work risks misunderstanding the theoretical orientation of its lodestar discipline of anthropology, without which all thick description would dissolve into perspectivist anecdote. While much of the criticism of the poverty of megatheory is well taken, dissatisfaction with Marxist or liberal synthesis does not obviate the need for generalizing human experience beyond the single individual. Instead of requiring a grand leap from a single, deeply explored example to universal truths, theoretically oriented quantitative history allows either the testing of propositions derived from larger theories or the elaboration of middle-range generalization about measurable behavior which can be falsified empirically. While numbers can seldom represent human feelings adequately, they do help resolve the bothersome issue of representativeness which undercuts much textually oriented research. Many pragmatic historians have begun to realize that interesting voices from the past need to be located in larger reference groups in order to understand for whom they speak. Instead of falling from one extreme of numerical zealotry into another extreme of textual fanaticism, researchers would do better to combine these methods judiciously. Reconstructing the past requires imaginative empathy as well as numerical generalization.

HISTORY AND THE SOCIAL SCIENCES

Many of the concepts applied by quantitative historians stem from the neighboring social sciences. Since they only rarely develop theories themselves, historians are often forced to borrow conceptually from sociology, economics, political science, or anthropology. Contrary to the expectation that the social sciences provide a gigantic toolbox containing some magic universal wrench applicable to all historical problems, the importing of constructs is in fact often dangerous. At least three obstacles confront a historian in search of theory: Social scientists generally work in a nomothetic fashion, trying to establish general laws, while historians tend to proceed ideographically, seeking to explain particular events. Moreover, concepts nurtured within other disciplines possess a logic of their own and cannot be lifted out of context without sacrificing some of their meaning. Finally, borrowers run the risk of seizing upon the fashion of yesteryear, discovering as brand new constructs which are already considered passé. While the importation of concepts from the social sciences may well continue to be necessary until historians develop more generalizations out of their own research, it is a hazardous enterprise which must proceed with great caution, lest it create more problems than it solves. Just as in selecting statistical techniques, the challenge for the historian is to find the appropriate set of theories in the neighboring disciplines (Tilly 1981).

Fortunately there are several strategies which can minimize the dangers of conceptual borrowing. Its pitfalls can be avoided through immersion in the internal dialogue of another discipline through conversation with colleagues, selective reading, etc., until researchers can be reasonably sure of their conceptual footing. More promising yet is interdisciplinary collaboration on the same data base or a shared research problem. The concrete discussion of a common interest, such as the first French settlement west of the Mississippi (St. Genevieve in Missouri), among anthropologists, sociologists, and historians facilitates entry into the strange world of other approaches (see the forthcoming study by S. Flader). Another all too rarely used possibility is the recourse to social science concepts with which contemporaries analyzed a problem, thereby reflecting an older horizon of consciousness. When dealing with turn of the century household structure, for example, it might pay to consult the first systematic writings on family problems from around 1900. Finally, quantitative methods themselves offer another bridge between disciplines. Since much of the social science debate is explicitly quantitative, only historians schooled in this vocabulary and rhetoric will be able to appreciate the theoretical implications of such presentist research for their own earlier interests. For instance, the recent sociopolitical debate about educational opportunities has yielded a number of indicators which, when measured historically by Fritz Ringer (1979), have made international historical comparisons possible. The great value of exploring the debate of a neighboring discipline lies in the clarification of the question, the stimulation of new analytical methods, and the suggestion of novel theoretical conclusions.

On a higher plane, the problem of conceptual borrowing involves the question of the relationship of history to the social sciences in general. The internal discussion among quantitative historians has produced three distinctive reactions: First, cliometricians like Robert Fogel (1982) insist on applying the quantitative methods and behavioral models of the social sciences to the study of history in order to make it truly "scientific." The proponents of QUASSH (*quantitative social scientific history*) promote the creation of a quantitative historical social science, more historically minded than the social sciences and more scientifically rigorous than history (Kousser 1980). The practical aim of these quantitative *enthusiasts* is to create statistically based models of the past. Second, supporters of formalized historical analysis such as Charles Tilly (1987) view quantitative methods as only one necessary component of theory-guided research, among others (such as systematic textual analysis). While endorsing the need for explicit hypothesis-testing and model building, these quantitative *moderates* also allow for the systematic use of nonquantitative evidence and theory in historical interpretation. Finally, in the last decade erstwhile pioneers of quantification like Lawrence Stone (1977, 1979) have become disappointed in the failure of quantitative methods to fulfill the great expectations of their initial discovery. In calling for "a revival of narrative," such quantitative *skeptics* have preached a return to qualitative sources and to the history of mentalities, while borrowing from anthropology instead of the harder social sciences. Though not excluding quantitative methods for small local studies, this "neo-narrativism" has tended to downgrade them to occasional illustrative use.

Given this division of opinion, the hope for a convergence of history and the social sciences into a historical social science seems somewhat premature (Landes and Tilly 1971). The ebbing of the behavioralist impulse and the rediscovery of qualitative documentation has created a return to time perspectives and developmental questions among some social scientists. Often using the past as a giant quarry for its conceptual building blocks, this emerging macrohistory sometimes pays too little attention to the internal consistency and reliability of the evidence on which it rests. Among quantitative historians, the conceptual borrowing of theoretical approaches from the neighboring disciplines has also improved conditions for a meaningful dialogue. But the lead discipline has shifted from political science to sociology and on to anthropology during the last two decades, while deconstructionist and postmodernist currents threaten the debate before it has begun to bear much fruit. Even if possibilities for well-meant misunderstanding abound, the increasing usefulness of historical evidence for social scientists and of theoretically oriented quantitative research for historians encourages a continuation of the difficult interdisciplinary discourse. Though this debate about the relationship between history and the social sciences may seem somewhat esoteric, it does have important implications for the practicing scholar: At the beginning of each project the investigator needs to decide upon a general style of argumentation, since that choice will govern not only one's research steps but also the presentation of results.

HYPOTHESES AND MODEL BUILDING

As mentioned perhaps ad nauseam, the hypothesis is central to the practice as well as interpretation of quantitative historical research. Derived from the thesis of medieval scholarly disputations, it is often misused by being left undefined and being simply taken for granted. In quantitative history a hypothesis is a statement about the assumed relationship between independent and dependent variables, linking potential causes with probable effects. According to

Johan Galtung it must meet the following criteria in order to be useful in research: It must be clearly *falsifiable* so as to be proven or disproven by logical argument. It must also be *testable* so that it can be compared statistically with empirical evidence. It is also desirable that a hypothesis be *general*, applying to a large number of cases, that it be *complex*, describing complicated relationships, and that it be *deterministic*, predicting results with a high degree of probability. In practical terms, it is necessary for a hypothesis to be *reproducible*, allowing the research steps to be retraced at least in principle, and to be *communicable*, making it possible for the procedures and conclusions to be communicated to other researchers. Though it is also helpful for hypotheses to permit predictions, this requirement is of only limited utility for historians preoccupied with the past rather than concerned about the future. Even if historical hypotheses will rarely meet all of the above criteria, they need to be stated as explicitly and clearly as possible in order to form the core of a quantitative analysis that transcends mere description. A hypothesis is the crucial link between question, data, statistics, and interpretation. (For more detail, see Galtung [1967] and Hoover [1988].)

Several hypotheses concerning a problem can be combined into a *model* which formulates the implications of a general theory for a specific historical situation. As applied theory, a model defines the relationships between a number of independent and dependent variables and specifies their causative interaction. Verbal models abound in history: For instance, any laundry list of presumed causes of the Civil War (abolitionism, slavery, sectionalism, capitalism, and so on) is an implicit model, especially if the relationship between the factors is also discussed. Statistical models are formulated more stringently, since they assign numerical weights to the expected connections and clarify their mutual interaction logically. Contrary to folklore, models possess no magical qualities. They are, however, quite useful in clarifying linkages between hypotheses and in generating new suppositions to be investigated empirically. Obviously, models are only as good as the hypotheses which they contain. They ought to be *general*, comprising as many hypotheses as possible, possess great *range*, including descriptive as well as analytical statements, and provide *criteria* for evaluating results logically or empirically. To increase their utility, models ought to be *formalizable, axiomatic,* and *compatible* with other theories. Even if combining hypotheses into exclusively quantitative models is difficult in areas outside econometrics, historians ought to strive for model building, since models provide a more stringent form of reasoning about the past than ordinary verbal statements. Moreover, only the construction of a quantitative model will permit an assessment of how much of a development still needs to be explained by qualitative factors.

One example taken from the "new political history" might illustrate the historical use of hypothesis and modeling. The most influential of the path-breaking behaviorist works on American political history was probably Lee Benson's *The Concept of Jacksonian Democracy,* published in 1961. Starting with a relatively conventional hypothesis that voting behavior in New York State during the 1830s was influenced primarily by economic factors, Benson, stimulated by Paul E. Lazarsfeld, took a rigorous quantitative look at the evidence. On the basis of a data set which included voting behavior, economic variables, and ethnoreligious factors, Benson probed voting cycles in local case studies. This fresh approach yielded the startling conclusion that not economic interests but rather ethnocultural influences determined party allegiances and voting behavior. The new model suggested that members of the same ethnocultural community in New York behaved politically in similar ways. In religious terms, "puritan" denominations tended to become Whigs in opposition to more latitudinarian groups which supported the Democratic party. All the essential elements —a clear hypothesis, a complex data set, rigorous statistical testing, and a fresh model, revising the original interpretation—are contained in this pioneering study. In the meantime, as the work of J. Morgan Kousser demonstrates, the style of argumentation among the "new political historians" has, if anything, become even more formalized and statistical (Kousser 1974 and Bogue 1983).

Interpretation is not a self-evident by-product of research but rather the most challenging aspect of the entire process. Since it involves formulating and communicating results, the scholar ought to spend more actual effort on this final stage of the work. Instead of being dead tired or frantic about a deadline, scribbling down almost anything that comes to mind, a quantitative historian needs to allow sufficient time for formalizing complex conclusions. It is a pity for grandiose data sets which have taken years to collect to be vastly underinterpreted. Greater care should also be taken in communicating the results. Reams of printout or mountains of tables document an impressive effort but do little to convey meaning. At the other extreme, an elegant phrase can lightly skate over an abyss of statistical difficulties. While undigested quantitative research offends by its lack of ideas and excess of figures, accomplished quantitative work impresses with the clarity of concepts and the economy of appropriate statistics. Instead of seeking to overawe the reader with strings upon strings of undigested figures, quantifiers need to polish their prose and design their tables carefully for instant intelligibility. With interesting hypotheses, presented persuasively, quantitative history need not lead to a terrible simplification of historical understanding, but rather to a clearer and more complex vision of the past.

The Role of Quantitative Methods in History

The successful application of quantitative methods requires not only sufficient mastery of their techniques but also a receptive scholarly climate. During the last three decades quantification in history has reached a certain maturity. Even traditionalists admit that the heated debate among historians has ended in the triumph of the innovators within the guild. Tentative beginnings in the 1950s gave way to exciting departures during the 1960s when quantitative methods were programmatically hailed as saviors or denounced as destroyers of the profession. In the 1970s the quantitative movement succeeded in institutionalizing itself and in transforming the research agenda in a variety of fields through major substantive contributions. During the 1980s the advance of quantitative methods among historians appeared to have stalled somewhat, since trendsetting scholars turned to other innovative methodologies. Nonetheless, recent surveys show that on the working level quantitative methods have been accepted by a considerable sector of the profession as practical and worthwhile additions to historical tools to be applied as a matter of course (Kousser 1989). But the rise of new, postmodern reservations against quantification makes one wonder about the future: Will quantitative methods continue to retreat, will they stabilize in partial acceptance, or will they begin another period of rapid advance?

A sober assessment of the problems and promises of quantitative methods within historical research is complicated by a triple jeremiad. With considerable relief, traditionalist observers assert that the vogue of quantification has passed, consigning computerized research to the failed fashions of yesteryear. In its extreme form, enunciated by the formidable Gertrude Himmelfarb (1987), this argument indicts all of the "new histories." At the same time, innovative deconstructionist, feminist, and everyday historians have turned away from quantification, charging it with reductionism, sexism, and elitism (Johnson 1990). Disoriented by the loss of avant-garde status, some quantifiers like Rolf Dumke (1985) have started to wonder about a certain loss of creative vigor, a climacteric of cliometrics. No longer do they see breathtaking breakthroughs, but rather, in Kuhnian terms, quantification seems to have settled into "normal science." In contrast to these impressionistic laments, measurable indicators such as citation indexes or tabulation of statistical articles seem to indicate unbroken progress. From the venerable SSHA to QUANTUM, INTERQUANT, and, most recently, the Association for History and Computing, quantitative organizations appear to be flourishing. The major quantitative journals such as *JIH*, *SSH*, *HM*, *HSR*, *HeM*, and *HC*, just to mention a few of the English, French, and German titles, are publishing increasingly sophisticated work. What is one, therefore, to make of the discrepancy between a subjective sense of stagnation and objective indications of continued success? Perhaps an international perspective with its common problems might suggest some fresh solutions and provide a clearer prognosis.

NATIONAL STYLES OF QUANTIFICATION

Although much of the computing hardware and many of the statistical methods are similar, quantitative history has developed a handful of distinctive national styles. Divergent historiographical traditions, contrasting modes of disciplinary institutionalization, and separate cultural, ideological, and political agendas have led to different forms of quantitative research in other countries. In spite of international communication in specific research fields, the intellectual presuppositions, technical procedures, and forms of presentation show substantial differences across cultures which complicate the transnational dialogue. Since most scholars think and write within one of these traditions, it is important to be aware of their strengths as well as limitations. National approaches such as the much discussed *Annales* paradigm cannot simply be transferred, since they also rest on metascientific foundations which need to be taken into account. It is no accident that in the United States quantitative methods flourished particularly in econometrics and produced a "social science history" not replicated elsewhere. Greater awareness of work in other styles might help in assessing current trends by escaping the implicit provincialism of a single tradition, no matter how important it might be.

The oldest and most influential form of quantification outside of the United States is the French *Annales* school. Since its accomplishments are justly famous, only a few rudimentary facts need to be recalled. Founded by M. Bloch and L. Febvre in 1929 in a new journal of that name, it attempted to break the dominance of event-oriented political history through concentration on "economic and social history." This shift in subject matter and methodology was carried further by F. Braudel (1976) and E. Labrousse in the 1950s and continued by E. LeRoy Ladurie (1966), F. Furet (1971), and others as *nouvelle histoire* in the 1960s. Since the Annalists were preoccupied with "structure and . . . the long term," the "very logic of such an undertaking inevitably meant working with figures and statistics." This *histoire sérielle* aimed at recreating the total history of a community through a layering of multiple time series in a statistically simple but documentarily complex fashion. In countless theses French historians explored the economic (price) and demographic (family reconstitution) structure or conjuncture of a locality (town, department), moving eventually to society, material culture, and mentality. In spite of their objectivist air, the Annalists also shared a generally progressive political outlook focused on "economism and the masses." Brilliant external (toward the social sciences) and internal (toward traditional historians) strategies enabled the *Annales* group to conquer the central academic institutions such as the Centre de Recherches Historiques and to achieve a hegemonic position in French intellectual life. Recently such success has begun to breed discontent from without (failure to write biography or political and diplomatic history) and within (lack of theory, statistical primitivism). But the *Annales* approach remains, in spite of its bias for preindustrial structures, a highly successful national style of quantitative history which is exerting increasing influence outside France. (See also Couteau-Begarie [1983] and Bourdelais [1984].)

In German-speaking countries, quantitative methods developed later and have yet to reach the same level of public acceptance. Interrupted by the Third Reich, the older tradition of statistical work metamorphosed into full-blown quantitative history only during the late 1960s. The general change of historical interest to social concerns (*Gesellschaftsgeschichte*), the renewal of the neighboring social sciences, the influence of American and French scholars, and the availability of sophisticated computing machinery stimulated the new approach (Wehler 1973 and Kocka 1977). In the mid-1970s a group of young historians and sociologists at the University of Cologne founded in quick succession an organization (QUANTUM), a journal (*Historical Social Research*), and a publication series (HSF). After fairly rapid initial gains, this momentum has now somewhat slowed, since the overcrowding of the profession and the reduction of research funding have hurt institutionalization. The emerging German style of quantitative history is more focused on politics than in France, since the turbulent political past of Central Europe makes it difficult to ignore this dimension. At the same time, it tends to be more theoretically oriented due to the distinguished philosophical tradition and to the lingering influence of Max Weber. Moreover, the German notion of *historische Sozialwissenschaft* is less behaviorist than American historical social science, because the connotation of *Wissenschaft* is more "systematic scholarship" than hard "science." With the recent foundation of the Cologne Center for Historical Social Research, Central European quantifiers are, in spite of their late start, often technically sophisticated and open to international scholarly dialogue (Best 1981 and Johnson 1988).

In the Soviet Union and to some degree in other Eastern European countries, a Marxist-Leninist approach to quantitative history has developed as well. Building on a long Russian tradition of statistical compilation for social reform, Soviet historians in the early 1960s became interested in applying mathematical and statistical methods to historical research. Led by I. Kovalchenko (1983) and J. Kahk (1982), efforts at the Soviet as well as the Estonian Academy of Sciences or at Moscow State University are being coordinated by a special committee within the Soviet National Committee of Historians. According to D. K. Rowney's anthology (1984), favorite topics are agricultural history, labor history, etc. Though employing similar statistical procedures, Soviet quantitative scholars seem to work more descriptively and use modeling in a different synthetical sense than their Western counterparts. Given the basic Marxist assumptions, their ultimate aim could not be to develop a general theory of human behavior, but rather to refine historical explanations of particular changes. With the arrival of glasnost, some quantifiers have joined the ranks of the critics by addressing such formerly forbidden topics as the victims of Stalin's purges, Kondratieff waves in the Soviet economy, and so on. While there are active pockets of quantitative interest in East Germany, Poland, Hungary, and even Romania, it is hard for an outsider to estimate how many scholars use quantitative methods in Eastern Europe. But it seems reasonable to assume that they constitute only a distinctive, if dynamic, minority (cf. Kuczynski 1985 and Wilke 1990).

Because of the interpenetration of the Anglo-American academic communities, it is difficult to define a separate British national style of quantitative history. Interest in quantitative methods began as early as the 1950s, reached considerable levels of sophistication by the 1970s (see, e.g., R. Floud's text [1979]), but could never completely overcome the skeptical resistance of traditional scholars. In the early 1980s computer use even in the departments of social and economic history remained relatively low. The Cambridge Group for Population Research, led by P. Laslett (1965), E. A. Wrigley (1971), and R. Schofield (with Wrigley 1981), became internationally famous for pioneering historical demography. But the leading quantitative efforts in political history were undertaken by American scholars like W. O. Aydelotte (1977), while the radical social historians like E. J. Hobsbawm (1971) or E. P. Thompson remained skeptical about quantification. Hence in Britain quantifiers appear to be highly respected in some fields but remain a limited group facing difficulties in increasing their influence in the near future (since they are also hampered by the severe budget cutting of the Thatcher government). Nonetheless, there are signs of closer cooperation in a new journal called *History and Computing*, edited by the Association for History and Computing. Perhaps one should, therefore, think of British quantitative history as a technically advanced variant of a common Anglo-American pattern.

In the smaller Western European countries the situation is similar, since their academic communities are not large enough to produce an independent national style. Oriented largely toward English language debates, some creative scholars have been employing quantitative methods for two decades. The especially rich records of Scandinavia have allowed the creation of a massive social data base for the last two centuries, which encourages advanced work on social mobility, literacy, and family reconstitution. As in the Benelux countries, technical standards are often quite high, and there is much interest in scholarly cooperation among economic and demographic historians. While there are some stirrings of interest in Mediterranean countries, surprisingly little Italian or Spanish quantitative work has become known internationally (Jarausch 1984).

In the Third World the position of quantitative history is more precarious. Precious computer time is rarely available to historians, the audience for quantitative work is limited, cultural bias militates against it, and documentary as well as political obstacles abound. Nonetheless, in Latin America an accomplished body of quantitative historical scholarship has crystallized in the last decade. Methods as well as methodologies are imported as technology transfer either from the *Annales* school in France or the econometricians in the United States. But Latin American historians have made impressive gains in collecting basic historical statistics and are beginning to make distinctive interpretative contributions (Perez-Brignoli and Ruiz 1984). In the Far East, there are promising pockets of highly sophisticated work in Japan, located in departments of economics. But in Third World countries quantitative history still seems to be struggling in isolation to close the gap between enormous promise and limited accomplishment. On the international scene, the progress of quantitative methods, therefore, ranges from dominance in France all the way to faint beginnings in Africa or Asia.

CURRENT PROBLEMS

In spite of their wide proliferation, quantitative methods have remained surprisingly problematic for the majority of professional historians. Shying away from quantification because of different interests or the amount of work involved, traditional historians react in several predictable ways: A few obscurantists like the intellectual historian Jacques Barzun (1974) completely reject the "quanto-maniacs," charging that they confuse vocabulary with method and try to make a humanities discipline into a natural science. The majority of the professional historians respond more ambivalently, on the one hand acknowledging in principle the usefulness of quantitative methods but on the other hand avoiding them in practice (Bailyn 1982). They are fond of citing Arthur Schlesinger's dictum that all really important historical questions cannot be quantified. Finally, more methodologically open scholars accept quantification in a lukewarm way, but concede it only a kind of subordinate, illustrative utility in their politically committed writings (Kousser 1989). Over the last two decades the balance of reactions has shifted toward greater tolerance of quantitative methods; at the same time, the partisans of quantification have grown less sanguine, admitting with David Herlihy (1981) that the promise of explicit argumentation leading to higher levels of explanatory certainty has not been entirely met. This decreasing stridency in the debate between detractors and zealots signals a normalization, a working acceptance by a significant part of the historical profession which shifts attention away from programmatic claims and counterclaims to actual research performance. While de-emotionalized, the controversy has left a legacy of suspicion and misunderstanding which complicates current concerns.

The chorus of qualitative criticism has pinpointed several real but surmountable difficulties for quantitative historians. A favorite charge, cropping up in different countries, is the contention that historical data are too incomplete and imprecise to allow quantification. Often true for social scientists who simply accept statistics at face value, this argument tends to assume a standard of accuracy and completeness which qualitative scholarship cannot meet either. Earlier census takers were not necessarily greater fools than present ones. There are many good qualitative sources (such as recruitment registers) which can be codified. Moreover, statistical sampling, variable transformation, and other techniques can help in assessing the problems of incomplete information. Another common objection is the incomprehensibility of a quantitative argumentation which transcends "common sense." In principle the resort to statistics is hardly different from a complex philological analysis of ancient Greek or Hebrew which the educated public does not grasp directly either. While understandable, the irrational animus of humanists against numbers is a highly regrettable self-limitation, since it renders them illiterate in an ever growing realm of contemporary information. The manipulation of statistics is similar to the tricks of verbal rhetoric—anyone with some training can easily see through it.

More serious than lingering prejudice is the methodological rejection of the results of quantitative work. Often opponents maintain that quantification merely yields trivial conclusions which were already suspected. However, falsification of some qualitative assertions and proof for another hypothesis represent considerable scholarly progress, even if it was known beforehand. Only in this way can some sacred cows be slaughtered and hoary errors be eliminated. Historicists object to the "extremely artificial character" of quantitative reasoning which reduces complex reality into a few factors. But this process of abstraction is common to all science, as long as it does not lose its relation to reality, can be tested, and so on. Theory need not be a reductionist "prison." Traditional historical interpretation with its laundry lists of one "cause" after another tends to be more imprecise and sloppy than quantitative modeling which specifies directions of relationships and their relative strengths. (See also Kousser [1984].) Postmodernists charge quantification with textual flatness, accepting categories of analysis at face value and reifying constructs without sufficient attention to their hidden meanings and ambiguities. While premature generalization indeed oversimplifies the contradictory nature of the past, the deconstruction of accepted meaning aims at discovering underlying patterns just as the numerical quest for regularities behind verbal claims does. Only a scholar acquainted with statistics can penetrate their rhetorical surface and begin to discover the hidden breaks and ambiguities in the language of numbers (Jarausch 1990).

Another major area of inconclusive debate is the ideological affinity of quantitative history. Feminist critics accuse quantifiers of male chauvinism, since much early quantitative work neglected to stress gender cleavages in historical development. In research practice, this fault is easy to remedy, since leading women's historians have themselves demonstrated the fruitfulness of taking females seriously as an empirical category (Tilly and Scott 1978). Time and again, quantitative investigation has shown gender to be a crucial social variable, be it in crime patterns, educational opportunities, or political attitudes. But the integration of quantitative results into the received body of male-dominated scholarship may prove somewhat more difficult, since it requires recasting accepted understanding of the past in a more fundamental way. Part of the problem derives from a structural asymmetry: Since the 175 women, at most, were a tiny minority of the 19,200 German lawyers before 1933, their imprint on the legal profession was slight—but the impact of this first cohort of female jurists for the rise of women professionals was enormous! Even if insufficiently expressing the hopes and aspirations of women as actors, quantitative evidence can be a considerable help in recovering female experiences, since figures cannot be quite as easily dismissed as a one-sided, partisan reading as can literary arguments.

The instinctive antipathy of radical "people's historians," whether explicitly Marxist (History Workshop in Britain) or more populist in bent, rests on a similar misunderstanding of quantitative history. Their main objections center on the class bias in statistical data, the impersonalism of quantification, the capitalist theoretical foundation of econometrics, and the difficulties of learning quantitative techniques (Floud 1984). In Germany the leftist proponents of *Alltagsgeschichte*, the everyday history of the little people, tend to reject quantification as dehumanizing, as incapable of grasping a social situation or consciousness of an individual worker, a housewife, etc. A similar split seems to exist in Latin America, where the radical historians prefer the *Annales* approach over econometrics precisely because of their political associations. This hostility is somewhat surprising, since many Western pioneers shared a leftist outlook (Ingham 1986) and in Eastern Europe Marxist historians use quantitative methods with little ideological compunction (Rowney 1984). In France both Marxists and non-Marxists employ quantitative methods with equal bravura, since the ideologically progressive cast of the founders of the *Annales* did not render them suspect. These reactions clearly demonstrate that there is no necessary connection between quantitative methods and reactionary politics. Moreover, it is relatively easy to refute the specific charges: Statistics are one of the few suitable approaches to the mute masses, quantitative data can be meaningfully complemented by qualitative evidence, there is a Marxist quantitative economic history, and so on. But it will take much convincing to change the deeply ingrained bias against quantitative history of the Western Left, which confuses method with commitment.

A more practical hurdle is the insufficient infrastructure for quantitative research. In spite of the progress of journals, organizations, or institutions, frustrating problems remain. While much of the hardware and a considerable amount of the software are American, nationalistic support for independent computer design makes machines incompatible and requires basic software to be translated. Therefore, many customized programs for specific tasks cannot be transported across frontiers. Moreover, the business market dominance leads to the proliferation of commercial packages ill-suited for historical research. While in the United States and some of the wealthier Western European countries computer access is relatively easy for historians, in Eastern Europe it is more restricted, and in Third World countries it is virtually nonexistent. Even under the best of circumstances, historians rank far below heavier users in informatics, medicine, or the hard social sciences. In practice this low priority means limited budgets and working in environments designed for other disciplines' problems. The considerable differences between the state-sponsored teamwork of the Europeans and the individualized cottage industry of the Anglo-Americans also produce distinctive problems. While it usually has more assistants and project supplies, collective research has difficulty in coordinating the work and in producing written results beyond mimeographed progress reports. In individual projects the lack of manpower often seriously restricts the size of the study or extends the work over so many years that the conclusions are outdated when they appear.

The current status of quantification in history is therefore not as rosy as some of its partisans claim. Despite considerable progress, quantitative historians continue to face a skeptical profession, suffer substantive criticisms, experience ideological objections, and encounter practical difficulties. While the passing of the computer fad is a relief, the sense of self-doubt among some practitioners combined with the renewed denigration of detractors raises some fresh dangers. The contraction of general support for historical research has tended to hurt quantitative projects more than traditional work because they are sometimes costlier and less well established within the discipline. While research is burgeoning, training in quantitative techniques is becoming more haphazard, since many departments have yet to offer formal course work and some of the earlier summer schools have been abandoned (Kousser 1989). Moreover, the leading textbooks in the English language are by now two decades old. Historical teaching software also tends to favor qualitative simulations over exercises in statistical analysis (Gutman, 1990). However, these critical observations are not meant to sound a note of pessimism. Instead of complacency, the minority status of quantitative methods in historical research requires redoubled efforts to involve more of the discipline, lest these techniques become encapsulated as a marginal *Hilfswissenschaft*, essential but inferior like a kind of modern paleography.

POTENTIAL SOLUTIONS

In order to overcome external attacks, quantitative historians need to develop a rigorous internal *self-criticism*. Nothing discredits a method more quickly than its faulty application. Each major step of quantitative research contains its own dangers. Just like the classical philological method, quantitative techniques require a rigorous source criticism. Process-produced statistics should never be accepted at face value, since they usually contain a hidden agenda of some kind. Moreover, the conversion of structured mass data into machine-readable form is also fraught with pitfalls, since coding, especially of nominal variables, always loses information which might be vital later on. Because many historians acquire statistical know-how secondhand, they often select the wrong procedure or use it inappropriately. The literature is full of examples of such errors as the "ecological fallacy" (in which conclusions about individual properties are based on group or ecological data). Sometimes a certain approach like factor analysis happens to be fashionable and the data are run through it whether this makes substantive sense or not. Often statistics are misused or their internal logic is violated. For instance, a chi-square is sometimes misinterpreted as an indicator of the strength of a relationship rather than as a test of significance, and the misuse of regression or multiple classification analysis on dichotomous dependent variables is also common. Hence it is vital to choose the appropriate statistic for a given problem and to document it clearly but economically. Finally, interpretation can also be troublesome. Often a scholar is content with description when the data would have permitted more elaborate analysis. At times researchers will also confine themselves to the factors contained in their data sets and ignore everything else, much as the drunk searches for his key under the streetlight, since it is too dark elsewhere. Hence it is essential to maintain analytical control. Only frank self-criticism of mistaken quantitative applications will increase this method's credibility (Clubb and Scheuch 1980).

In order to convince the skeptics, the results of quantitative research also need to be communicated effectively. The most elaborate research design, comprehensive data set, discerning statistics, and imaginative interpretation are of little use unless they can be conveyed in such a manner as to interest and convince the reader. At this point quantitative historians often have their greatest difficulties. Confidently at home with numbers, they are sometimes at a loss for words. Some simple suggestions might help to overcome this hurdle. Before writing, scholars have to decide which audience they wish to address, since each public comes with different expectations: Quantitative specialists will want to savor the technical details and qualitative historians would like to follow the logic of the argumentation, whereas the mythical general reader might only be interested in the results. This initial choice governs the manner of quantitative documentation. Fellow quantifiers will expect enough justification of crucial coding decisions, detailed tabulations, and inferential statistics as well as explicit modeling so that they might be able to replicate the study themselves. Qualitative historians need to know only the general line of reasoning (with technical matters consigned to footnotes or an appendix), while interested laymen will enjoy an occasional table as illustration and take the rest on faith. Third, the drama of numbers which is apparent to the trained eye must be made exciting for the uninitiated. It takes so much effort to penetrate large columns of figures that most readers will soon give up. Hence the salient features and the startling changes ought to be summarized and paraphrased, not in a murky morass of percentages but in a few pithy sentences. A statistically representative quotation or an apt graph can make a complex relationship intuitively come to life. Unless they want to talk only to other cognoscenti, quantitative historians must abandon their penchant for leaden prose and relearn how to write (Rabb 1983a).

A recent development which promises to overcome many of the practical problems is the microcomputer revolution. Even after discounting some technological hype, software, access, project size, and cost problems have been significantly reduced by the advent of powerful third-generation micros. Even the most traditional historians have adopted the microcomputer for its superior word processing, giving an author greater flexibility and control. The arrival of free-field filing and self-indexing software also has rendered the card file obsolete, since information retrieval is quicker and more accurate by machine than by memory. In many research projects micros serve as data-entry terminals, eliminating coding on paper and keypunching computer cards. This not only speeds up the work but makes it more reliable. Finally, a growing minority of quantifiers also use the micro for statistical manipulation of moderate size data sets, trading off the ease of working in comfortable surroundings and the lack of cost for computer time with the somewhat slower speed of downsized mainframe packages. Once bought, a PC lowers the cost of computing (to buying occasional diskettes and paper) and reduces access barriers (as long as it can be wrested away from one's game-playing children). Moreover, micros are also more compatible with the individualized research style of Anglo-American scholars. This is not to say that they do not create problems of their own, such as misaligned floppy-disk drives, crashed hard disks, and so on. But on balance the micro might well lead to another quantum jump in the dissemination of quantitative methods, since students (through games) and scholars (through word processing) find them more friendly to use than mainframes (Jensen 1983).

The related advance of data bases and specific historical software might further reduce the barrier between qualitative and quantitative computer applications. More and more research institutions and megaprojects are developing their question-specific data sets into integrated data bases combining textual and statistical information. These large accumulations of evidence from a number of different sources, such as the Philadelphia Urban History Project, are amenable to repeated analyses from different disciplinary perspectives that blend literary with statistical approaches. The development of historical software for source-oriented data processing by Manfred Thaller (1989), called KLEIO, also promises to tear down the artificial qualitative/quantitative divide. Another innovation which holds great promise for quantitative history is the extension of multivariate analysis to nominal variables. In the recent past the mathematical testing of models through multiple regression techniques had been confined to factors which could be measured in numerical terms, such as population size or economic growth, thereby limiting applications to econometrics, demographics, and some areas of the new political history. During the last decade statisticians have developed new forms of linear and logit modeling that extend the principles of powerful multivariate analysis to categorical variables, such as social class, religion, and the like. Just beginning to be perceived by historians, this advance in statistical techniques is likely to open up fresh areas of social and political history to stringent modeling (Kousser 1989).

The dual hard- and software impetus is currently creating the possibility of overcoming the misleading distinction between qualitative and quantitative approaches. During the next decade historians will use integrated work stations with data sets on optical disks, on terminals connected to powerful mainframes via broadband or fiber-optic networks and hooked up to scanners for text entry and laser printers for beautiful output. While such technological advances will command a considerable price, and the European chair structure with its secretarial emphasis will continue to retard development, the combined hardware improvement and software innovation is likely to open up new vistas for computer-assisted historical research. The renewed interest of social scientists in qualitative data may well yield further statistical innovations. Since the dynamism seems to be greatest on the textual or database end, this development will need to broaden quantitative methods into formal analysis. Increasingly complex data bases are becoming more compatible with anthropologically inspired cultural studies. Recent collective volumes by M. Thaller on data banks (1986) and by P. Denley and D. Hopkin on *History and Computing* (1987) reflect this widening range of historical applications. Instead of replacing quantification, such extension of computer use will not only stimulate linguistic methods but also make statistical analysis even more compelling for historical research.

THE QUANTITATIVE CHALLENGE

In many ways quantitative methods present a continuing challenge to historians. Traditional qualitative scholars will need patient tolerance toward the not always successful experiments of a new approach. Only a willingness to inform themselves about some of the idiosyncrasies of quantitative research and to discuss quantitative findings rather than ignore them will lead to constructive interchange. Innovative historians willing to run the risks of quantification will require enough stamina to master the novel techniques so as to use them correctly. Moreover, they ought not to encapsulate themselves as a new sect but rather confidently search for substantive dialogue with their colleagues. Neither the time-honored hermeneutic method nor the newer social science approach is a priori superior to the other—the historical question must have priority. Inasmuch as quantifiers address the "core questions" of their discipline, their work will be discussed and accepted. When dealing with fundamental issues of the past such as industrialization, family life, political allegiance, or social conflict, quantitative historians will have an opportunity to reshape historical understanding. If their work is of high quality, opens new insights into the past, and is communicated effectively, it will be read and appreciated. It is pointless to continue the sniping between "quantifiers" and "qualifiers"; instead, the profession needs a more tolerant and substantive dialogue between them on the big historical questions (Tilly 1987).

A healthy development of quantitative methods also requires further improvement of scholarly infrastructure. To begin with, the teaching of quantitative methods to historians must be upgraded dramatically. It is not enough to mention these techniques briefly in a general historiography course. It is also ineffective to abandon all responsibility for quantitative training and to turn it over to other disciplines with different needs and priorities. Every history department offering graduate work must have a course on quantitative methods. In cases where such research skills can be substituted for a second language, there needs also to be a coherent program of additional statistical or computer work as well as a standardized testing procedure. The arrival of microcomputers is even making introductory training in undergraduate courses possible, since some teaching software will involve quantitative procedures. Secondly, the publication of quantitative research can be improved further. Outside of the specialized quantitative journals, the refereeing of manuscripts needs to involve quantitative specialists on a regular basis. University presses also need to be educated to understand the greater requirements of quantitative documentation. Finally, in spite of the current fiscal crisis, it is imperative to strengthen financial support for quantitative research. Since many fields are unthinkable without them, quantitative methods are not a luxury which one can afford in fat years and cut back in lean ones. Only with a greater commitment to training, publication, and funding will quantitative methods be able to fulfill their expectations (Clubb 1986).

In the final analysis, quantification is only a method—but an extraordinarily powerful one. Since they are more used to addressing substantive issues, historians tend to have some difficulty in assessing the role of quantitative methods correctly. While quantification should never be an end in itself, quantitative methods have not only their own technique to be mastered but also their own internal logic to be followed. The tension between research problem and method can best be illustrated by the "tool" analogy. On the one hand, an ax is only useful if employed for a purpose for which it was designed, such as chopping down trees rather than digging trenches. On the other hand, the task of felling timber is more easily accomplished with the correct instrument, since trees are hard to tear out by hand and spades do not cut particularly well. Correctly applied, a method like quantification makes possible the solution of certain problems which were intractable before. Thereby it also opens up entire new directions of questioning. This *enormous potential of quantitative methods* is often underestimated by its detractors and supporters alike. This is not to say that quantification is about to spread to all areas of historical inquiry, since it is clearly irrelevant for many concerns. But the boundaries of its appropriate use are expanding all the time through the ingenuity of researchers, and even prima facie nonquantitative fields like diplomatic history (e.g., the study of arms races or of diplomatic personnel) contain more questions amenable to quantitative analysis than one might imagine. Moreover, historical data bases, comprising qualitative data subject to systematic analysis, are mushrooming everywhere. As the coeditor of one of the leading journals, Theodore K. Rabb, asserts, quantification has already changed entire areas through statistically based studies, from education to elections, from agriculture to fertility (1983a). The greatest challenge of quantitative methods therefore consists of applying them correctly and developing them further in order to extend the range, precision, and power of historical research.

Appendix A

The Fort Moultrie and New England Data Sets

by Dale Steinhauer

The text has made frequent reference to data on the inhabitants of Fort Moultrie, South Carolina, in 1850, and on the population, economic activity, and political behavior in Massachusetts, Rhode Island, and Connecticut in 1860. The purpose of these two data sets is to serve as didactic examples for explaining the relationships among variables rather than to introduce new historical interpretations. These case studies were intentionally kept small and simple. Since the questions raised in the text continually relate to Fort Moultrie's population and the characteristics of New England counties, the reader should take careful note of the data presented in this appendix. A secondary objective of this material is to illustrate the mechanics of putting together a data set, from the discovery of a source of data through its preparation for entering in the computer.

FORT MOULTRIE SOLDIERS

Though historians know a great deal about the composition of the United States Army after the Civil War, they have not paid much attention to its makeup in the antebellum period. Where were the soldiers born? How old were they? What was their social status, based on their occupational skills and the wealth they had accumulated? Historians have also sometimes failed to take into account the social environment of the army post. Besides officers and enlisted men, each post had a population of women and children who were usually dependents of the soldiers.

Fort Moultrie was just one of about 75 army posts in the United

States in 1850. In terms of the army as a whole at midcentury, the single company of the Second Artillery Regiment stationed at the post was only one company of over 150. Though Fort Moultrie was by no means representative or typical of the entire army, it offers one case study which provides a good example of research techniques.

The choice of Fort Moultrie was based on the easy availability of the microfilmed population schedules of the 1850 census for South Carolina. Since a typical university library holds the historic population schedules of federal censuses for the state and sometimes the region, a student could create a similar data set for another post. Under ideal conditions the researcher would use the readily available census records in conjunction with less accessible military files, such as enlistment registers and muster rolls, in order to link records and explore other characteristics of the soldiers of Fort Moultrie.

Since 1790 the United States has taken a census every ten years. While the first six censuses contained only the names of heads of household, with the other members simply referred to by their race, sex, and age categories, the censuses since 1850 have listed the names and selected information on each person in the household. In 1840 an entire military post might simply be given under the name of its commanding officer; a decade later, the census included the name of each person living there at the time the census enumerator made his count. The population schedules of the 1850 census include ten pieces of information about each person in a household: age; sex; color (white, black, or mulatto); occupation of males over 15 years of age; value of real estate owned; birthplace; married within the year; attended school within the year; literacy; and disability, such as deaf and dumb, blind, insane, lunatic, pauper, or convict. Excluding the columns that the enumerator left blank and the attended school column, the census roughly looks like this:

Fort Moultrie
Charleston Harbor, South Carolina
1850

Name	Age	Sex	Occupation	Birthplace
Erving, John	50	M	Lieut. Colonel	Massachusetts
Elisa	35	F	—	"
William	17	F?	—	"
Elisa	13	F	—	"
Anna	7	F	—	"
Luther, Roland	35	M	Captain	Pennsylvania
Wild, T. B. I.	28	M	1st Lieut.	Maine
Benson, Henry	25	M	2d Lieut.	New Jersey
Wagner, George 0.	26	M	Sergeant	Georgia
Mary	21	F	—	Ireland
Lucius	1	M	—	South Carolina
Mahoney, John	26	M	Sergeant	Ireland
Makwell, James	22	M	"	"
Anderson, John	23	M	"	"
Anna D.	21	F	—	New Brunswick
M.	1	F	—	South Carolina
Dornan, Henry	36	M	Corporal	Ireland
Catherine	30	F	—	"
Henry	5	M	—	New York
Elizabeth	1	F	—	South Carolina
Tullan, H.	25	M	Corporal	Hannover
Dole, Jacob	26	M	"	Germany
Mary Ann	20	F	—	Maryland
M. L.	1	F	—	South Carolina
Connelly, H.	20	M	Fifer	Ireland
Alger, L.	22	M	Private	"
Barnett, James	30	M	"	Tennessee
Bele, C. H.	28	M	"	Maine
Bitz, C.	27	M	"	Germany
Binley, A. B.	28	M	"	Ireland
Boyle, Catherine	33	F	—	"
Michael	31	M	Private	"
M. A.	9	F	—	New York
C. M.	5	F	—	South Carolina
Brennan, M.	25	M	Private	Ireland
Brondman, H.	32	M	"	Germany
Curry, J.	33	M	"	Maryland
Delano, D.	29	M	"	New York
Fleming, J.	29	M	"	Ireland
Flynn, P.	31	M	"	"
Henderson, R.	23	M	"	Scotland

Fort Moultrie Inhabitants (continued)

Name	Age	Sex	Occupation	Birthplace
Hymes, R.	29	M	"	Ireland
Johnson, A.	32	M	"	New York
Keirly, U.	26	M	"	Ireland
Lynch, P.	25	M	"	"
Martin, J.	20	M	"	"
McCourt, C.	33	M	"	England
McCoy, T.	28	M	"	Massachusetts
Neimyer, H.	28	M	"	Germany
Nieland, P.	19	M	"	Ireland
Osborn, T.	34	M	"	"
Redwine, G.	34	M	"	North Carolina
Stuart, W.	24	M	"	Scotland
Wagner, W.	25	M	"	Pennsylvania
Westerfeldt, P.	25	M	"	New Jersey
Williams, H.	40	M	"	Germany
Woodbury, E.	23	M	"	Ohio
Zimmerman, A.	23	M	"	Germany
Moore, C. N.	23	M	"	North Carolina
Brunsman, Catherine	32	F	—	Prussia
C.	4	M	—	New York
M.	1	F	—	South Carolina
Gruber, Sarah	30	F	—	Ireland
A.	3	M	—	New York
Masterson, N.	30	F	—	Ireland
Margaret	15	F	—	Michigan
Martha	9	F	—	New York
James	16	M	—	"
Michael	3	M	—	"
Martin, Alice	40	F	—	Ireland
Obydon, Cathrn.	17	F	—	Connecticut
Martin, Richard	14	M	—	Louisiana
Mary	8	F	—	Florida
Harris, Mathias	31	M	Clergyman	Maryland
Catherine	30	F	—	"
A. B.	13	F	—	"
H. J.	11	M	—	"
Burger, Mary	20	F	—	South Carolina
Porter, John B.	40	M	Physician	Connecticut
Anita A.	35	F	—	Florida
Francis B.	6	M	—	unclear

In addition to the four given variables—age, sex, rank, and birth-place—one can also create two new variables simply by looking at age and the order in which names are presented: marital status and number of dependents.

For the sake of demonstrating statistical techniques, two fictitious variables have been added. Since the census enumerator left blank the column for real estate, perhaps because no one living on the post owned local property or slaves, the authors have artificially assigned a value of real estate to certain residents of the post. Also, because an enlisted man would have been employed in civil life before joining the army, the authors have ascribed an occupation to each. Remember that real estate and occupation are variables conceived simply for didactic purposes.

The next step is to create a codebook that provides a guide for rendering all of the variables in numeric form. It could have the following structure:

Fort Moultrie Codebook

Variable	Description
ID	An identification number, beginning with 1, assigned sequentially to each case as it appears in the census.
AGE	The age of each person as given in the census. Those infants who are under the age of one and whose age is given as a fraction are regarded as zero years old.
SEX	1 = Male 2 = Female
RANK	0 = no rank (all nonsoldiers) 1 = private or fifer 2 = corporal 3 = sergeant 4 = 2d lieutenant 5 = 1st lieutenant 6 = chaplain (includes clergy) 7 = physician (includes surgeon) 8 = captain 9 = major and above (includes lieutenant colonel)

Fort Moultrie Codebook (continued)

Variable	Description	
BPL	Birthplace	
	NATIVE-BORN	
	1 = Connecticut	New England states
	2 = Maine	
	3 = Massachusetts	
	4 = New Hampshire	
	5 = Rhode Island	
	6 = Vermont	
	7 = New Jersey	Middle Atlantic
	8 = New York	states
	9 = Pennsylvania	
	10 = Ohio	Other free states
	11 = Michigan	
	12 = other free states	
	21 = Florida	Slave states
	22 = Georgia	
	23 = Louisiana	
	24 = Maryland	
	25 = North Carolina	
	26 = South Carolina	
	27 = Tennessee	
	28 = Virginia	
	29 = other slave states	
	FOREIGN-BORN	
	31 = England	British Isles
	32 = Scotland	and dominions
	33 = Ireland	
	34 = other	
	35 = Canada (includes New Brunswick)	
	41 = Germany (includes Hannover, Prussia, and Brunswick)	Europe
	42 = Austria	
	43 = Switzerland	
	44 = France	
	45 = other Europe	
	50 = all other	Other

Fort Moultrie Codebook (continued)

Variable	Description

MAR | Marital status
0 = single, aged 1 to 17
1 = single, aged 18 and above
2 = married

DEP | Number of dependents for married male heads of household.
All single soldiers have no dependents.

REAL | Value of real estate owned.

OCC | Occupation

0 = no occupation	
1 = professional	High white-collar
2 = physician	
3 = lawyer	
4 = clergyman	
5 = teacher	
6 = public official (higher level)	
7 = army officer	
8 = planter	
9 = merchant	
21 = grocer	Low white-collar
22 = storekeeper	
23 = bookseller	
24 = barkeeper/tavernkeeper	
25 = clerk	
26 = musician	
27 = student	
28 = army noncommissioned officer	
29 = public official (lower level)	
30 = large farmer	
40 = mechanic/machinist	Skilled blue-collar
41 = baker	
42 = butcher	
43 = brewer	
44 = cabinetmaker	
45 = carpenter	
46 = cooper	
47 = blacksmith	
48 = mason	

Fort Moultrie Codebook (continued)

Variable	Description	
	49 = stonecutter	
	50 = bricklayer	
	51 = bookbinder	
	52 = saddler	
	53 = painter	
	54 = miller	
	55 = printer	
	56 = weaver	
	57 = shoemaker	
	58 = tailor	
	59 = carter	
	60 = landowning farmer	
	71 = soldier	Semiskilled blue-collar
	72 = sailor	
	73 = fisherman	
	74 = servant	
	75 = nonlandowning farmer	
	81 = laborer	Unskilled blue-collar
	82 = farm laborer	

Note: The five general classes are derived from Stephan Thernstrom (1973, pp. 289–92). Since his ordering is intended to suit only an urban setting, agricultural occupations have been added to each of the categories.

The final step in creating a data set involves transforming the original document into numeric form through coding. A raw data set based on the Fort Moultrie census would look as follows:

ID	AGE	SEX	RANK	BPL	MAR	DEP	REAL	OCC
1	50	1	9	3	2	4	2500	7
2	35	2	0	3	2	0	0	0
3	17	2	0	3	0	0	0	0
4	13	2	0	3	0	0	0	0
5	7	2	0	3	0	0	0	0
6	35	1	8	9	0	0	1500	7
7	28	1	5	2	0	0	800	7
8	25	1	4	7	0	0	500	7
9	26	1	3	22	2	2	400	28
10	21	2	0	33	2	0	0	0

Fort Moultrie Raw Data Set (continued)

ID	AGE	SEX	RANK	BPL	MAR	DEP	REAL	OCC
11	1	1	0	26	0	0	0	0
12	26	1	3	33	0	0	450	28
13	22	1	3	33	0	0	250	25
14	23	1	3	33	2	2	300	57
15	21	2	0	35	2	0	0	0
16	1	2	0	26	0	0	0	0
17	36	1	2	33	2	3	400	28
18	30	2	0	33	2	0	0	0
19	5	1	0	8	0	0	0	0
20	1	2	0	26	0	0	0	0
21	25	1	2	41	0	0	200	28
22	26	1	2	41	2	2	200	40
23	20	2	0	24	2	0	0	0
24	1	2	0	26	0	0	0	0
25	20	1	1	33	0	0	0	81
26	22	1	1	33	0	0	0	81
27	30	1	1	27	0	0	75	47
28	28	1	1	2	0	0	0	45
29	27	1	1	41	0	0	0	25
30	28	1	1	33	0	0	0	81
31	33	2	0	33	2	0	0	0
32	31	1	1	33	2	3	100	60
33	9	2	0	8	0	0	0	0
34	5	2	0	26	0	0	0	0
35	25	1	1	33	1	0	0	81
36	32	1	1	41	1	0	150	45
37	33	1	1	24	1	0	175	71
38	29	1	1	8	1	0	50	25
39	29	1	1	33	1	0	0	75
40	31	1	1	33	1	0	100	40
41	23	1	1	32	1	0	50	81
42	29	1	1	33	1	0	100	25
43	32	1	1	8	1	0	150	40
44	26	1	1	33	1	0	0	81
45	25	1	1	33	1	0	0	81
46	20	1	1	33	1	0	0	81
47	33	1	1	31	1	0	200	75
48	28	1	1	3	1	0	0	40
49	28	1	1	41	1	0	0	81
50	19	1	1	33	1	0	0	81
51	34	1	1	33	1	0	0	40
52	34	1	1	25	1	0	25	75
53	24	1	1	32	1	0	0	81
54	25	1	1	9	1	0	0	57

Fort Moultrie Raw Data Set (continued)

ID	AGE	SEX	RANK	BPL	MAR	DEP	REAL	OCC
55	25	1	1	7	1	0	0	81
56	40	1	1	41	1	0	300	75
57	23	1	1	10	1	0	0	75
58	23	1	1	41	1	0	0	81
59	23	1	1	25	1	0	0	81
60	32	;	0	41	1	2	75	0
61	4	1	0	8	0	0	0	0
62	1	2	0	26	0	0	0	0
63	30	2	0	33	1	1	50	0
64	3	1	0	8	0	0	0	0
65	30	2	0	33	1	0	75	0
66	15	2	0	11	0	0	0	0
67	9	2	0	8	0	0	0	0
68	16	1	0	8	0	0	0	0
69	3	1	0	8	0	0	0	0
70	40	2	0	33	1	0	100	0
71	17	2	0	1	0	0	0	0
72	14	1	0	23	0	0	0	0
73	8	2	0	21	0	0	0	0
74	31	1	6	24	1	0	1000	4
75	30	2	0	24	1	0	0	0
76	13	2	0	24	0	0	0	0
77	11	1	0	24	0	0	0	0
78	20	2	0	26	1	0	0	0
79	40	1	7	1	2	2	1500	2
80	35	2	0	21	2	0	0	0
81	6	1	0	50	0	0	0	0

NEW ENGLAND COUNTIES

Who were the members of the new Republican party on the eve of the Civil War? Historians can approach this problem by attempting to trace the political roots of individual Republicans from the other contemporary parties and by identifying their common characteristics. An alternative method would be to look not at individuals but rather at geographic units. The populations of these units would differ from each other in the strength of their enthusiasm for the Republican party and the degree to which they represent other characteristics. From this sort of ecological analysis, the historian can conclude that where the Republicans were strong, certain other characteristics are also to be found.

In 1860 the Republican presidential contender Abraham Lincoln received a large vote in Connecticut, Massachusetts, and Rhode Island, easily carrying each of them. When focusing on geographic divisions within the three southern New England states, one finds that his success varied considerably. W. Dean Burnham has compiled the results of presidential elections at the county level (1955). This standard work presents the figures of the 1860 returns for the 27 counties of the three states.

Which other characteristics of these counties may or may not have helped to shape the voting habits of the inhabitants? The best source for information on the county, state, and national levels is published census records. While the population and other schedules from which the census data are drawn are available on microfilm, the aggregated statistics are even more easily accessible in bound volumes. By 1860 the scope of the census had expanded so that four volumes were necessary to contain the population, mortality, agriculture, and manufacturing statistics. A century later, of course, the Census Bureau's even more voluminous output makes the 1860 effort seem meager and incomplete.

Though one could indiscriminately search the available statistics for any influence on voting behavior, it would be preferable to start with some idea about what might be important. In terms of the population, one might want to consider the total number, the density, the proportion of the population that lives in urban areas, and the share of foreign-born and African-Americans. With respect to the economic activity of the population, one might explore the leading industry of each county, the number of persons employed in manufacturing, capital invested in manufacturing, and the cash values of farms in the county. In addition, one might take into account whether or not the county is located on the coast or in the interior, factual information that can be obtained from a map. One might also wish to know the area of the county in square miles, a piece of information readily available in guides to the states. Having decided on the variables, one can create a codebook:

New England Counties Codebook

Variable Short Name	Descriptive Name Coding	Explanation
NO	Number	A number from 1 to 27 0–14 Massachusetts counties 15–22 Connecticut counties 23–27 Rhode Island counties
CO	Name	The first five letters of the name of each county
P	Population	1860 population (in hundreds)
SQ	Square Miles	The area in square miles (to be used in determining population density)
FBP	Foreign-Born	Foreign-born population in 1860 (in hundreds)
AAP	Afro-American	Afro-American population in 1860 (in hundreds)
UP	Urban Pop.	The number of people living in cities with a population of 7,500 or more (in hundreds)
FW	Female workers	Women employed in manufacturing (in hundreds)
MW	Male workers	Men employed in manufacturing (in hundreds)
IN	Industry	Leading industry 0 = no industry with more than 20 percent of the work force 1 = fisheries, 40 percent or more of the work force 2 = boots & shoes, 40 percent + 3 = boots & shoes, 20–39 percent 4 = cotton goods, 40 percent + 5 = cotton goods, 20–39 percent 6 = woolen goods, 40 percent + 7 = woolen goods, 20–39 percent 8 = clothing, 20–39 percent 9 = other, 20–39 percent

New England Counties Codebook (continued)

Variable Short Name	Descriptive Name Coding	Explanation
MC	Manufact. Capital	Amount invested in manufacturing (in hundred thousands)
FC	Farm Cash Value	Value of farms (in hundred thousands)
GL	Geogr. Location	Coastal or Interior 1 = Coastal 2 = Interior
V	Voters	Total number of votes in 1860 presidential election (in hundreds)
RV	Republican Vote	Votes for Abraham Lincoln (in hundreds)
DV	Democratic Vote	Votes for Stephen Douglas (in hundreds)

From the above variables, one can create new variables through data transformation: density of population; percent urban population; per capita manufacturing capital; per capita farm value; percent Republican vote. The coded data set looks as seen on the following page.

ID	CO	P	SQ	FBP	AAP	UP	FW	MW	IN	MC	FC	GL	V	RV	DV
1	BARNS	360	400	16	1	0	1	33	1	18	21	1	32	24	1
2	BERKS	551	929	98	12	80	25	42	7	54	99	2	85	52	29
3	BRIST	938	557	167	19	517	47	213	1	242	69	1	107	80	17
4	DUKES	44	102	2	0	0	0	2	1	3	6	1	6	3	1
5	ESSEX	1656	495	295	7	1009	154	310	2	209	103	1	226	148	38
6	FRANK	314	702	23	1	0	7	18	9	14	76	2	54	40	9
7	HAMPD	574	618	121	5	152	59	51	4	85	74	2	81	52	20
8	HAMPS	378	528	53	3	0	16	25	5	26	77	2	56	46	6
9	MIDDL	2164	822	502	9	1044	146	222	3	269	244	1	306	178	71
10	NANTU	61	47	3	1	0	0	6	1	9	2	1	5	4	0
11	NORFO	1100	400	263	2	426	60	117	3	80	155	1	159	89	36
12	PLYMO	648	655	67	4	85	17	97	2	36	76	1	103	67	14
13	SUFFO	1927	57	673	24	1912	50	141	8	145	8	1	225	110	49
14	WORCE	1597	1514	319	8	419	129	185	3	139	222	2	248	173	52
15	FAIRF	775	632	121	17	209	20	60	0	43	159	1	161	70	32
16	HARTF	900	739	195	13	292	39	84	0	112	199	2	152	85	33
17	LITCH	473	922	53	11	0	10	35	0	37	144	2	82	48	17
18	MIDDL	309	373	44	3	0	8	31	9	28	57	1	55	29	12
19	NEWHA	973	610	224	21	493	65	123	0	118	140	1	165	87	29
20	NEWLO	617	669	98	13	242	25	58	5	65	95	1	95	55	26
21	TOLLA	207	412	25	3	0	13	18	6	19	38	2	41	25	11
22	WINDH	347	515	47	5	0	24	30	4	35	76	2	54	36	15
23	BRIST	89	26	17	3	0	3	7	4	8	12	1	11	7	5
24	KENT	173	172	32	3	89	18	20	4	28	22	1	19	12	7
25	NEWPO	219	107	37	8	105	8	4	5	8	48	1	25	16	9
26	PROVI	1078	416	274	20	916	79	159	5	180	79	1	121	72	49
27	WASHI	187	333	14	6	0	12	15	6	19	35	1	24	15	8

Appendix B

Choosing Statistical Techniques for Bivariate Relationships

Level of Measurement of the Dependent Variable	Level of Measurement of the Independent Variable		
	Categorical	Ordinal	Continuous
Categorical	Chi-square	Chi-square	Logistic Regression
	Cramer's V Lambda	Cramer's V Lambda	
Ordinal	Mann-Whitney U	Chi-square	Ordered Logistic Regression
	Kruskal-Wallis H	Gamma Tau c, Spearman's r_s	
Continuous	ANOVA	ANOVA	Least Squares Regression
			Pearson's r

Selected Bibliography

Akademija Nauk SSSR, ed. 1987. *Kompleksnye metody v istoricheskikh issledovaniiakh*. Moscow.

Aldrich, J. H., and F. D. Nelson. 1984. *Linear Probability, Logit, and Probit Models*. Beverly Hills.

Alexander, T. B. 1967. *Sectional Stress and Party Strength*. Nashville.

Allison, P. D. 1989. *Event History Analysis: Regression for Longitudinal Event Data*. Beverly Hills.

Andrews, F. M. 1981. *A Guide for Selecting Statistical Techniques for Analyzing Social Science Data*. Ann Arbor.

Aydelotte, W. O. 1977. *The History of Parliamentary Behavior*. Princeton.

———. 1971. *Quantification in History*. Reading, England.

Aydelotte, W. O., A. G. Bogue, and R. W. Fogel, eds. 1972. *The Dimensions of Quantitative Research in History*. Princeton.

Bacher, J. 1989. "Einführung in die Clusteranalyse mit SPSS-X für Historiker und Sozialwissenschaftler." *Historical Social Research* 14, no. 1:6–167.

Bailey, R. W., ed. 1982. *Computing in the Humanities*. Amsterdam.

Bailyn, B. 1982. "The Challenge of Modern Historiography." *American Historical Review* 87:1–24.

Barzun, J. 1974. *Clio and the Doctors*. Chicago.

Belsley, D. A., E. Kuh, and R. E. Welsch. 1980. *Regression Diagnostics*. New York.

Benson, L. 1964. *The Concept of Jacksonian Democracy*. Pbk. ed. New York.

Bentler, P. W. 1985. *Theory and Implementation of EQS: A Structural Equations Program*, version 2.1. Los Angeles.

Berkhofer, R. 1969. *A Behavioral Approach to Historical Analysis*. New York.

Best, H. 1981. "Quantifizierende Historische Sozialforschung in der Bundesrepublik Deutschland." *Geschichte in Köln* 9:121–57.

Best, H., et al., eds. 1989. "Computer Applications in the Historical Sciences: Selected Contributions to the Cologne Computer Conference 1988." *Historical Social Research* 14, no. 3:5–104.

—————. 1988. *Cologne Computer Conference: Volume of Abstracts.* Cologne.

Blalock, H. M., Jr. 1972. *Social Statistics.* 2d ed. New York.

—————. 1964. *Causal Inference in Nonexperimental Research.* Chapel Hill, N.C.

Bogue, A. 1983. *Clio and the Bitch Goddess: Quantification in American Political History.* Beverly Hills.

—————. 1978. *The History of American Electoral Behavior.* Princeton.

Bollen, K. A. 1989. *Structural Equations with Latent Variables.* New York.

Botz, G., et al., eds. 1988. *'Qualität und Quantität.' Zur Praxis der Methoden der Historischen Sozialwissenschaft.* Frankfurt.

Bourdelais, P. 1984. "French Quantitative History." *Social Science History* 8:179–92.

Bourdelais, P., and J.-Y. Raulot. 1987. *Une Peur bleue: Histoire du choléra en France.* Paris.

Brand, S., ed. 1984. *Whole Earth Software Catalogue.* Garden City, N.Y.

Braudel, F. 1976–78. *La Méditerranée et le monde méditerranéen à l'époque de Philippe II.* 3d ed. 3 vols. Paris.

Burnham, W. D. 1955. *Presidential Ballots, 1836–1892.* Baltimore.

Carlin, M. 1989. "The Medieval and Early Modern Data Bank." *Perspectives* 27:12.

Childers, T. 1983. *The Nazi Voter: The Social Foundations of Fascism in Germany, 1919–1933.* Chapel Hill, N.C.

Clausen, A. R. 1988. "Social Science History: Citation Record, 1976–1985." *Social Science History* 12:197–215.

Clegg, F. 1982. *Simple Statistics.* Cambridge, England.

Clubb, J. M. 1986. "Computer Technology and the Source Materials of Social Science History." *Social Science History* 10:97–114.

—————. 1985. "Murray Murphey and the Possibility of Social Science History." *Social Science History* 9:93–104.

Clubb, J. M., and E. K. Scheuch, eds. 1980. *Historical Social Research: The Use of Historical and Process-Produced Data.* Stuttgart.

Cohen, J., and P. Cohen. 1983. *Applied Multiple Regression/Correlation Analysis for the Behavioral Sciences.* 2d ed. Hillsdale, N.J.

Conover, W. J. 1980. *Practical Nonparametric Statistics.* New York.

Cooper, R. A., and A. J. Weeks. 1983. *Data, Models and Statistical Analysis.* Totowa, N.J.

Couteau-Begarie, H. 1983. *Le Phénomène 'nouvelle histoire.'* Paris.

Crew, D. 1979. *Town in the Ruhr.* New York.

Daniel, C., and F. Wood. 1980. *Fitting Equations to Data.* Rev. ed. New York.

Denley, P., and D. Hopkin, eds. 1987. *History and Computing*. Manchester.

Desai, M. 1976. *Applied Econometrics*. New York.

Doan, T. A., and R. B. Litterman. 1983. *User's Manual RATS*, version 4.11. Minneapolis.

Doane, D. P. 1976. "Aesthetic Frequency Classifications." *The American Statistician* 30, no. 4:181–83.

Dollar, C. M., and R. Jensen. 1971. *Historian's Guide to Statistics: Quantitative Analysis in Historical Research*. New York.

Dumke, R. 1985. "Clio's Climacteric? Bemerkungen und Thesen zum Stand und zu den Entwicklungstendenzen der Cliometrischen Wirtschaftsgeschichte." Münster. Manuscript.

Duncan, O. D. 1975. *Introduction to Structural Equation Models*. New York.

Engerman, S. 1977. "Recent Developments in American Economic History." *Social Science History* 1:72–89.

Everitt, B. S. 1984. *An Introduction to Latent Variable Models*. London.

———. 1980. *Cluster Analysis*. 2d ed. London.

———. 1977. *The Analysis of Contingency Tables*. London.

Everitt, B. S., and G. Dunn. 1983. *Advanced Methods of Data Exploration and Modelling*. London.

Falk, J. D. 1989. "OCLC and RLIN: Research Libraries at the Scholar's Fingertips." *Perspectives* 27:1–17.

Fienberg, S. E. 1980. *The Analysis of Cross-Classified Categorical Data*. 2d ed. Cambridge, Mass.

Flanigan, W., and N. Zingale. "Alchemist's Gold: Inferring Individual Relationships from Aggregate Data." *Social Science History* 9:71–91.

Floud, R. 1984. "Quantitative History and People's History." *Social Science History* 8:151–68.

———. 1979. *An Introduction to Quantitative Methods for Historians*. 2d ed. London.

Fogel, R. W. 1982. " 'Scientific' History and Traditional History." In *Logic, Methodology and Philosophy of Science*, ed. L. Cohen et al. Amsterdam.

———. 1964. *Railroads and American Economic Growth*. Baltimore.

Fogel, R. W., and G. R. Elton. 1983. *Which Road to the Past? Two Views of History*. New Haven.

Fogel, R. W., and S. Engerman. 1974. *Time on the Cross*. Boston.

Furet, F. 1977. *Lire et écrire: L'Alphabetisation français*. Paris.

———. 1971. "Quantitative History." *Daedalus* 100:151–67.

Galtung, J. 1967. *Theory and Methods of Social Research*. Oslo.

Genet, J.-P., ed. 1988. *Standardisation et échange des bases de données historiques*. Paris.

Graff, H. 1980. *Quantification and Psychology: Towards a 'New' History*. Washington.

————. 1979. *The Literacy Myth*. New York.

Greenstein, D. I. 1989. "A Source-Oriented Approach to History and Computing: The Relational Database." *Historical Social Research* 14, no. 3:9–16.

Gujarati, D. 1988. *Basic Econometrics*. New York.

Gutman, M. P. 1990. "Computer-Based History Teaching in Higher Education: The United States." *History and Computing* 2:24–30.

Haberman, S. 1978. *Analysis of Qualitative Data: Introductory Topics*, vol. 1. New York.

Hammarberg, M. 1977. *The Indiana Voter*. Chicago.

Hareven, T. 1978. *Family and Population in Nineteenth Century America*. New York.

Harrell, F. E., and K. L. Lee. 1985. "A Comparison of the Discrimination of Discriminant Analysis and Logistic Regression under Multivariate Normality." In *Biostatistics*, ed. P. K. Sen. New York.

Härtel, R. 1989. "To Treat or not to Treat: The Historical Source before the Input." *Historical Social Research* 14, no. 2:25–38.

Hayduk, L. 1987. *Structural Equation Modelling with LISREL*. Baltimore.

Heffer, J., J.-L. Robert, and P. Saly. 1981. *Outils statistiques pour les historiens*. Paris.

Heise, D. R. 1975. *Causal Analysis*. New York.

Herlihy, D. 1981. "Numerical and Formal Analysis in European History." *Journal of Interdisciplinary History* 12:115–36.

Hershberg, T. 1981. *Philadelphia: Work, Space, Family and Group Experience in the Nineteenth Century*. New York.

————, ed. 1975/76. "A Special Issue: The Philadelphia Social History Project." *Historical Methods* 9, entire.

Hexter, J. 1971. *Doing History*. Bloomington.

Hickey, A. A. 1986. *An Introduction to Statistical Techniques for Social Research*. New York.

Himmelfarb, G. 1987. *The New History and the Old*. Cambridge, Mass.

Hobsbawm, E. J. 1971. "From Social History to History of Society." *Daedalus* 100:20–45.

Hockey, S. 1980. *A Guide to Computer Applications in the Humanities*. Baltimore.

Hoffman, P. T. 1984. "Wills and Statistics: Tobit Analysis of the Counter Reformation in Lyon." *Journal of Interdisciplinary History* 14:813–34.

Holtfrerich, C.-L. 1986. *The German Inflation, 1914–1924: Causes and Effects in International Perspective*. New York.

Hoover, K. R. 1988. *The Elements of Social Scientific Thinking*. 4th ed. New York.

Horan, P. M. 1987. "Theoretical Models in Social History Research." *Social Science History* 11:379–400.

Horan, P. M., and P. G. Hargis. 1989. "The Anatomy of a Measurement Model." *Historical Methods* 22:45–53.

Hubbard, W., and K. H. Jarausch. 1979. "Occupation and Social Structure in Central Europe: Some Notes on Coding Professions." *Historical Social Research* 11:10–19.

Iggers, G. G. 1984. *New Directions in European Historiography.* 2d ed. Middletown, Conn.

Ingham, J. N., ed. 1986. "Thernstrom's Poverty and Progress: A Retrospective after Twenty Years." *Social Science History* 10:1–44.

Jaffe, A. J., and H. F. Spirer. 1987. *Misused Statistics: Straight Talk for Twisted Numbers.* New York.

Jarausch, K. H. 1990. "Towards a Social History of Experience: Postmodern Predicaments in Theory and Interdisciplinarity." *Central European History,* forthcoming.

———. 1986. "Some Reflections on Coding." In *Datenbanken,* ed. M. Thaller, 175–78. St. Katherinen.

———, ed. 1984. "Quantitative History in International Perspective." Special issue of *Social Science History* 8:123–215.

———. 1982. *Students, Society and Politics in Imperial Germany: The Rise of Academic Illiberalism.* Princeton.

———, ed. 1976. *Quantifizierung in der Geschichtswissenschaft.* Düsseldorf.

Jarausch, K. H., and G. Arminger. 1989. "The German Teaching Profession and Nazi Party Membership: A Demographic Logit Model." *Journal of Interdisciplinary History* 20:197–225.

Jarausch, K. H., G. Arminger, and M. Thaller. 1985. *Quantitative Methoden in der Geschichtswissenschaft.* Darmstadt.

Jarausch, K. H., and W. H. Schroeder, eds. 1987. *Quantitative History of Society and Economy: Some International Studies.* St. Katherinen.

Jendrek, M. P. 1985. *Through the Maze: Statistics With Computer Applications.* Belmont, Calif.

Jensen, R. 1983. "The Historian and the Microcomputer." *Journal of American History* 14:91–111.

———. 1971. *The Winning of the Midwest.* Chicago.

Johnson, E. A. 1990. "Reflections on an Old 'New History': Quantitative Social Science History in Postmodern Middle Age." *Central European History,* forthcoming.

———. 1988. "Counting 'How It Really Was': Quantitative History in West Germany." *Historical Methods* 21:61–79.

Jöreskog, K. G., and D. Sörbom. 1988. *Lisrel 7: A Guide to the Program and Applications.* Chicago.

Kahk, J. 1982. *Peasant and Lord in the Process of Transition from Feudalism to Capitalism in the Baltics.* Tallinn, Estonia.

Kalton, G. 1983. *Introduction to Survey Sampling.* Beverly Hills.

———. 1977. "Practical Methods for Estimating Survey Sampling Errors." *Bulletin of the International Statistical Institute* 47, no. 3:495–514.

Kamphoefner, W. 1987. *The Westfalians: From Germany to Missouri.* Princeton.

Kater, M. H. 1983. *The Nazi Party: A Social Profile of Members and Leaders, 1919–1945.* Cambridge, Mass.

Katz, M. 1975. *The People of Hamilton, Canada West: Family and Class in a Nineteenth Century City.* Cambridge, Mass.

Kershaw, I. 1985. *The Nazi Dictatorship: Problems and Perspectives of Interpretation.* London.

Kim, J.-on. 1978. *Introduction to Factor Analysis.* Beverly Hills.

Kim, J.-on, and G. D. Ferrer. 1981. "Standardization in Causal Analysis." In *Linear Models in Social Research,* ed. P. V. Marsden. Beverly Hills.

Kirk, R. E. 1982. *Experimental Design: Procedures for the Behavioral Sciences.* Monterey, Calif.

Klecka, W. R. 1980. *Discriminant Analysis.* Beverly Hills.

Kmenta, J. 1986. *Elements of Econometrics.* New York.

Kocka, J. 1984. "Theories and Quantification in History." *Social Science History* 8:169–78.

———. 1982. "Theorienorientierung und Theorieskepsis in der Geschichtswissenschaft." *Historical Social Research* 23:4–19.

———. 1977. *Sozialgeschichte.* Göttingen.

Kousser, J. M. 1989. "The State of Social Science History in the Late 1980s." *Historical Methods* 22:13–19.

———. 1984. "The Revivalism of Narrative: A Response to Recent Criticism of Quantitative History." *Social Science History* 8:133–49.

———. 1980. "Quantitative Social Scientific History." In *The Past Before Us: Contemporary Historical Writing in the US,* ed. M. Kammen, 433–56. Ithaca.

———. 1974. *The Shaping of Southern Politics.* New Haven.

Kovalchenko, I. D., and V. A. Tishkov. 1983. *Kolichestvennye metody v sovestskoi i amerikanskoi istoriografii.* Moscow.

Kuczynski, T., ed. 1985. *Wirtschaftsgeschichte und Mathematik. Beiträge zur Anwendung mathematischer, insbesondere statistischer Methoden in der wirtschafts- und sozialhistorischen Forschung.* Berlin.

Landes, D. S., and C. Tilly. 1971. *History as Social Science.* Englewood Cliffs, N.J.

Laslett, P. 1965. *The World We Have Lost.* New York.

Lee, E. S., R. N. Forthofer, and R. J. Lorimer. 1989. *Analyzing Complex Survey Data.* Newbury Park, Calif.

Lefkowitz, J. M. 1985. *Introduction to Statistical Computer Packages.* Boston.

LeRoy Ladurie, E. 1979. *The Territory of the Historian.* Chicago.

————. 1966. *Les Paysans de Languedoc.* Paris.

Lindblad, J. T. 1984. *Statistiek vor Historici.* Muiderberg.

Long, J. S. 1983. *Confirmatory Factor Analysis: A Preface to LISREL.* Newbury Park, Calif.

Long, J. S., and T. D. Miethe. 1988. "The Statistical Comparison of Groups." In *Common Problems—Proper Solutions,* ed. J. S. Long. Newbury Park, Calif.

Lorwin, V. R., and J. M. Price. 1972. *The Dimensions of the Past: Materials, Problems and Opportunities for Quantitative Work in History.* New Haven.

McCaa, R. 1984. "Microcomputer Software Design for Historians." *Historical Methods* 17:68–74.

McCleary, R., and R. A. Hay. 1980. *Applied Time Series Analysis for the Social Sciences.* Beverly Hills.

McWilliams, P. A. 1983. *Word Processing on the IBM.* Los Angeles.

Maddala, G. S. 1983. *Limited-dependent and Qualitative Variables in Econometrics.* Cambridge, England.

Maynes, M. J. 1981. "Demographic History in the United States." *Historical Social Research* 19:3–12.

Meddis, R. 1984. *Statistics Using Ranks: A Unified Approach.* Oxford.

Mendenhall, W., and L. Ott. 1976. *Understanding Statistics.* 2d ed. North Scituate, Mass.

Monkkonen, E. H. 1984. "The Challenge of Quantitative History." *Historical Methods* 17:86–94.

Morris, R. J. 1990. "Occupational Coding: Principles and Examples." *Historical Social Research* 15:3–29.

Murphey, M. 1973. *Our Knowledge of the Historical Past.* Indianapolis.

North, D. 1981. *Structure and Change in Economic History.* New York.

Norton, P. 1983. *Inside the IBM PC: Access to Advanced Features and Programming.* Bowie, Md.

Norusis, M. J. 1988a. *SPSS/PC+ Advanced Statistics V2.0.* Chicago.

————. 1988b. *SPSS/PC+ V2.0: Base Manual.* Chicago.

Ohler, N. 1980. *Quantitative Methoden für Historiker.* Munich.

Ostrom, C. W. 1978. *Time Series Analysis: Regression Techniques.* Beverly Hills.

Pedhazur, E. J. 1982. *Multiple Regression in Behavioral Research: Explanation and Prediction.* 2d ed. New York.

Perez-Brignoli, H., and E. A. Ruiz. 1984. "History and Quantification in Latin America." *Social Science History* 8:201–15.

Phillips, J. A. 1979. "Achieving a Critical Mass While Avoiding an Explosion: Letter-Cluster Sampling and Nominal Record Linkage." *Journal of Interdisciplinary History* 9:493–508.

Possekel, R. 1990. "Die Notwendigkeit der Vermittlung unterschiedlicher theoretischer Ansätze für die Erklärung eines historischen Prozesses: unter besonderer Berücksichtigung von Erfahrungen bei der Anwendung quantitativer Methoden in den USA." Dissertation, Berlin-East.

Press, S. J., and S. Wilson. 1978. "Choosing between Logistic Regression and Discriminant Analysis." *Journal of the American Statistical Association* 73:699–705.

Rabb, T. K. 1983a. "The Development of Quantification in Historical Research." *Journal of Interdisciplinary History* 13:591–601.

————, ed. 1983b. "The Measure of American History." Special issue on quantitative methods in American history of the *Journal of Interdisciplinary History* 13, no. 4.

————. 1967. *Enterprise and Empire*. Cambridge, Mass.

Rinearson, P. 1986. *Word Processing Power with MICROSOFT WORD*. 2d ed. Redmond, Wash.

Ringer, F. 1979. *Education and Society in Modern Europe*. Bloomington.

Rosenburg, M. 1968. *The Logic of Survey Analysis*. New York.

Rowney, D. K., ed. 1984. *Soviet Quantitative History*. Beverly Hills.

Rowney, D. K., and J. Q. Graham, eds. 1969. *Quantitative History: Readings in the Quantitative Analysis of Historical Data*. Homewood, Ill.

SAS Institute. 1988. *SAS/STAT User's Guide*. Release 6.03 ed. Cary, N.C.

————. 1985a. *SAS Introductory Guide for Personal Computers*. 6th ed. Cary, N.C.

————. 1985b. *SAS User's Guide: Basics*, version 5. Cary, N.C.

————. 1985c. *SAS User's Guide: Statistics*, version 5. Cary, N.C.

Schaeffer, R. L., W. Mendenhall, and L. Ott. 1979. *Elementary Survey Sampling*. 2d ed. North Scituate, Mass.

Schiffman, S. S., M. L. Reynolds, and F. W. Young. 1981. *Introduction to Multidimensional Scaling*. New York.

Schroeder, W. H. 1988. "Historische Sozialforschung." *Historical Social Research*, supp. no. 1.

————, ed. 1989. "Methoden der Multivariaten Analyse Nominal- und Ordinalskalierter Daten." Special issue of *Historical Social Research* 42–3:3–189.

Schwob, A., K. Kranich-Hofbauer, and D. Suntinger, eds. 1989. *Historische Edition und Computer*. Graz.

Sheshkin, D. 1984. *Statistical Tests and Experimental Design: A Guidebook*. New York.

Shockey, J. W. 1988. "Latent Class Analysis: An Introduction to Discrete Data Models with Unobserved Variables." In *Common Problems— Proper Solutions*, ed. J. S. Long, 288–315. Newbury Park, Calif.

Shorter, E. 1971. *The Historian and the Computer: A Practical Guide*. Englewood Cliffs, N.J.

Siegel, S., and N. J. Castellan. 1988. *Nonparametric Statistics for the Behavioral Sciences.* New York.

Silbey, J. 1967. *The Shrine of Party: Congressional Voting Behavior, 1841–1852.* Pittsburgh.

Smith, P., ed. 1984–85. "Statistics, Epistemology and History." Special issue of *Historical Methods* 17 (Summer, Fall, and Winter).

Sprague, D. N. 1978. "A Quantitative Assessment of the Quantification Revolution." *Canadian Journal of History* 13:177–92.

SPSS. 1988. *SPSS User's Guide.* 3d ed. Chicago.

Stearns, P. 1980. "Towards a Wider Vision: Trends in Social History." In *The Past Before Us: Contemporary Historical Writing in the US,* ed. M. Kammen, 205–30. Ithaca.

Stier, W. 1989. "Basic Concepts and New Methods of Time Series Analysis in Historical Research." *Historical Social Research* 14, no. 2:3–24.

Stone, L. 1979. "The Revival of Narrative: Reflections on a New Old History." *Past and Present* 85:3–24.

———. 1977. "History and the Social Sciences in the Twentieth Century." In *The Future of History,* ed. C. F. Delzell. Nashville.

Sudman, S. 1976. *Applied Sampling.* New York.

Swafford, M. 1980. "Three Parametric Techniques for Contingency Table Analysis." *American Sociological Review* 45:664–90.

Swierenga, R. P., ed. 1970. *Quantification in American History.* New York.

SYSTAT. 1984. *The System for Statistics.* Evanston, Ill.

Temin, P. 1981. "Economic History in the 1980s." *Journal of Interdisciplinary History* 12:179–97.

Thaller, M. 1989. *Kleio: Ein Datenbanksystem,* version 1.1.1. Göttingen.

———, ed. 1986. *Datenbanken und Datenverwaltungssysteme als Werkzeuge Historischer Forschung.* St. Katherinen.

———. 1982. *Numerische Datenverarbeitung für Historiker.* Vienna.

———. 1980. "Automation on Parnassus. CLIO—A Databank Oriented System for Historians." *Historical Social Research* 15:40–65.

Thaller, M., and A. Müller, eds. 1989. *Computer in den Geisteswissenschaften.* Frankfurt.

Thernstrom, S. 1973. *The Other Bostonians.* Cambridge, Mass.

———. 1964. *Poverty and Progress: Social Mobility in a Nineteenth Century City.* Cambridge, Mass.

Thome, H. 1989 and 1990. "Grundkurs Statistik für Historiker." *Historical Social Research,* supp. no. 2:1–147 and no. 3:1–271.

Tilly, C. 1987. "Formalization and Quantification in Historical Analysis." In *Quantitative History of Society and Economy: Some International Studies,* ed. K. H. Jarausch and W. H. Schroeder. St. Katherinen.

———. 1981. *As Sociology Meets History.* New York.

————. 1972. "Quantification in History, as Seen from France." In *The Dimensions of the Past: Materials, Problems and Opportunities for Quantitative Work in History*, ed. V. R. Lorwin and J. M. Price, 93–125. New Haven.

Tilly, C., R. Tilly, and L. Tilly. 1975. *The Rebellious Century*. Cambridge, Mass.

Tilly, L., and J. W. Scott. 1978. *Women, Work and Family*. New York.

Tilly, R., and G. Hohorst. 1975. "Sozialer Protest in Deutschland im 19. Jahrhundert." In *Quantifizierung in der Geschichtswissenschaft*, ed. K. H. Jarausch, 232–78. Düsseldorf.

Tufte, E. R. 1983. *The Visual Display of Quantitative Information*. Cheshire, Conn.

Tukey, J. W. 1977. *Exploratory Data Analysis*. Reading, Mass.

Vinovskis, M. 1980. *Education and Social Change in 19th Century Massachusetts*. Cambridge, Mass.

Walker, H. M., and J. Lev. 1953. *Statistical Inference*. New York.

Wehler, H.-U. 1973. *Geschichte als Historische Sozialwissenschaft*. Frankfurt.

Wilcox, R. R. 1987. *New Statistical Procedures for the Social Sciences: Modern Solutions to Basic Problems*. Hillside, N.J.

Wilke, J. 1990. *Datenbanken in der Geschichtsforschvng*. Berlin.

Williams, F. 1968. *Reasoning with Statistics*. New York.

Wrigley, E. A. 1971. *Population and History*. New York.

Wrigley, E. A., and R. Schofield. 1981. *The Population History of England, 1541–1871*. Cambridge, Mass.

Ziegler, H. F. 1989. *Nazi Germany's New Aristocracy: The SS Leadership, 1925–1939*. Princeton.

Index

Alexander, Thomas B., xv
Alltagsgeschichte. See Everyday
  history
American Historical Association
  (AHA), quantitative methods
  committee, xv, 8
Analysis of covariance, 146
Analysis of variance (ANOVA), 128,
  130–31, 139, 147, 169, 229; fixed
  effects, 130; one-way, 128, 147,
  155–56; random effects, 130; re-
  peated measures, 130, 169
Analytical control, 185–89
Analytical statistics, 31, 43, 64–66,
  186
Annales, 5, 199–200, 206–7
Antiquarianism, numerical, 4, 188
Arminger, Gerhard, xii, xv, 28
ASCII, 46
Assembly language, 19
Association for History and Com-
  puting (AHC), 9, 24, 199, 203
Assumed error, 66–67
Autoregressive regressions, 173
Aydelotte, William O., 9, 202

Bar chart, 85, 87, 102
Barzun, Jacques, 204
BASIC, 19, 23
Behavioralism, 5. *See also* Social
  scientific methods
Benson, Lee, 196

Best, Heinrich, 10
Beta coefficients, 151–53
BITNET, 13
Bivariate analysis, 80, 111, 118, 229.
  See also Relationship
Bloch, Marc, 200
BMPD, 22
Bogue, Allan, 6
Box-Jenkins time series, 174
Box plot, 97, 102, 126
Braudel, Fernand, 200
Brigham Young Concordance, 21
Burnham, W. Dean, 225

C, 19
Cambridge Group for Population
  Research, 5, 60, 202
Cases, 2, 5, 7, 17, 30, 64
Causal model, 142, 144
Causation, 104
Censored dependent variable, 173
Census, 22, 38. *See also* U.S. census
Central tendency, 88–89; mean, 89;
  median, 89; mode, 89
Centre de Recherches Historiques,
  200
Chi-square, 108, 114, 135, 161–66,
  168, 209, 229
Civil War, 195, 215, 224
Classification, problem of, 26, 39–
  41, 44
Cliometrics, 4, 199

Cluster analysis, 171, 180–81, 183–84

Cobb-Douglas production function, 172

COBOL, 19

Cochran-Mantel-Haenszel statistic, 138

Codebook, design of, 42–44, 219–22, 226–27

Coding, 22, 38–44; diary of, 43; errors in, 53–55; rules of, 38–39; schemes for, 39–40; sheets for, 45

Coefficient of determination, 151

Coefficient of variability, 98

Compiler programming language, 19. See also BASIC; C; COBOL; FORTRAN

Computers in the study of history, 2, 12, 210; applications, 13–15; hardware, 16–19; software, 19–24

Concept of Jacksonian Democracy, The, 196

Concordance. See Brigham Young Concordance; Oxford Concordance Program

Contingency table, 105. See also Crosstabulation

Correlation, 65, 104. See also Relationship

Counter-factual analysis, 4

Covariance structure analysis, 178

Cramer's V, 110, 112, 138, 229

Crosstabulation, 105–12, 116

Data: cleaning of, 53–55; entry of, 45–47; modification of, 55–58; source-oriented processing of, 20–21; storage of, 14, 46

Data bank, 186

Data base, 19–24, 30, 37–38, 50–62; hierarchical, 40, 60; relational, 61

Data set: creation of, 27–28, 37–41;

property of, 48–49, 60

dBase IV, 14, 48, 61

De-bugging, 17

DEC, 17, 22

Deconstruction: critique of quantification, 8, 199, 205–6

Degrees of freedom, 78

Democratic party, 196

Demography, 5, 202

Denley, Peter, 9, 212

Dependent variable: defined, 32, 105

Descriptive statistics, 31, 43, 63–67

Dimensions of a table, 106

Discriminant function analysis, 182

Documentation of a project, 35–36

Dollar, Charles, 6

DOS, 16, 19

Dumke, Rolf, 199

Dummy variable, 127, 149, 157–58, 165–66, 168

EARN, 13

Ecological fallacy, 209

Econometrics, 4, 7, 206. See also Cliometrics

EDLIN, 46

Elton, G. R., 1, 9

E-mail, 13, 15

EQS, 178

Error correction: logical, 54; random, 55; visual, 53

Error sum of squares, 124

Estonian Academy of Science, 201–2

Eta, 127

Euclidean space, 181

Event history models, 174–75

Everyday history: critique of quantification, 199, 206

Factor analysis: confirmatory, 178–79; exploratory, 178; factor loadings, 178; factor score coefficients, 177

Family reconstitution, 5

Febvre, Lucien, 200

Feminism: critique of quantification, 1, 8, 199, 206

Flader, Susan, 192

Floud, Roderick, 9

Fogel, Robert, 19, 193

Formalized research procedure, 2, 28–32, 185–89

Fort Moultrie, S.C., 22, 38, 56, 116, 118, 215, 222; census of, 217–24; officers of, 131, 136, 157, 165, 215–17, 222; soldiers of, 58, 131, 136, 157, 165, 215–17, 222

FORTRAN, 19, 22

Frequency distribution, 83; bimodal, 89; joint, 105; skewed, 89; symmetric, 89

Furet, François, 200

FYI 3000, 14

Galtung, Johan, 195

Gamma, 114, 138, 229

Geschichte und Gesellschaft, 6

Gesellschaftsgeschichte, 201

Gettysburg address, 3

GLIM, 23

Goodman and Kruskal's lambda, 110, 229

Graphics, 188–89

Great Depression, 3, 32–33

Hardware. See Microcomputer

Herlihy, David, 204

Hermeneutics. See Historical methods

Hershberg, Ted, 186

Hexter, Jack, 9

Hilfswissenschaft, 208

Himmelfarb, Gertrude, 198

Histogram, 86–87

Histoire et Mesure, 9, 199

Historical methods, 1, 10–11, 26, 36, 189–97; hermeneutic, 9, 212–13; statistical, 64–68

Historical Methods, 9, 199

Historical Social Research, 9, 199, 201

Historical work station, 18, 212

Historische Sozialwissenschaft, 201

History and Computing, 9, 199

Hobsbawm, Eric J., 202

Hollerith, Herman, 16

Homoscedasticity, 125, 131

Hoover, Kenneth R., 25

Hopkin, Deian, 9, 212

Hypothesis testing, 28–31, 49, 76–80, 189–91, 194–97; null hypothesis, 30, 77–78; one-tailed test, 101–2; two-tailed test, 101–2

IBM, 17–19, 22

Independent variable: defined, 32, 105

Inferential statistics, 63, 67, 74

Institute for Research in Social Science (IRSS), xiv–xv

Interaction, 147, 154; one-way, 147, 155–56; two-way, 147, 157–56; variables, 163, 165

International Commission for the Application of Quantitative Methods in History (INTERQUANT), xv, 9, 199

Interquartile range, 93

Inter-University Consortium for Political and Social Research, 8

Jarausch, Konrad H., xiii, 9, 28

Jensen, Richard, 9

Johnson, Eric, xv
Journal of Interdisciplinary History,
9, 199

Kahk, Juhan, 201
Kamphoefner, Walter, xv
Kater, Michael H., 28
Katz, Michael, 7
Kendall and Stuart's tau c, 113, 229
KLEIO, 21, 61, 211
Kocka, Jürgen, 189
Kousser, J. Morgan, 196
Kovalchenko, Ivan D., 201
Kruskal-Wallis H, 118, 130, 138,
229

Labrousse, Ernest, 200
Lambda, 138
Laslett, Peter, 202
Latent variable structural equation
modeling, 177–78, 180
Lazarsfeld, Paul E., 196
Least squares regression, 119, 122,
172, 229
LeRoy Ladurie, Emmanuel, 200
Level of confidence, 67
Level of significance, 79
Levels of measurement, 31, 63, 74–
76. See also Measurement
Lincoln, Abraham, 3, 225
Linear additive models, 140
LISREL, 23, 118, 171, 178
Logistic regression, 132, 134–36,
162, 164, 182, 229
Logits, 133, 135, 137, 139, 162, 164,
168
Log-linear models, 163
Lotus 1-2-3, 15, 48

Mann-Whitney U, 118, 122, 138,
229
MANOVA, 139, 169
Mapping, 20, 188. See also Graphics

Marxism: attitude toward quantifi-
cation, 6, 201, 206–7
Maximum likelihood estimation,
134, 160
Mean deviation, 96,
Mean deviation coding, 149
Measurement: interval, 31, 75;
nominal, 31, 74–75; ordinal, 31,
75; ratio, 31, 75–76
Measurement rule, 74
Medieval and Early Modern Data
Bank (MEMDB), 14–15
Mentalité history, 4, 10, 191
Microcomputer, 16–17, 210–11
Missing values, 27, 41, 48, 83
Mode, 83–85
Models: building of, 32, 194–96;
causal, 174–76; hierarchical, 155;
linear additive, 140; multiequa-
tion, 178; nonlinear, 172; recur-
sive, 176; statistical, 77; verbal,
195
Monkkonen, Eric, 3
Moscow University, 173
Multicollinearity, 157
Multidimensional scaling, 180–81
Multiple logistic regression, 160,
161, 166, 167
Multiple R, 128, 134, 150
Multivariate statistics, 80, 171

Narrative, revival of, 3, 8
New economic history, 4
New England counties, 57, 215,
224–27
New political history, 5–6
New social history, 6–7
North, Douglas C., 4
NSDAP, support of, 28–30, 32–33,
40

Occupation, coding of, 22, 40–41,
86

OCLC, 13
Odds, 133–34, 160, 162–63
Ordered response model, 137
Outliers, 125
Oxford Concordance Program, 21

Parameter estimate, 158
Partial regression coefficients, 152, 158
PASCAL, 19
Path models, 153
PC, 12. *See also* Microcomputer
Pearson chi-square, 107, 165
Pearson's r, 122, 229
Philadelphia Urban History Project, 60, 186, 211
Pilot study, 34–35, 44, 73
Population transition, 5
Postmodernism: critique of quantification, 1, 198, 205
Precoding. *See* Coding
Princeton Population Research Center, 5
Probabilities, 162–63
Probit models, 172–73
Program packages: statistical, 14–15, 19–24, 50–53; word processing, 13. *See also* Software
PROLOG, 61
Prosopography, 7
P-STAT, 22
P Value, 67

Quantifiability, 25–28, 49
Quantitative historians, 204, 210
Quantitative history: acceptance of, 1–11, 191, 194, 199, 203; criticism of, 1, 3, 8, 204–7; definition of, 1–4; infrastructure for, 207–8, 213; literature on, 8–11; national style of, 8–11; varieties of, 4–7
Quantitative methods, xiii, 26; analytical possibilities of, 2, 198, 200–201, 204, 214; challenge of, 214; communication of results, 209–10; self-criticism of, 208–9; sources for, 26–27, 37; training in, xiii, 208, 213
QUANTUM, 199, 201
Quartile, 96
QUASSH, 193. *See also* Social science history

Rabb, Theodore K., 9, 214
Random Access Memory (RAM), 16, 18
Random error, 66–67, 78
Range, 93
Read Only Memory (ROM), 16
Recoding, 56
Record linkage, nominal, 20, 58–62; difficulties of, 58–60; techniques of, 60–62
REF 11, 15
Register, creation of, 20
Regression: bivariate, 119–25; multiple, 147–60
Regression diagnostics, 125, 139
Relationship, 104, 141; chain, 145; curvilinear, 114, 119; linear, 119; negative, 112, 119; positive, 112, 119; spurious, 143
Replicability, 39, 195
Representativeness, 27, 69
Republican party, 224–25
Research design, 28–36, 64
Residuals, 125
Results, interpretation of, 31, 185–87, 196–97
Ringer, Fritz, 7, 193
RLIN, 14
Roll call analysis, 5
Rowney, Don K., 202
R squared (coefficient of determination), 151, 157

St. Genevieve, 192
Sample size, 33, 68–72
Sampling, 33, 63, 68–74; alphabetical, 33; cluster, 70; error, 33; random, 33; simple random, 69; source bias in, 73; stratified, 70; systematic, 33, 69
Scales of measurement, 74–76
Scanners, 45–46
Scatterplot, 118–19
Schlesinger, Arthur, 204
Schlözer, August Ludwig von, 11
Schofield, Robert S., 202
Schroeder, Willy H., xv
Screen formatting, 46
Semipartial R, 152
Shorter, Edward, 9
Significance test, 67
Smith, Peter, 9
Social mobility, 7
Social science history, 10, 28–32, 36, 191–94, 196, 200
Social Science History, 9, 199
Social Science History Association (SSHA), 8–9, 24, 199
Social scientific methods, 3, 32–36, 76–79, 189–97
Software, 21, 102–3
—data-base, 50–62; KLEIO, 21, 61, 211; KWIC, 21
—historical teaching, 208
—statistical, 14–15, 19–24; SAS, xiii, 14, 23, 47–48, 51–53, 138–39, 169, 183; SPSS, xiii, 14, 23, 51–53, 138–39, 169, 183; SYSTAT, 22–23
—word-processing, 13; Microsoft Word, 13; Nota Bene, 13; Word-Perfect, 13; WordStar, 13
SOUNDEX, 60
Soviet National Committee of Historians, 202
Soviet Union, 201
Spearman's r_s, 116, 229

Spengler, Oswald, 190
SPIRES, 14
Standard deviation, 93; mean squared deviation, 96
Statistical analysis, 15, 64–65; fear of, 1, 3
Statistics: analytical, 64–65; cooking of, 187; descriptive, 63–67, 74, 83–85; inferential, 74
Stearns, Peter, 9
Steinhauer, Dale, xiv, 215
Stone, Lawrence, xv, 3, 193
Stuart's tau c, 113
Student's t distribution, 98
Sum of squares: error, 124; explained, 124
System file, 47–49

Tau c, 113–14, 138
Textual analysis, 20–21. See also KLEIO; SPIRES
Thaller, Manfred, xii, xv, 21, 212
Theory, 189–91, 205. See also Social science history
Thernstrom, Stephan, 7, 222
Third World countries, 203, 206
Thompson, E. P., 202
Tilly, Charles S., 6, 27, 193
Time series, 173; Box-Jenkins technique for, 174
Tobit estimator, 173
Toynbee, Arnold, 190
Type I error, 79
Type II error, 79

U.S. census, 216–19, 225
Univariate statistics, 80, 86–103, 171; descriptive analysis, 82
University of Cologne, 201
UNIX, 16

Variability, 85
Variables, 30, 47–49, 64; categorical,

83, 182; continuous, 86–87, 180;
dependent, 32; endogenous, 174,
176, 178; exogenous, 175, 178; independent, 32; intermediate, 144;
label for, 48; latent, 177; naming
of, 47–48; suppressor, 140
Variance, 93, 193
VMS, 16
Voting behavior, 6, 196

Wallerstein, Immanuel, 190
Weber, Max, 201
Wehler, Hans-Ulrich, 6
Whigs, 196
Wilcoxon test, 118
Word processing, 13
Wrigley, E. A., 202

Z distribution, 98